£16.95

City and Islington Sixth Form College
283-309 Goswell Road
London
EC1V 7LA
020 7520 0652

CITY AND ISLINGTON
COLLEGE

This book is due for return on or before the date last stamped below.
You may renew by telephone. Please quote the Barcode No.
May not be renewed if required by another reader.

Fine: 5p per day

To India and Nathaniel.
Follow your dreams and
reach for the skies.

Millennium People
the soul of success

Photographs and text
by Derek Burnett

Hibiscus Books
London

Front Cover Images: (L-R) Trevor Phillips, Kanya King, Lennox Lewis
Oona King MP, Major Ezenwa Ugwuzor & Marianne Jean-Baptiste.

Back Cover Image: Derek Burnett

Text by Derek Burnett

Foreword by Professor Chris Mullard of the Focus Consultancy Ltd. UK.

Photography by Derek Burnett

Additional photographs by kind permission of the owners—
see acknowledgements.

Photographic images sponsored by the kind support of
Paterson Group International.

Revised and updated edition 2003
First edition published 1999
Publisher: Hibiscus Books
122-124 High Road, London NW6 4HY,
United Kingdom
www.hibiscusbooks.com

Artwork: Interactive Marketing, Malaysia
Typesetting: Art Revo Studio, Malaysia.
Book jacket styling by the Millennium Consultancy, UK.
Printed in Malaysia.

British Library Cataloguing in Publication Data.
A catalogue record for this book is available from the British Library.

ISBN 0 9535383 2 X

A range of related products and support materials based on
Millennium People is also available from Hibiscus Books —
see page 150 for a full list of the *Millennium People Series.*

Contents

Preface to Updated Edition

Some three years on since *Millennium People – the soul of success* was first published, it is my belief that the key issue I sought to highlight then, is today, all the more evident, if not irrefutable. Namely, that ever more growing numbers of black British people are rising to make their mark, and in so doing, are leaving their indelible footprints on the rich tapestry of British life and culture, as we sojourn into the twenty-first century.

Is this then the awaited confirmation that Britain is now a truly pluralist, multicultural society with all that is implied by this? Sadly not, as the wealth of other socio-economic indicators would surely tell us. But it is undoubtedly, and at the very least, I believe, a highly encouraging and welcome trend towards this declared societal goal.

To quote the rather apt words of Baroness Patricia Scotland, one of the *Millennium People* featured, and who is today a Junior Minister of growing stature in Her Majesty's Government:

> 'We cannot pretend that all the challenges have been met and all the demons overcome. There is still much to do, but we are getting there. Britain is no longer a mono culture and barriers to ethnicity and gender are being dismantled.'

Since the publication of the first edition I have received much welcome feedback, and have myself observed various pointers to that which Baroness Scotland so eloquently refers.

The number of people who, for example, in commending me on the book have yet also rejoined me for not including this or that person amongst those profilled, have in my mind only served to reinforce the very point I sought to make. This belief is perhaps further supported by the steady progress and upward rise, in just these few short years, of many of the individuals featured in the book. A fact which was instrumental in prompting this updated edition.

At the same time, however, data and experience from schools, colleges and across the British education sector more generally—and not overlooking the overwhelming response to *Millennium People* from this very sector—underlines that the struggle for equality of opportunity is far from over. There remains a significant task ahead to further raise the aspirations and potential, as well as the opportunities afforded to the younger black British generation, if we are to reap the harvest of a genuinely diverse and multicultural British society.

Clearly, the broader challenge still exists. But, as I indicated in the first edition of *Millennium People*, let us not forget to take stock and heart from the gains and in-roads that are being made, as exemplified by the inspiring and uplifting stories of those portrayed in the pages of this book.

If the individuals featured are, as is suggested, people whom to look out for in the new millennium, and yet, at the same time, are also representative of a wider and steadily growing trend, what has been their fate since the publicalion of the first edition of *Millennium People*? How have those featured fared in their chosen fields over the intervening period?

In an effort to shed some new light on them for this updated edition, those featured were canvassed to see how, if at all, their respective careers and business paths may have changed since the first edition. A summary of what was discovered in this process is contained in the new Epilogue section which can be found at the rear of the book (see pages 147-149).

Additionally, I am pleased and privileged to report that a new profile has been added to this updated edition, namely that of Lenny Henry, comedian, actor and hugely popular entertainer, whom I had so wanted to include from the outset.

By the same token, however, I must also record, with great sadness, the untimely death of one of the individuals featured in *Millennium People*. Val McCalla, the founder and Chairman of the Voice Newspaper Group, regrettably passed away in 2002.

If I may be so bold as to say, I feel Val McCalla's helmsmanship, his indomitable spirit, energy and vision for the future lives on in the character of so many of those found within the pages of this book and a good many others besides.

The course which has been so well and truly set by these *Millennium People*, is now forging a path for the many other young black Britons who also dream of success and achievement in today's Britain.

Derek Burnett

Foreword

There has been a black presence in the British Isles for over two millennia, even before the English (and the Normans) came here. From the 'Division of Moors' marooned on the most northern point of the Roman Empire, 'Hadrian's Wall', in the third century AD, to the growing London population of 'Negras' in the late sixteenth century, our presence had become sufficiently disturbing for Queen Elizabeth I to deport 'those kinds of people' from the realm. Her proclamation in 1601, in which she declared herself 'highly discontented to understand the great numbers of Negras and Blackamoors which [had] crept into this realm' marked the end of tolerance and the beginning of contemporary racism.

Against rising xenophobia at home, colonialism abroad, and more than three centuries of thought and social practice in which blacks were considered congenitally inferior, the beginnings of the making of today's multi-cultural Britain started to take shape. In the taverns of the slave ports of London, and to a lesser extent in

Professor Chris Mullard

Liverpool and Bristol, an early sense of community was forged, one which generated support, space and strength which, in turn, allowed our forebears to make direct political, economic and cultural contributions to eighteenth- and nineteenth-century Britain.

Some of the more well-known contributors in the eighteenth century included Ukawsaw Gronniosaw, who wrote an account of his experiences in Portsmouth and London in 1770; Phillis Wheatley, the black poet, whose *Poems* was published in London in 1773; Ignatious Sancho, the writer, musician and businessman whom Gainsborough painted in 1768; the political activist and abolitionist Ottobah Cugoano who, in effect, coined the phrase 'stand up and be counted'; and Olaudah Equiano, arguably the first political leader of Britain's black community, who toured the length and breadth of the country campaigning vigorously for the abolition of slavery.

The nineteenth century witnessed the contributions of William

Cuffay who, born in Kent, became one of the leaders of the Chartist Movement before being transported to Australia in 1848; Mary Seacole, who was not only as famous as Florence Nightingale in the 1850s but who, according to some, must be credited with the development of modern nursing; Ira Aldridge, the first black actor who played not only Shakespeare's Othello, but also Hamlet, Lear and Macbeth; and the concert musician Samuel Coleridge-Taylor who, born in London in 1875, epitomised through his 'open house' hospitality what in the twentieth century became known as 'racial solidarity'.

The more recent black history of the twentieth century was built upon this foundation of struggle and contribution. Indeed, the Pan-Africanists of the first half of the century, from Archer through to Charles Moody and George Padmore, and the campaigners against racial discrimination in the second half, from Sir Leary Constantine and Lord David Pitt to blacks born in Britain like myself, all acknowledge this distinguished past.

The contribution we have made since the 1960s, in particular, has been no less significant. The National Health Service would not be what it is today without our nurses, doctors and ancillary workers. The textile industry on both sides of the Pennines would have been non-competitive if it had not been for the labour of those early Indian and Pakistani workers in the 1960s. Similarly, many metropolitan transport systems would have ground to a halt if workers from Asia and the Caribbean had not been persuaded to migrate. And so the story continues....

But if this were the only story, then the main thrust of this imaginative book would be lost. The expanse of our contribution in every area of modern life—politics, business, law, fashion, education, entertainment, science, local government, civil service, medicine, media, sport, etc.—suggests that we are now part of the cultural fabric of a Britain which is beginning to recognise itself as being multi-cultural. To even start to appreciate nearly all areas of sport, from football to karate, athletics to cricket, requires an understanding of this transition: the extent to which our presence has started to make an impact. In the case of politics and public life, as witnessed by those profiled in *Millennium People* (for example, Baroness Valerie Amos, Oona King MP, and Sir Herman Ouseley) or the news media and business (Trevor Phillips, Val McCalla, Verna Wilkins, Rene Carayol, etc.), it is clear that at the end of the second millennium we are here to stay.

We have broken the mould that has stereotyped us for so long—as only being successful in sport, music and other forms of entertainment. It would have been unimaginable just ten years ago to think that the Army, for instance, would be actively seeking black and Asian soldiers and officers today or that the Chief of the Defence Staff would be launching a 'war against racism'. But at the end of the second millennium and the beginning of the third, this is not only imaginable, it is happening. Indeed, in nearly every walk of life represented in Derek Burnett's book, and triggered by our own contributions as much as by the current government's initiatives and commitment to racial justice, obstacles which have hitherto restricted our successes are gradually being removed.

So what can one expect in the new millennium? First, our

material base, and hence our role in wealth creation, will improve significantly; secondly, the flame of resilience and imagination we have kept alive since that black soldier 'of great fame among clowns and good for a laugh anytime' marched along Hadrian's Wall in AD 210 will continue to burn brightly in all that we do: as spiritual leaders, civil servants, plumbers, doctors, lawyers, politicians, entertainers, scientists, accountants, police chiefs, mechanics, fashion designers, soldiers, sailors, airmen and women, writers, sportsmen and women, businessmen and women, and so on. Our numbers, along with our contributions to these and other career areas, will continue to grow. Thirdly, given that for the first time in 2,000 years a real window of opportunity exists, I believe that those profiled in this book, together with many, many others will, over the decades, help to dismantle the practices of institutionalised racism and replace them with those of institutionalised equality of opportunity.

Lastly, it does seem likely that the 'soul of success' which glows throughout this book will become the bedrock on which Britain's black population will flourish in the third millennium. For our soul of success has been created out of the experiences of our past, and our contributions in both the past and present will shape and help to secure our future as tomorrow's truly equal citizens.

Professor Chris Mullard

Introduction

The people portrayed in this book are all successful and influential decision-makers as well as charismatic and impressive achievers. All of them are black and all of them are making their mark in Britain.

When I set out to portray these leading black role models, most of whom, in my view, will reach the pinnacle of their success in the next millennium, I knew little of the personal struggles and hurdles they have had to overcome on their way to the top. Having now met and interviewed these *Millennium People,* I feel compelled to highlight the heart and humanity behind their stories, or, to put it another way, the soul of their success.

This book has been a long time in gestation. I had pondered the idea for many years, but it was only after I had finally committed myself to action that close scrutiny of my early research material, collection of press cuttings, and scribbled notes on possible subjects and the treatment for the book, revealed that some of the items were almost ten years old.

As black and British myself, and an avid consumer of information on the black presence in the UK, not to mention my professional background and work which involved more than a slight consideration of the subject, I had longed to see a book which positively recognised and indeed, celebrated the black population's contribution to British life. In particular, I wanted to see a British book which squarely addressed the issues of black success and black achievement as opposed to one which focused on the 'problems' and 'difficulties' encountered by black people—important though this is—or, as in the eyes of some, those 'associated with' black people.

As a keen, amateur photographer who appreciates the power and potency of the photographic image, I had also longed to see images of black British people presented in a positive, uplifting manner, and for those images to encompass not only the fields of music, sports and entertainment—significant though they are—but also the myriad of fields which make up British life.

In formulating my ideas for this book, I have, of course, been inspired by books and magazines which cover these themes, although these were invariably produced overseas, and thus have an overseas focus to their content. Such treatments, for example, of or by African Americans are now so commonplace that it is readily recognised both in the United States and elsewhere that there are a multitude of successful African Americans to be found in all areas of American life. One such book which inspired and indeed helped me to crystallise my thinking on *Millennium People,* is *I Dream a World* by Brian Lanker. This superb book, interestingly by a white American photo-journalist, celebrates the role played by African American women in helping 'to change and shape the America we know today'. Another excellent book in this genre— again American-published—is *Face Forward* by Julian Okwu. Okwu chose for his subjects African American men, whom he engagingly portrays in a laudable effort to counter the myths and stereotypes associated with this group.

It is not that British literature, or the UK media in general, does not portray any positive images or give any coverage to the contribution of black people in British society. Indeed, there are many notable exceptions, one being the recent coverage of the fiftieth anniversary of the arrival of the ship 'Empire Windrush', which brought some of the early Caribbean settlers to Britain. But the overwhelming bulk of the coverage is negative, and what positive images there are tend to be swamped by those less positive ones. Moreover, the positive images that do emerge often tend to be narrowly focused and concentrated on particular fields, or on a small and sometimes predictable number of well-known individuals. The general impression one gains as a result of this filtering process—both at an individual level and at the wider societal level—is that there are few black people worthy of special note in the UK, and that its black population has still to make any significant impression on the wider British canvass.

Millennium People - the soul of success is a book which unashamedly seeks to acknowledge and celebrate the growing emergence and success of black people in virtually all aspects of mainstream British life. In it, I have sought to make the very simple but, I believe, nonetheless telling statement that black people can and do achieve. To borrow the term coined by the Phillips brothers in their excellent book, *Windrush, the irresistible rise of multi-racial Britain,* this 'irresistible rise' has led to an ever expanding tranche of black individuals who have already achieved a critical level of success, or have made a significant contribution in their respective fields, and who are, in my view, poised to help carry Britain forward into the next millennium.

Although those featured in the book are all individuals who have made a mark on some aspect of British life, and whose other common denominator is that they are members of Britain's black population, it should be emphasised that they are merely representative of a much larger group of talented, creative and forward-looking individuals. There are many other equally successful black Britons who could have been portrayed on these pages. I hope readers will realise that this is my very personal view of the subject, and one which was never intended to be an exhaustive 'who's who' nor a scholarly survey.

Time, resources, opportunity and, of course, the number of pages in the book, were all constraints on the number of people who could be featured. More importantly, I wanted to find examples that offered difference—to identify and select people from as wide a range of professional fields and disciplines as possible, and within each field to seek variation and difference whenever possible.

In addition to my own research on possible subjects, I received recommendations and referrals from various professional bodies and organisations, as well as suggestions from friends and colleagues. Access to the subjects' own contacts and network of black peers and professional colleagues was another much appreciated source of information. There were also a small number of subjects with whom I was already acquainted, either having known them on a professional basis or through personal friendship.

Perhaps my biggest regret in carrying out this project is that I did not have the opportunity to personally interview a number of individuals whom I was especially determined to feature in the book. Although most expressed a willingness to participate, their schedules and other commitments did not in the end enable us to meet in the time allowed. However, because I felt that a *Millennium People* book of successful black British individuals would be lacking if certain people were not included, I decided to add a short selection of brief profiles to bridge this gap.

This book has been a labour of love. It was conceived as a personal mission rather than a commercial venture. Some twenty months of my life, and that of my family (both vicariously and directly), were ultimately devoted to the project. Much effort was put into each of its various stages—from the initial background research and groundwork preparations to writing up the interviews. The intermediate stages involved establishing contact with my chosen subjects, persuading them—sometimes through their agents or representatives—to participate, and finding time in their busy schedules to carry out the interviews. The interviews themselves presented their own challenges. The subjects were invariably pressed for time and I also needed to get a satisfactory photographic image from the session.

The pleasures derived from the project were gained in many ways and from many sources. I gained, of course, much satisfaction in simply knowing that I had finally found the courage, made the time—initially by taking a year's career break from my job at the BBC—and committed the necessary resources to get the project off the ground. Sponsorship from Paterson Group International, the UK photographic equipment manufacturers (who were at the time launching their new black and white film product), was not only of great practical help in reducing project costs, but was important for the morale-boosting endorsement that it offered in the initial stages. I am indebted to Paterson for their kind support.

Another satisfactory aspect of the project was the opportunity it gave me to meet and engage with a talented and inspiring group of people, many of whom I had long admired but, in most cases, from a distance. The effort and chase of securing an interview, and then the logistics of getting from one interview to another (occasionally at opposite ends of the country), were more than compensated by the inspiring life stories of each of my subjects and by the warmth, openness and generosity of spirit in which they responded to my verbal and photographic probings. In some cases, the interviews allowed me to renew and strengthen long-standing friendships, in others it was a pleasure and a privilege to be able to form new friendships.

At every interview I learnt a great deal about the line of work or business in which each was engaged, and felt privileged to be given a glimpse into their personal and professional lives, and to learn how they got to where they are today, the goals they had set out with and the issues they had had to deal with along the way, as well as to explore their personal vision for the future—all the more poignant as we enter a new millennium. My hope is that I have done justice to the wealth of information which they entrusted to me, and that I have also adequately reflected, both pictorially and through the written profiles, something of the remarkable personal qualities and the energy and drive of my subjects.

Whilst not intending to produce any blueprint or write a text on the drivers for achieving professional success, I believe readers—whether black or white—can gain insight and inspiration from the various profiles on what it takes to climb the ladder of success and, in the process, remain human and aware of the needs of others.

Another pleasure derived from undertaking this project was the chance to renew contact with Professor Chris Mullard, who has written the Foreword for *Millennium People.* My acquaintance with Professor Mullard and his work goes back almost twenty-five years, to 1975 when I chose his book, *Black Power in Britain,* as a prize on winning my school's award for economics—the choice of which I recall raised a few eyebrows in the predominantly white grammar school which I attended. Some fifteen years later, when our paths crossed professionally, I surprised him by asking him to sign my still treasured copy. Ten years later, and still greatly impressed by his learned vision and his now international work and standing in the field of equality and diversity, it seemed wholly appropriate and something of a completing of the circle, to ask Professor Mullard to provide the Foreword for my own book. This he has done with great insight.

Readers will note that I use the term 'black' throughout the book, and I feel I should explain what I mean by this term and why I selected subjects within this definition. For *Millennium People,* I have purposely used the term 'black' to denote people of African and Caribbean origin—that is, people of colour from the wider African diaspora—rather than the broader, more political definition of 'black' (to which, in other contexts, I wholeheartedly subscribe) as denoting all peoples of colour, regardless of their national or ethnic origins.

I deliberately chose to focus on the black British population of African Caribbean origin, in part for practical and logistical reasons, but also - more fundamentally - because I believe there to be a more pressing need for the achievements of this group to be highlighted. On a practical level, being black British myself—I was born in the Caribbean, on the island of Curaçao, and brought up in London from the age of four—enabled me to identify with many of the individuals featured in this book, to establish rapport with them, and to relate to many of the experiences they recounted. My links with other people of African Caribbean origin, both personal and professional, of course, also provided me with helpful contacts and inroads to my target group.

On a more fundamental level, however, I felt that there was a great need for a book of this nature, and at this point in time, which focused on Britain's black African Caribbean population, because of the countless and often negative stereotypes which still exist about this section of the population, even as we move towards the twenty-first century. Ours is a community which is, at times, still struggling to break free from the debilitating impact of low expectations and negative opinions imposed on it by others, as witnessed by some of the experiences recounted by the *Millennium People* subjects.

Although there is another publication with a somewhat similar treatment, a British book published in 1997 entitled *Women of Substance* by Pushpinder Chowdhry, which profiles over *200* Asian women who have made their mark in British society, nothing comparable has been written on, or for, Britain's African Caribbean population. I hope, therefore, that this book will help to redress the balance, and that the results will shed some light and possibly provoke some discussion on a subject too often overlooked or not seen as important: the 'irresistible rise' of Britain's black population.

For those interested in the practical and technical aspects of the project, the basic details were as follows: All the interviews and photographic sessions took place during 1998. I used two cameras for the photographic work - a single lens reflex Canon EOS camera and a Bronica ETRS medium format camera - together with a variety of portable studio flash lights for inside shots. Virtually all of the portraits shown in the book were in fact taken with the more adept medium format camera. There was a great challenge in turning up at an unknown location and trying both to interview and capture photographically, my subject in as meaningful way as possible, all against the unrelenting pressure of the clock. In most cases I only had the one opportunity—usually consisting of no more than an hour or two—to get what I wanted and be gone. I received invaluable help and technical support in selecting and presenting the photographs in the book from what must be the best-equipped photo studio of its kind in South East Asia. I am particularly indebted to Mr Teik Teo, of Sungrafix and Lingo Sdn. Bhd., Malaysia, for his superb technical assistance and unceasing good nature in the face of my continued needs and requests.

One of the topics which I explored in my discussions with the subjects portrayed in the book was their view of the present position of black people in British society as we near the end of the twentieth century, and how they see that position changing, if at all, in the new millennium. Were they optimistic, or perhaps fearful, of what the future holds for Britain's black population? I offer my personal thoughts and observations as we approach the twenty-first century.

This last year of the twentieth century has, if anything, seen an added focus on 'race relations' issues within British society. Tension was briefly and dramatically heightened by the bombings which occurred in areas distinctly associated with London's black and Asian communities, and more tragically, in the heart of London's gay community. The Macpherson report issued in 1999 by the Home Secretary's appointed Inquiry into the Death of Stephen Lawrence, and the resultant Government response to its findings and recommendations, also received considerable media coverage and public airing. The murder by racist thugs of Stephen Lawrence, a young black schoolboy, on the streets of London, and the inept handling of the investigation by the Metropolitan Police, graphically revealed that the ghosts of racism have not been laid to rest.

However, the response of the Government and other authorities to these incidents did at least indicate that they recognised there is still much to be done to make Britain a truly multi-racial and multi-cultural society, and one which genuinely embraces and values diversity. Further evidence that the twin adversaries of discrimination and disadvantage are still alive and well in British society, is also regularly confirmed by statistics and surveys. Indeed, without seeking to dwell on the topic in my interviews, many of the *Millennium People* nonetheless volunteered their personal experiences of this issue.

Despite this situation, which clearly should not and cannot be ignored, and which needs to be properly addressed, I share the optimism expressed by many of my *Millennium People* subjects. I feel we should not be blind to the many advances made by black people in Britain. To acknowledge and celebrate this does not deny the persistence of some of the barriers which still stand in the way of progress. Rather, it demonstrates that talent, creativity and energy, if properly channelled, will find ways round whatever obstacles are put in the way.

I believe that there is an almost tangible, surging self-confidence and self-belief rising amongst black people in Britain. Over the last two decades, many breakthroughs and firsts have been achieved by black people eager to give expression to their skills and talents across a multitude of fields. In many cases, these breakthroughs have been achieved despite the obstacles, rather than because of their absence, and owe much to the tenacity, determination and drive of the individuals concerned, as witnessed by some of the examples portrayed in this book.

The question that arises is how much richer might that contribution have been if it were truly nurtured, and if whatever barriers still in existence were removed once and for all. It is crucial to the future well-being of Britain's black and other ethnic minority communities, and to the greater good of Great Britain PLC, that all talents be allowed to flourish and to reach their highest potential.

If *Millennium People - the soul of success* offers anything, I would like to feel it will be a message of hope to its readers, and especially to young black British people, those of the millennium generation, that they can do it. If their hearts and souls are really committed to achieving their goals, they will do it. To them, I offer these few parting words which sum up the essence and soul of *Millennium People:* Dream...create...excel!

Derek Burnett

Millennium People

Marianne Jean-Baptiste
Actress

Evan Williams
Dancer

Marianne Jean-Baptiste from Peckham, south east London, earned a place in British film-making history in 1997 when she was nominated for an Oscar as Best Supporting Actress in Mike Leigh's hit film, *Secrets and Lies,* the first black British artiste to be nominated for this coveted award. The nomination clearly marked her out and confirmed long-standing opinion that she is a considerable talent to note.

What further distinguishes her as a quite exceptional creative talent is that besides being an accomplished actress of both stage and screen, she composes musical scores—she co-wrote the score of a subsequent Mike Leigh film, *Career Girls,* of which she is as proud as of her acting—and she is also a playwrite. If that were not enough, she is no mean singer and musician. This basket of talent is held by someone who initially wanted to become a barrister, and who had quite a pivotal decision to make about whether to go to university to study law or to opt for acting and go to drama school. Marianne Jean-Baptiste modestly says, 'I am only now coming to terms with being an actress.'

In fact, Marianne's professional destiny may have been mapped out from an early age. She recalls doing drama at seven and being asked at primary school to play the guitar to the rest of her class. She was frequently told by teachers and other observers how good she was at both music and drama.

She smilingly adds, 'My family are all quite "theatrical", though none of them work in the business.' This did not stop her parents—who came from the Caribbean islands of Antigua and St Lucia—from giving Marianne constant encouragement and practical support, allowing her to attend a variety of after-school and weekend dance and drama classes. Marianne also fondly remembers the help she received from certain teachers at school who took an interest in nurturing and encouraging her talent, and laments the closing down of the children's drama groups which she attended.

Having taken the decision not to go to university, Marianne chose instead to apply to RADA, although, she says, 'some people tried to deter me from even auditioning

there on the basis that RADA reputedly didn't take black people, but that for me was all the more reason why I wanted to try to get in there!' Marianne did indeed secure a place at RADA, and whilst still a student got her first acting job at the Lyric Theatre, Hammersmith. She also earnt her actor's Equity card and wrote the first of her plays to be professionally performed.

Reflecting on her career to now, Marianne Jean-Baptiste comments on how relatively naïve she was about the significance of the Oscar nomination. 'What immediately came into my mind was that being nominated for an Oscar meant that people whom I greatly admire, such as Robert De Niro and Samuel L. Jackson, had seen me act,' she says, 'and that meant a lot to me!' Indeed, one of the career highlights Marianne mentions was when the actor Samuel L. Jackson came over to her at the Golden Globe award ceremony to say how much he had enjoyed seeing her work. Marianne is very proud of the African American Award for Excellence which she received for her performance in *Secrets and Lies,* which was presented to her by the famous American writer Maya Angelou.

Marianne is honest about the fact that being a black British actress has at times been difficult. She cannot help contrast the lacklustre attention she believes she receives from the British media and the sporadic offers of work which she gets in Britain with those of some of her white female RADA contemporaries. It is a situation she hopes will improve for herself and other black British artistes in the new millennium.

Likewise, Marianne hopes that she might one day get an opportunity to try directing films, and laughingly confesses, 'I would really love to write and direct a film... now that would be a real achievement!' The Oscars had better take note, Marianne Jean-Baptiste is planning to be back, either as an actress, a musical score composer, director or writer, or just possibly combining all these roles in the one film. It is neither a secret nor a lie to say we are going to hear a lot more of Marianne Jean-Baptiste in the future.

I was fortunate to catch up with Evan Williams when he was spending precious time at home with his actress wife—Marianne Jean-Baptiste—and their lovely baby daughter. Over the past few years, Evan Williams has spent a great deal of time with various dance companies, taking dance productions to the distant corners of the world. He is a classically trained and highly accomplished dancer who has spent time with the Alvin Ailey American Dance Theater—the prestigious contemporary dance company of New York—a dance company in Switzerland, and with the Birmingham Royal Ballet, where he started his professional career.

'I started dancing at twelve, in the mid-1980s, when there was something of a dance boom in the UK. Fame was on television and a BBC documentary series was aired portraying the life of dancers called On the Male Dancer. Both programmes really inspired me,' says Evan Williams, although he candidly admits that since none of his friends or family danced or had any experience of professional dancing, he still had to overcome a certain amount of reticence, as well as plain prejudice, in choosing to make dance his career, especially as a male dancer. 'But I am quite strong-minded,' says Evan, 'and didn't feel that I had to follow the masses. Initially, it was not even about making a career, but simply that I liked doing it.'

At school, with his interest in dance already wetted, he was fortunate to be able to choose dance as one of his O level options. The opportunity this afforded him to go to see dance companies and drama productions perform in theatres and auditoriums, to which, as a black working class boy he had never previously had such exposure confirmed what Evan wanted to do with his life. 'I was totally mesmerised by the idea of being in a theatre, the lights, the stage... the whole magical experience of it.'

At sixteen, Evan Williams successfully auditioned for the Royal Ballet School where he spent three years learning his craft. On graduation, he was invited to join the Birmingham Royal Ballet company—a significant achievement given the very few contracts offered to the many applicants who try to get into the company, and the further

and The Dancer

number who occasionally get to dance with the company but are not taken on permanently. He became the first black dancer to join the company. But, undoubtedly, Evan Williams's boldest career move was made some years later when, as he says, 'I literally got myself on a plane to New York and turned up at the acclaimed Alvin Ailey dance company and asked for an audition.... I arrived as a complete nobody... And I got in! It really boosted my self-esteem and gave me confirmation of my talents'.

All of the dance companies with which Evan Williams has performed have been touring companies, and of the many countries he has visited and the numerous productions he has danced, Evan cites a tour of China as the real highlight. He also recalls the sheer thrill and emotion of dancing the ballet 'Revelations', of which he says proudly, 'Dancing that piece and feeling the audience's reaction is incredible. The reception is the same all round the world; it really moves people'.

Evan Williams acknowledges some of the great classical choreographers as people who most inspire him, such as the American Ulysses Dove. Closer to home, he also expresses admiration for the Lawrence family—whose son Stephen was killed in a racist attack—whose determined action and faith in persisting with the tragic issue of their son's untimely death, he believes, forced it to national attention.

'It has not been easy being a black dancer,' admits Evan. 'Racism can sometimes be very blatant in this profession.' That said, he remains optimistic about the future in the field of dance, and in society more generally. 'Things are changing, and will change more rapidly as our generation emerges and gets into positions of power and influence. It's already happening but will gather pace in the future,' asserts Evan. He also hopes that the millennium will see dance receive more attention and exposure by the media, commensurate to that given to other art forms. With his acknowledged talent and a determination to succeed, the elegant form of Evan Williams is clearly intent on being visible, not only on dance stages of the world, but in other mediums as well.

Artistic partnership

Dotun Adebayo
Publisher, The XPress

I interviewed Dotun Adebayo for *Millennium People* on a Saturday morning at The XPress offices in east London. After a typically busy week attending to the company's core business of publishing books, Dotun was running a weekend workshop for new and aspiring black writers, one of the company's initiatives to develop black literary talent and, as Dotun Adebayo says, 'because we want to give something back to the community'. Listening to the session whilst waiting for the opportunity to interview and photograph him, what became abundantly clear was not only Dotun Adebayo's easy rapport with those attending, but his infectious enthusiasm for the written word. If his passion for literature is transferred to the next generation of writers, along with his practical advice and suggestions, Dotun Adebayo will rightly be able to take credit for fostering a number of budding literary talents, and The XPress may one day receive their manuscripts for consideration and possible publication.

Dotun Adebayo is one of the co-founders of The XPress publishing house. Starting very modestly in 1992, The XPress has forged a niche for itself by providing popular fiction for a previously ignored black readership. Although still a relatively small publishing house, the company has nonetheless published over forty titles under its three imprints and has sold thousands of copies of each title. The XPress represents the company's main business, although it also publishes the '20/20' and 'Nia' imprints which cater to a slightly different readership. Their products, however, are still essentially 'black books'. The XPress's biggest selling book, *Baby Father* by Patrick Augustus, although out of print for over two years at one stage, sold over 25,000 copies, whilst its first book, *Yardie* by Victor Headley, sold 12,000 copies largely through word-of-mouth before being reprinted in paperback by Pan Books. It went on to sell another 50,000 copies.

The XPress is unashamedly commercial in its approach, although as Dotun points out: 'We have the potential to influence a whole generation of the black community. We can and do give messages through our books.' With most of its books being written by first-time authors. The XPress has, in its seven years of operation, succeeded in providing a much needed outlet for black literary talent, one which other publishers have since recognised and have now also begun to trawl. Dotun Adebayo's enterprise has also given literary expression to aspects of the black British cultural experience, since many of the novels are written in a black street language style or else reflect, though fiction, issues of concern and interest to a predominantly young black readership. This focus has, however, also attracted a certain amount of controversy from the standpoint that it glorifies only one narrow view of black British culture.

If his company is now established in the British literary market, Dotun Adebayo freely admits that it was by no means easy. 'We started out with £1,500, each putting in what we could, and you cannot really start a company with that little capital without going through some pain, and we did go through a lot of pain. But', he adds with evident pride, 'we have turned a corner and I now feel that I have the best job in the world.'

The XPress was born 'by luck' says Dotun. He was working at the time as the Music Editor of *The Voice* newspaper, where Steve Pope was Editor, when they were approached by a mutual friend—Victor Headley—seeking advice on getting a screenplay he was writing into film. With no experience of the film industry, but having read and liked what Victor had scripted, Dotun and Steve agreed to help him. They decided that the best way to create interest would be to bring the screenplay out initially as a novel. Together with the author they set about editing and reshaping it into book form and then prepared it for print on a computer at home. Whilst maintaining their day jobs and working through the night to produce the book. The XPress's first novel, *Yardie,* was born.

Again, with no real knowledge of sales, marketing or distribution, Dotun recalls that he sold copies of the book from the boot of his car, or turned up at bookshops with copies in a plastic bag. Hoping to sell about 1,000 copies to make the venture worthwhile, they eventually sold 12,000 copies. *Yardie* was subsequently made into a film.

Victor Headley, the author of *Yardie,* is still with The XPress, declining to go elsewhere when it would perhaps have been more lucrative for him to do so. He has since written two sequels. The success of *Yardie* attracted other aspiring black writers, and with the experience gained from their first venture—although Dotun adds 'we are still learning every day'—both Dotun Adebayo and Steve Pope decided that they had a business in the making and gave up their day jobs to properly establish The XPress. Dotun says, 'I could have stayed in journalism and probably had an easier life, but nothing beats working for yourself. The sum total of our success is that there are now many authors out there whom we have helped get started, and whose livelihoods are now tied up with our business.'

While luck played a hand in getting The XPress started— 'if Victor had not come to me with his manuscript I might not be in publishing today'—Dotun believes that the key to the success of the venture was that he and Steve had spent many previous years in journalism learning their craft. 'It was that background which made it feasible for me to go into publishing,' says Dotun. He reflects with admiration and gratitude on the approach taken by his Nigerian parents when he was growing up. Dotun, who came to the UK at six, and the other Adebayo siblings, were made to go to their local library each day whilst their friends were out playing. 'And', says Dotun, 'we were made to give our father a synopsis of each book we had read and be prepared to be quizzed about it. We virtually read the entire library! I didn't appreciate it at the time but I can certainly see what it did for me now.' There was also a high value placed on education in the Adebayo household, and all five children went on to university. Indeed, it was whilst he was studying at Stockholm University that he was given his first break in journalism—'writing a music article for a newspaper in Danish!'

Of his goals and hopes for the future, Dotun says, 'Our agenda was never to be "get rich quick merchants" but to do something positive for ourselves and for our community,' though he adds for good measure, 'But it would be nice to one day be able to walk into Penguin Books and make a down payment to buy the company!' His personal goal, he says, is simply 'to be a good role model', and he hopes that the millennium will bring with it the reality that every black child in the UK will have the opportunity to explore and exploit their individual talents. Dotun Adebayo is making his personal contribution to that goal by providing a vehicle for black literary expression and is smart enough to make The XPress a very successful business enterprise as well.

The success xpress

Richard Adeshiyan
Journalist and Media Consultant

'**I** have my fingers in a lot of pies,' says Richard Adeshiyan. This is indeed true. His various work commitments and professional projects span all the main news mediums. 'In essence', Richard asserts, 'I am a media man. I like to work across the whole spectrum rather than be confined to one particular discipline or field.'

Although Richard Adeshiyan is by profession a print journalist, with experience at various levels in that medium, he has also worked as a television producer. Yet his real forté is due largely to the fact that he has amassed an extensive range of contacts across the media. Richard Adeshiyan is hired by television companies, independent production houses, newspapers and publications to help facilitate their projects—especially where there is a black or ethnic minority perspective involved— by utilising the expertise, skills and innumerable contacts he has accumulated over the years.

He gives some examples of recent projects. One was with a well-known television company where the production team put together a major documentary on the sensitive topic of juvenile gang rape. Through Richard's careful and considered approach, and his innumerable contacts, a potentially controversial topic was dealt with sensitively. He was also involved, from the development stage as an Associate Producer, in putting together a television documentary series due to be aired in autumn 1999, on the impact and legacy of slavery as it relates to Britain.

Of the niche which he has created for himself, and which he hopes to develop into a larger, more fully-fledged consultancy employing the skills and expertise of others, he believes he has simply recognised and is selling his uniqueness. As a black person operating in the media, he asserts, 'Beyond the specific skills we have to offer—in my case as a journalist—we also have unique experiences and contacts, and it is this which gives us added value.'

My own dealings with him in relation to *Millennium People* shed some light on that uniqueness. His extensive knowledge of Britain's black community, including how or where to make contact with particular individuals, was not only impressive but of practical benefit to the *Millennium People* project. Moreover, whenever Richard Adeshiyan's name came up in conversation in the course of my research, I heard nothing but praise and high commendation about him. He is clearly held in very high regard, testimony to his personable nature and highly developed skills as a networker.

Prior to his role as a media troubleshooter and facilitator, Richard Adeshiyan was first the Sports Editor and then the Deputy Editor of The Voice newspaper. Spending some eleven years in total with the Voice Group, he was also for a time the Managing Editor of the *Weekly Journal*—the broadsheet sister paper of *The Voice*. He followed this by becoming the founding Editor of the then new black weekly newspaper, the *New Nation*. All of these positions contributed to his wide-ranging knowledge and extensive contacts across Britain's black communities. Furthermore, as the London correspondent for the American *BET Weekend* magazine (part of the US Black Entertainment Television network), and a member of the US National Association of Black Journalists—not forgetting the time he spent as the Foreign Editor of The *Weekly Journal*—he has developed equally extensive contacts across America and elsewhere.

Richard smiles as he shares with me the story of his entry into the media. Having left school not knowing what he wanted to do for a career, he trained for several years as an athlete with the well-known Haringey Athletic Club, where he got to know many of the prominent British athletes and sporting people of the day, including Daley Thompson and the then emerging Linford Christie. He explains, 'I was reading *The Voice* one day, and on looking at the sports pages thought I could do this, especially given the people that I knew and the inside perspective to stories that I felt I could get.' He went along to see *The Voice's* Editor, Sharon Ali, and although nothing emerged at the time he began, he says, to hang around *The Voice* offices. In the end, they gave him the odd assignment— 'probably', he laughs, 'just to get me out of the way'.

He fondly remembers his first real assignment, to cover a cricket match at Lords—England versus a World XI. 'It was only a small report but it was a start,' says Richard proudly. After that he was given more regular assignments on the sports section, and years later, when the Sports Editor left, he was asked to fill the position. 'I particularly loved being able to cover all types of sports, whether boxing, athletics, football, cricket, judo—unlike the Fleet Street journalists who usually cover only one.' Developing his journalism skills as he attended all the major sporting events in the UK and worldwide, he quickly made a name for himself through his reports.

Although in his element as a Sports Editor, Richard mentions two other career highlights. As the Foreign and Managing Editor of *The Weekly Journal*, he covered the build-up to the first democratic elections in South Africa in 1994. He movingly describes the experience of being there as 'momentous, and a once-in-a-lifetime experience'. Staying at the black township home of the Political Editor of the major black South African newspaper, *The Sowetan*, while most other foreign journalists were in downtown international hotels, enabled him to cover the story from a black perspective. Another highlight of his career, he says, was the personal mountain he climbed on being appointed Editor of *The New Nation*. At the behest of the newspaper's owner, the then son-in-law of Rupert Murdoch, Richard recruited the paper's staff, found premises and produced the first edition of the new weekly in just two months. He regards it as his 'ultimate challenge'.

Needless to say, Richard Adeshiyan views himself as self-driven and declares that he does not really have role models. He nevertheless mentions two professionals whom he holds in especially high regard: Trevor Phillips for his journalistic talents, and Sharon Ali for giving him his break with *The Voice*. He also adds warmly, 'My career would not have been possible without the support of my long-suffering wife and media widow, and my daughter who have helped put the balance between my life and career in better perspective.'

Of Nigerian parentage, Richard Adeshiyan has no hesitation in referring to himself as black British. 'This is home whatever we think, or whether we feel truly accepted or not.' In Richard's view, major in-roads have been made by black people into the British mainstream. 'Things are changing,' he says, 'but it's slow.' On a personal level, Richard Adeshiyan says his goal for the future is to develop his wide-ranging media brief and establish a full media consultancy offering specialist advice to television programme makers and to the media more generally.

The photograph of Richard in this book was taken at his home. After we had finished the photo session, he started to show me some of the interesting pictures and photographs he owned. His fondness for this particular picture—of a black woman, created from hundreds of small pieces of painted paper—was so apparent that I felt compelled to show him in this light.

Heart to art

Educating the future

Keith Ajegbo
Headteacher

Twelve years in almost any job is excuse enough for being somewhat fatigued, if not a little jaded, all the more, so if those twelve years have been spent as a headteacher of a tough inner-city state secondary school. But when I met and talked with Keith Ajegbo about his school and educational matters in general, as I did at the end of a school day and the back end of a long school week, what became apparent was his good nature, enthusiasm and commitment, and how forward thinking he remains for the task and the challenges which lie ahead.

Keith Ajegbo is headteacher of Deptford Green Secondary School in the borough of Lewisham, south east London. Even in an area like Lewisham, with its strong policies and declared commitment to equal opportunities, Keith Ajegbo is still the only black headteacher of a Lewisham secondary school, although there are one or two black headteachers of primary schools. Nationwide, the figures on black headteachers, although improving, indicate that Keith Ajegbo is still one of a small minority across the country.

When Keith Ajegbo was appointed to Deptford Green Secondary School as its headteacher in 1986, its reputation with local parents was so poor that many avoided sending their children there. Keith recalls, for example, how twelve years ago its intake of new pupils would be grossly under-subscribed. For the 120 places available, the school would be lucky to receive seventy applications.

Twelve years later, under Keith's headship, the school has been significantly transformed. He takes evident pride in explaining that 'a lot of hard work was put in by everyone involved, but the effort has brought a lot of pluses'. One of those pluses, Keith points out, is that 'the school has become massively more popular. People actually compete now to get into Deptford Green. We have built a reputation with the local feeder primary schools and parents in the area as a school where children will get a good education, and that is immensely satisfying.' This has occurred despite a virtual doubling of its student size, from 600 pupils in the mid-1980s to nearly 1,200 today. Around sixty per cent of the pupils come from ethnic minority groups. The intake figures confirm this trend. In 1997, there were some 380 children applying for the school's 208 available places.

Beyond managing a school of choice, Keith Ajegbo also takes satisfaction form other key indicators that the school is on the right track. He points to the improving examination performance of the upper school, with more pupils now achieving five or more GCSE examination passes at A - C grades than ever before; the higher ratio of fifth-year pupils who now choose to stay on in the school's sixth form; and the school's commended record for retaining potentially disruptive pupils within the school, where staff help them work through their difficulties, rather than exclude them. Indeed, Deptford Green Secondary School was cited in a recent OFSTED school inspection report as being a school which offers 'good value for money'. Particular practices of the school were also singled out for special praise, most notably the school's ethos and adherence to multi-cultural education.

What makes the school's transformation and Keith's headship of it all the more notable is that the school draws its pupils from a solidly working-class inner-city area, with all the attendant issues of social deprivation and low socio-economic status. For instance, many children arrive at the school with reading ages far below average, and for many others English is often a second language. The school also caters for children with learning difficulties and those with special needs.

The difficult environment does not stop Keith Ajegbo from looking ahead with enthusiasm and resilience. To him, these issues are challenges, not problems. His goal is to raise the academic achievement of the school even further. 'I feel that there are things I can still do towards attaining our goals and I have not lost any enthusiasm for the challenge,' he declares.

It is perhaps Keith Ajegbo's own background which gives him the necessary motivation. Keith—of mixed African and white parentage—lived the early part of his life on a council housing estate not dissimilar to those where many of his pupils live, and indeed he grew up only a few miles from where he now teaches. But with support and encouragement, especially from his mother, and later a teacher who took him under his wing—whom Keith fondly remembers for helping to build his self-esteem through sport (Keith was introduced to tennis and subsequently went on to play at national level), as well as encouraging him academically—Keith Ajegbo went on to read English at Cambridge University.

Keith Ajegbo admits that at university he had no particular vocation or interest in becoming a teacher, much less a headteacher. He decided to do a post-graduate teaching diploma as a 'holding operation' whilst considering his career options. But having gone into a school as part of the training and started to teach, he recalls, 'I found I enjoyed it and decided that this was what I wanted to do.'

After teaching for a few years in an all-white grammar school in the leafy suburbs of London, Keith decided that he would prefer to teach in a school with some black pupils, not least 'for my own identity and self-fulfilment'. He jokingly recounts how he went through 'a year of hell' when he moved to his next school, an inner-city comprehensive in Wandsworth, south London, such was the vast difference. He obviously rose to the challenge because, without setting any definite career goals, he began to rapidly climb the career ladder and was appointed headteacher at the relatively young age of thirty-nine.

Keith says that the person whom he found most inspiring as he grew up was the late Arthur Ashe, then the only black tennis player on the top flight circuit, who went on to win the Wimbledon singles title in 1975. Besides meeting Arthur Ashe very briefly during his own involvement in tennis, Keith cites Arthur's great tennis skills and quiet dignity as being particularly inspiring at a time when few black people were in such prominent positions.

Looking forward to the new millennium, Keith has mixed emotions. On one level he says, 'Being in a school makes you optimistic. Ninety per cent of the children you deal with are fine, hard-working, cheerful and nice to talk to. And you are impressed with the thought that these are going to be the people who shape the future. It is why I enjoy being with young people, and why I feel so committed to education.' Equally, he declares, across London and the UK, issues of race relations and equality are improving and that too lends itself to optimism. But where he does express a level of concern is with respect to some of the issues which he believes still confront young people, such as the pressures of advertising and the damaging drug culture, as well as the wider global issues of the environment and international relations.

With committed and forward-looking people responsible for educating the millennium generation, we can look forward to the achievements and the contributions to society from a well-nurtured and well-prepared group of young people who will build on the solid foundations laid by today's educators such as Keith Ajegbo.

Parliamentary poise

Baroness Valerie Amos
Minister of State and Peer, House of Lords

Baroness Valeric Amos is one of three black peers who sit proudly in the House of Lords. Valerie Amos was created a life peer (upon which she was conferred the title 'Baroness') and introduced to the upper legislative chamber, the House of Lords, in October 1997.

Not for her a title of mere status or symbolism, Valerie is what is referred to as a 'working peer', which means that she is actively involved in all aspects of the legislative business of the House. Sitting on the Labour Government bench, she brings her expertise and experience to debates in Chamber and the Committee work of the House.

Regardless of her recent elevation to the Lords, Valerie Amos was, and is, precisely the sort of person whom I wanted to profile in this book. Her standing, reputation and record of achievement are such that when *Millennium People* was merely the seed of an idea, Valerie Amos was a name that had been slated for inclusion. Her introduction to the House of Lords simply underlines Valerie's standing and stature and, in my view, provides her with a further platform, at the very highest level, from which to make her mark.

Valerie sums up her thoughts on what it is like to be a member of the House of Lords: 'It's quite awe-inspiring ...there is something about seeing the sun shining on the Palace of Westminster, and the Lords' Chamber is really beautiful in a very ornate way. There is also a feeling of being privileged, and special, and being involved in something positive and worthwhile. But this brings with it a sense of responsibility. I am conscious of the wave of expectation from people outside. I am bringing some of the experience of what is happening to black people to the House of Lords and I do not want to let myself or other people down.'

There is, in my view, little chance that this will ever happen. Valerie Amos is one of those people who seem to take everything in their stride. Having known and observed Valerie in her professional capacity for some years, she has what I would describe as a calm, dignified, yet powerful way of getting things done. This is someone who is currently, as she says herself, 'putting down markers, getting to grips with the business of the House and its process and procedures,

learning about its conventions'. I have no doubt that once these are indeed learnt, Valerie Amos will prove to be a truly formidable parliamentarian.

What drives Valerie Amos? 'I am not a believer in standing still. I like to know what I am doing is making a difference,' she explains. Whilst at school, Valerie's early career ambition had been to be a doctor. But a strong interest in social justice and social policy led her in a somewhat different direction. Graduating with a Bachelor of Arts in Sociology from the University of Warwick and a Master's degree from Birmingham University, she found herself working as an equalities adviser within local government. After rapid promotion through the local government management chain, Valerie quickly climbed to the position of Head of Management Services for Hackney Council, one of the inner London local authorities.

In 1989, Valerie Amos was appointed Chief Executive of the Equal Opportunities Commission (EOC), a prominent national position which she occupied for four years. Valerie looks back on her time at the EOC as a period of which she is particularly proud. Certainly by the time Valerie moved on from the EOC she had succeeded in raising the organisation's profile and in building its reputation as an effective law enforcement and campaigning body.

The EOC experience also gave Valerie an opportunity and a platform from which to work at the international level, something which she continues to do privately as a development and management consultant. As one of the founding directors of an international consultancy and training partnership, Amos Fraser Bernard, Valerie acted for several years as an adviser to President Mandela's government in South Africa on public service transformation, human resources development and employment equity.

Holding positions as chairperson, deputy chair or board member on a range of committees and charities, Valerie's breadth and depth of experience, whilst still at a relatively young age, clearly marked her out for nomination to the upper house.

Asked if she ever dreamt of being where she is today, a member of the House of Lords, her instant response is 'Never. It came as a big surprise!' She admits that for her parents, who came to England as teachers from Guyana, determined to see that their children got a good education, it was a great thrill for them to see Valerie, as indeed all their children, succeed.

'When I was introduced to the Lords, friends and family from many different parts of the world came in for the ceremony,' Valerie recalls, adding ruefully, 'For me, I just wanted to get through the day without falling over my gown.'

Family support has been important to Valerie and she attributes a major part of her success to her parents, citing 'the stable, warm and loving home environment' which they provided as being the foundation upon which everything else has been built. She also fondly remembers two other positive influences in her early life. 'There were two particular teachers at school, who allowed me to flourish, one of whom especially helped me to further my love of literature which became my great interest at school and remains so today.'

Of her thoughts for the future, Valerie is forthright and upbeat. 'I am optimistic. I have to be to do what I do.' Apart from wishing to see equality and social justice issues placed higher up the political and economic agenda, she is particularly heartened by what she observes as the changed and improved relationship between young women and young men and, allied to this, the enhanced relationship between young people across all ethnic boundaries.

'This is the society I have grown up in. It's what I know and where I am comfortable, but I also have strong links with the Caribbean and with Africa and feel comfortable in all these places. A piece of me belongs to all these places I feel connected with, more than just Britain,' says Valerie.

One gets a sense that Baroness Valerie Amos is someone poised to make a significant difference at national level and beyond, but that she will continue to do so in her typically quiet and unassuming, but effective, way.

Metropolitan manager

Derrick Anderson

Chief Executive, Wolverhampton Metropolitan Borough Council

When 'DJ Dee' took second place in the 1997 national 'Revive Music' championships, few seeing him spinning his sounds would have been aware that in his other life DJ Dee is more usually known as Derrick Anderson, Chief Executive Officer (CEO) of a local authority employing over 12,500 staff and responsible for an annual budget of around £250m.

In talking to Derrick Anderson, I sense that his disk jockey interludes give him almost as much pleasure and satisfaction as his professional responsibilities and accomplishments, and that he thrives on not being pigeon-holed or restricted to a conventional career path. 'I don't like labels,' he says. 'My vision in life is about growing as a person rather than aspiring to hold a particular job....I try wherever possible to immerse myself in situations where I am going to learn and grow.'

Derrick Anderson has been CEO and Policy Adviser to Wolverhampton Metropolitan Borough Council since 1996. At forty-one he is the youngest CEO of any metropolitan local authority in the UK. He is also the CEO for the West Midlands local authorities joint pension fund, a body which administers and determines the investment policy for the £4 billion pension fund, as well as Chairperson of the West Midlands local authorities' Chief Executives' Group.

Born in the East End of London but spending most of his formative years in Handsworth, Birmingham, Derrick's route to the top (like his musical interests) did not follow a conventional path. From the age of nine he set himself the goal of going to university. The young Derrick Anderson decided that he wanted to study psychology. Troubled by the events of his childhood, when issues of 'race' often bubbled on or near the surface, he believed psychology held the key to understanding people and was a tool for making sense of the world about him.

Derrick Anderson did indeed go on to achieve his desired goal of getting to university, graduating in 1978 in his chosen field of psychology. After studying for a postgraduate qualification, he embarked on a career in the probation service. But it was not long though before his idealism and enthusiasm for this work began to become blunted by what he saw as institutional inertia and inflexibility. Disillusioned, he left the service after a couple of years.

For a while, Derrick considered the notion of working abroad, but decided instead to look for a new challenge in the UK. This came in the form of a music studio, Delkas Community Music Project, in partnership with his brother. Apart from satisfying his love of music, the aim was to help young people find a creative outlet for their talents and aspirations, and provide them with skills and know-how for possible careers in the music industry.

Such was its success that before long the studio's work, and the name of the Anderson brothers, received wider publicity. After two or three years running the music studio, Derrick Anderson was approached by the West Midlands arm of the UK national sports body—the Sports Council—to run a similar project, known as Action Sports, with an emphasis on outreaching to young people through sports development.

Still only in his mid-twenties, Derrick found himself managing some thirty-eight professional staff and being responsible for over 300 sports trainees. Although possessing no formal management qualifications or experience, Derrick felt that what he had to offer and what set him aside from others, was his passion for the value of outreach and his background and training in social intervention. Not only did he acquire the tools and experience which were to lay the foundation for the position he now occupies, but he also established a professional mentoring relationship with the then Director of the project, Charlie Burnup, a relationship which Derrick warmly acknowledges has helped shape and guide him to this day.

'I believe in this thing called "happen-stance", where things happen at the right time for the right reasons,' he explains. Charlie Burnup was, he believes, one of those happen-stances, 'someone who helped frame my view of the world and my understanding of what I could and could not achieve. He became a tremendous teacher for me.'

In addition to Charlie Burnup, Derrick attributes his accomplishments to the strong support and encouragement of his family, in particular his mother. 'I watched her struggle and make all the sacrifices that mothers do to keep the family together....I am driven now to make a contribution which she can feel proud of,' says Derrick. And on a lighter note, perhaps emphasising his wish not to be pigeon-holed, Derrick admitted that another source of inspiration for him as a youngster was the comic strip character, 'the Black Panther', found in the Marvel comics, whom he describes as the only black superhero figure of his day that he could relate to.

After Action Sports, Derrick held various management positions in the arts field, eventually becoming Director of Leisure Services at Wolverhampton Council—itself a chief officer position—while still only in his early thirties. Five years later, he was appointed to the top job of CEO and Policy Adviser for the Council despite coming from a non 'front-line' department.

He feels it a definite advantage that the Council, perhaps by virtue of the location, size and political make-up of the city of Wolverhampton, has stayed out of the media limelight. This, according to Derrick, does not reflect the regard with which the city and its local authority is held in official or governmental circles. He points out that in several service fields Wolverhampton is acknowledged as being at the forefront of pioneering and innovative work. He is, for example, particularly proud of the work done to regenerate the inner city area of Wolverhampton, aspects of which were started by Derrick himself in his former capacity as Director of Leisure Services. 'This work', he says, 'has brought a sector of the town back to life that had effectively been dead.'

Derrick also proclaimed his pride in getting the Council committed to providing a leadership challenge to other private and public sector employers across the city, the aim being to get them to achieve genuine diversity in their employment practices in order to better reflect the multi-cultural make-up of the city's population. 'There is still far too much to do to be complacent or self-satisfied. I feel I need a further two or three years before a proper assessment can be made of what has been achieved during my time as CEO,' says Derrick. 'I am not looking for greatness but neither am I a martyr. I view myself as the cement in the wall and my task is to hold the wall together rather than to be the more evident or decorative brickwork,' he adds.

That wall—today in the case of Wolverhampton local authority, but tomorrow quite possibly some other part of UK PLC—is undoubtedly stronger because of Derrick Anderson's contribution, and will continue to be strengthened by his continued presence. Perhaps when he has finished making a difference in his professional capacity, Derrick Anderson might be tempted to try and match, if not surpass this in his other, less formal pursuit - his love of music. Certainly, Derrick remains very positive for the new millennium. 'It fills me with great optimism to see where and how black people are making a difference to the public and private life of the UK.'

Team maker

Viv Anderson

Football Manager

Viv Anderson is one of those familiar names, particularly to sports or football enthusiasts, that suggests it has been around for a long time. At the same time, his is not a name to be found occupying as much space on the news, gossip or social pages as on the sports pages. For here is a person who does not court controversy, seek the limelight or hire a phalanx of public relations agents. He has, instead, over the years simply got on with, and applied himself diligently to his sporting life. He is also someone who has remained decidedly modest about his considerable sporting accomplishments.

My own efforts to persuade him to allow me to interview him for inclusion in *Millennium People* certainly bear witness to this observation. It took numerous telephone calls and a brisk exchange of correspondence to convince him that I was serious in wishing to have the privilege of featuring him in the book.

Viv Anderson, the football player, made his league debut for Nottingham Forest football club in 1974, aged seventeen, and went on to win virtually every honour in football over a distinguished playing career spanning more than twenty years. Amongst his many achievements was being the first black football player to play for England at the international level. At the time, this represented a milestone in the development of English football, the impact of which cannot be fully appreciated today when football fans are used to seeing three or four black players at any one time playing on the England team with such frequency that we no longer need to count.

Although he has now retired from playing, it is Viv Anderson, the young and still emerging football *manager,* that I especially wanted to portray in *Millennium People.* For it is as a football manager that Viv Anderson is someone to watch as we enter the new millennium.

The reality, of course, is that Viv Anderson, the player, goes hand in hand with Viv Anderson, the manager. One follows and flows from the other in a logical career development path. My selected photographic portrait of Viv shows him still bedecked in kit, holding aloft a football much as he would were he still a player, because one cannot portray Viv Anderson, the manager, without reference to Viv Anderson, the player.

'Long legs and longevity' is how one football commentator summed up Viv Anderson, while another described him as a 'winner and model professional'. In my view, he was, and is, all of these.

In over twenty seasons as a professional footballer, Viv saw and did it all, playing for some of the biggest clubs in English football, including Manchester United, Arsenal and Nottingham Forest. He won European Cup, League Championship, FA Cup and League Cup winner's medals, all of which no doubt sit nicely in his trophy cabinet alongside the thirty caps he gained for England.

Indeed, Viv is particularly well remembered for winning his first England cap. As both a black man and a football enthusiast of much the same age as Viv, I remember well the feeling of pride it raised in me at the time, and I asked Viv for his own recollections of the occasion. 'I knew it was a big issue,' he explained. 'There were debates about it on the television, and I remember receiving a congratulatory telegram from Elton John. But for me, I just wanted to do well on the night for my father who was there in the stands, the rest of my family watching on television, and most importantly, for myself.'

Viv acknowledges the vital role played by his family in helping him to where he is today. In acknowledging the many people who have helped him along the way, he cites an impressive list of names that would grace any 'Who's Who' of football greats—from the scout who first saw him, aged thirteen, playing with his father on a beach, through to Dave McKay who gave him his first break in football, to the likes of Brian Clough, Alex Ferguson, and Ron Greenwood—but he says proudly that over and above all these his parents were the backbone of his career.

My discussion with Viv shed light not only on his enduring success as a player but also gave a glimpse of the character and focus which no doubt provide the foundation for his continuing success as a manager. 'I am a very single-minded person. The desire or fire to succeed can only come from within,' he says as he shares with me the story of how, not long after getting over the disappointment of being rejected as a schoolboy by the club for which he had set his heart on playing (Manchester United), Viv was advised by a doctor that he would have to give special attention to a knee injury to prevent his knee from collapsing, thus ending his career before it had even properly started.

For the next twenty years, Viv Anderson made it his business to be the first player at training sessions each morning to carry out special strengthening exercises for his knee. In all his years as a professional player, not only did his knee not collapse but Viv Anderson only ever missed one day of training.

On retiring from his playing career, Viv found himself once again in a pioneering role. He became only the third black manager of any English football league team when he was appointed manager of Barnsley Football Club, and later, the first black manager in the top flight when he joined his good friend, Bryan Robson, as assistant manager at Middlesbrough Football Club. 'We have a unique relationship here where we share the management responsibility. I feel I therefore have an impact on everything that goes on at this club,' Viv explains.

Six years into football management, after a long playing career, but still as enthusiastic and fresh as ever, Viv revealed the secret of his staying power: 'As a manager you have to eat, sleep and drink football,' he says. 'I still have a great love and passion for the game.' As a management pair, he and Bryan Robson have already chalked up significant achievements at Middlesbrough. The club has been twice promoted to the premier league and has secured a brace of cup final appearances to complement the big names they have attracted to play for the club. But perhaps the most telling achievement for a club not really used to winning trophies is the fact that in a relatively short space of time Viv Anderson and his management colleagues have awakened a sleeping giant and have turned what was a fairly average club into one which now has the third highest crowd attendances in all of English football.

Asked about his experiences as one of the few black football managers in England, Viv's response was characteristic: 'Being a black manager has not been an issue, respect is the key issue, and I have earned that by what I have already achieved in the game.'

While Viv Anderson's parents are from Jamaica, England is very much this football great's home. 'I don't know any other culture,' he says. This is fortunate for England (and Britain) because, just as he led the quiet revolution of black British footballers so that they have now become an integral part of the multi-racial fabric of the game, Viv Anderson is once again in his quiet and unassuming way taking the revolution forward into the management of the game.

Fitzroy Andrew

Chief Executive Officer, the Windsor Fellowship

Fitzroy Andrew is the likeable and charismatic Chief Executive Officer of the acclaimed Windsor Fellowship, a charitable enterprise which conducts training programmes for high-achieving black and Asian graduates. Fitzroy Andrew is himself a high-flying black management executive who has devoted much of his own career to 'trying to make a difference'. Ignoring the lure of higher monetary rewards in management in private industry, Fitzroy is committed to developing the work of the Windsor Fellowship and, as he puts it, 'making it a brand name or byword for quality professional development'.

The Windsor Fellowship was established in 1986 following a major conference in Windsor attended by, amongst other influential participants, HRH The Prince of Wales. The conference was convened in the aftermath of the urban riots and social unrest which had erupted in many of the major cities throughout England and Wales in the mid-1980s. One of the practical initiatives which arose from the conference was the establishment of the Windsor Fellowship, which seeks to bridge the gap between companies and organisations committed to ensuring equal opportunities and diversity within their workforce, and the many black and Asian graduates who, despite such commitment, still have difficulty securing good employment. Through the Fellowship, black and Asian graduates are linked with an affiliated employer which undertakes to sponsor them by offering training or work placements in their company for a designated period.

In nearly fourteen years of operation, the Windsor Fellowship programme—with Fitzroy Andrew as its Chief Executive for the last two years—has had several hundred black and Asian graduates successfully complete the programme and go on to secure good career positions with either their sponsoring companies or elsewhere in industry, commerce or the public sector. The success of the Windsor Fellowship, Fitzroy explains, is such that places on the programme are now highly competitive. Moreover, affiliated companies are involved less for reasons of social responsibility than in the past, and more for straightforward business reasons. 'Today's perspective is more market driven—it's about getting good people into jobs,' says Fitzroy Andrew, adding that 'employers are now given access through the Windsor Fellowship to quality people whom they might otherwise have found difficult to attract.'

Fitzroy and his team of twenty-five staff have a specific goal in sight. They are working towards successfully recruiting the thousandth graduate of the Windsor Fellowship programme—the only one of its type in Europe—by the end of the year 2000. 'That would convey something quite powerful about the Windsor Fellowship,' says Fitzroy proudly. 'It would also, hopefully, begin to create a critical mass of black and Asian alumni of the programme out there in industry, many of them in senior decision-making positions. We might then begin to see things take off.'

Fitzroy Andrew oozes leadership qualities, and indeed was told as much at the grammar school he attended in east London. He recalls happily how one teacher in particular, Alan Chidwick, would single him out for special praise and encouragement, telling the young Fitzroy, 'You have got something special, you're a natural leader.' As the eldest of eight children whose parents separated when he was still at school, Fitzroy decided at eighteen not to go on to university despite his strong academic achievements, because he wanted to make a contribution to the household income. As an early sign of his leadership potential, within a year of starting his first job as an accounts clerk with the London Electricity Board, Fitzroy was promoted to office manager and given responsibility for the whole department, recognition indeed for the youngest member of staff. Fitzroy's leadership qualities and accumulation of practical experience have served him well in his working life.

Periods spent with McDonalds and then in local government in his twenties led him to realise that he especially liked the people development side of business. Fitzroy confesses that it was also the one and only time he engaged in a concrete piece of career planning, setting himself the goal of becoming a personnel director by the time he was thirty. Smiling broadly, Fitzroy recalls how just three months prior to his thirtieth birthday, he was appointed personnel director for an Area Health Authority in south east London which employed several thousand staff. He was subsequently head-hunted to set up and manage the national fast-track graduate development scheme for the National Health Service, before moving on to become a management consultant with the Office of Public Management—a well-known and respected independent think-tank and research body.

Taking stock of his career, besides his present work with the Windsor Fellowship, Fitzroy takes particular pride and satisfaction in his work as personnel director with another training and development organisation. Project Fullemploy, which aimed to increase the skills base of black and ethnic minority young people. 'Linbert Spencer, then Chief Executive of the organisation, was the first black person I had actually worked for in a line management capacity, and he was a great role model and inspiration.' Fitzroy also draws satisfaction from a research report he wrote whilst at the Office of Public Management. Not only did the report—*Not Just Black and White*—win an award and attract acclaim for quality research of its type, but its subject—the differences in career development between black and white managers in the UK—was, and remains, a topic close to his heart. Fitzroy is similarly pleased that he had the opportunity, albeit fifteen years after leaving school, to complete a part-time Master's degree at Bristol University.

Fitzroy is quick to acknowledge that probably the most influential people in his life have been his mother and his close-knit family. 'I am though essentially self-reliant, as I believe that fundamentally you have to be your own role model.' He laughs as he jokingly makes the point, 'I believe in myself. I have a big mouth and I am pushy, although I would like to think that as I have got older I also know a little better when to keep my mouth shut.'

Of his future plans, Fitzroy Andrew says he wants to develop further the Windsor Fellowship and to set a good example for his children. He also expresses optimism for the millennium. 'The most damaging thing for black people is to be pessimistic. It's not to deny reality—yes, racial discrimination is around and real—but as a community we are at a turning point. I hope the millennium will bring with it a demonstration of the black community's maturity and our coming of age.' He adds, 'I have no trouble calling myself a black Londoner—London is my home and I love the place.'

With his undoubted leadership qualities and vision for the way ahead, there is, I am sure, much more to be heard from this assured and accomplished black Londoner—Fitzroy Andrew.

In fellowship

Sky Andrew

Football Agent

Listening to Sky Andrew speak about his work as a football agent is as refreshing as it is revealing. Sky Andrew is Britain's sole black football agent, operating, some would say, in a field and at a time when commercial considerations are often to the fore, if not all important. This is not altogether surprising given the huge sums of money at stake in professional football, the very competitive environment and the relatively short professional lifespan of today's players. One would think that if anyone in the realm of professional football is going to espouse such pecuniary considerations it will be 'the football agent'. Yet Sky Andrew defies this popular, if not stereotyped, impression of a football agent. He is, in many respects, everything that the fictitious American football agent, Jerry Maguire (played by Tom Cruise in the film of the same name), aspires to be. Sky Andrew's conversation, for example, is littered with expressions like 'having good Karma', 'the importance of morality, integrity and sense of duty' and 'doing good in society'.

Sky Andrew is the football agent for Sol Campbell, England and Tottenham Hotspurs' rising star, and acts on behalf of a string of other young, emerging professional football players whom he describes as 'great prospects for the future'. Alongside his work representing professional footballers, Sky also handles corporate promotions and public relations projects for major UK companies such as British Airways, Heinz and One to One. He sees synergy between the two services his agency provides; he believes his corporate clients and contacts offer potential sponsorship opportunities for his football clients, and that his football contacts similarly offer interesting marketing opportunities for his corporate clients.

Although his is still a small sports management and public relations firm, this has not stopped Sky from receiving what he describes as 'two huge offers' from major American concerns to buy out his company while retaining him as managing director. 'Although other UK football agents have already chosen to go down that route', says Sky, 'that is not what I am about. I don't want to be successful but have to change who I am, and how I do things. I have dreams but I want to achieve those dreams my way.'

What, then, is the Sky Andrew way? To understand that, one has to look at his background. Sky Andrew was himself a major sporting figure in the field of table tennis during the 1980s and early 1990s. Of his own sporting past,

he says modestly, 'I was fairly successful.' The reality is that although table tennis may be a low-profile sport, Sky Andrew was a regular fixture in the England national team for over ten years. He represented Great Britain at the 1988 Olympics in Seoul, and won a cabinet full of medals and titles at various World, European or Commonwealth championships. He reached the pinnacle of his sporting career in 1992 when he became the highest ranked black table tennis player in the world.

The significance of Sky's earlier sporting achievements on his subsequent career as a football agent is made more apparent when he declares, 'I could not do my work anywhere near as effectively if I did not have my own sporting experience.' He adds, 'I never had an agent when I performed. It was something I missed out on, having someone whom I could speak to and who could help me with my career.'

Beyond helping him understand what his sporting clients are experiencing, and the pressures and strains of being at the top of one's game—few other agents have any sporting experience of their own—Sky Andrew also credits his table tennis background with honing his public relations skills. He says bluntly, 'Since I had no agent, and I was in a borderline sport, I could not afford to be borderline in my attitude....I had to push for sponsorship, and push for any television or magazine coverage that I received. I was constantly seeking PR opportunities.'

Even so, he admits that he still had no idea he would go into sports management at the close of his own sporting career. The ambition he really harboured was to be a television presenter, having already written one or two scripts for the acclaimed television satire, 'Spitting Image'. Alternatively, he thought, he would get more involved in the company he had started earlier with another British table tennis star, Desmond Douglas, importing table tennis equipment into the UK.

However, a chance encounter in 1994 with a former acquaintance, Sol Campbell, an already noted footballer with Tottenham Hotspurs football club, would totally change his career direction. Aware of Sky's contacts and know-how, Sol asked Sky if he would help him in his upcoming negotiations with his club. A good relationship was quickly established between the two and the one-off request for help became a regular feature, though still on a friendship footing rather than on a professional business

basis. Other footballers also began seeking Sky's help and he started to assist a range of people. He worked on a no-fee basis for almost two years before finally deciding that he had to put things on a more professional footing, and so began, somewhat casually, Sky's sports management and public relations agency.

Some five years later, Sky elaborates on some of the philosophies and principles which guide his work and business dealings. 'To be a good agent', he says, 'you have to be a good counsellor, negotiator, adviser and, especially, a good friend. If you only do business and nothing else, then at some stage someone else will come along and say to your client, "I can do better business for you", and chances are you will lose your client.' Sky maintains that it is important that he gets to know his clients first, to care about them, and to understand what they are trying to achieve. He adds, 'I will not get involved in money matters until we have built a proper client relationship; only then can you put the money side in its proper context.'

Sky has very strong views about the type of people he takes on as clients and the need for them, as he says, 'to give something back to society. No amount of money could get me to work for someone who I felt had no morality, integrity or sense of well-being, however big their name or future prospects. It might be bad business', he adds, 'but that's me.' He makes the further point that 'I want my people to have others look up to them and for them to be good role models with a sense of duty. You can earn money and have purpose. It's about doing some good in society.'

Sky attributes his approach and his success to the influence of his mother, whom he says told him as a youngster so repeatedly that he was going to be successful that he just had to succeed, whatever the field. The fact that there are no other black football agents in top-flight football does not bother Sky Andrew in the least. 'I am black and love being black, and it has never been a barrier to doing anything,' he asserts. 'I take a positive attitude to everything I do, and never look at anything negatively.'

For the future, Sky says simply, 'I will be striving to continue to work with good people.' He hopes to expand the company by training other people around him to look after people the way he does. Characteristically, he feels the key to the future growth and success of his business is in helping his clients to be successful, not just in their careers, but as people.

Calling Agent Andrew

A millennium recipe

Michelle Bartlett

Restaurateur

Little did Michelle Bartlett imagine, on admiring an attractive gallery-restaurant set in an old colonial cottage in Ocho Rios in her native Jamaica, that she would some years later become the owner of a similarly stylish enterprise in the heart of London. Today, Michelle Bartlett is the co-owner and the driving force behind London's best-known and most celebrated Caribbean restaurant.' Cottons, located in the trendy Camden Lock area of north London.

Just as London has built an outstanding culinary reputation for itself in the 1990s, Cottons restaurant has secured a niche within that competitive market, offering quality Caribbean, and more specifically Jamaican, cuisine in an attractive setting. Where other restaurants of its type have come and gone, Cottons has remained and thrived. Apart from being a favourite with its regular clientele—who, Michelle proudly says, span the ethnic spectrum—it also has a reputation as 'the place to go' for many celebrities who are in town. Michelle informs me that only the previous evening the actor Wesley Snipes had eaten at the restaurant, while other celebrity customers have included Tom Cruise, Stevie Wonder and Mary J. Blige.

Michelle points out that in comparison to the gastrodomes—the term given to some of the huge eateries that have sprung up across London—Cottons is still a small minority restaurant catering to the ethnic end of the market. And unlike certain other ethnic cuisines, such as Chinese or Indian, which are now as well-known in Britain as fish and chips, the general public is less well-acquainted with Caribbean food. Her 100-seat restaurant, which has a picture gallery on an upper floor—much like the Ocho Rios restaurant which first inspired her—managed to weather the cold winds of recession in the early 1990s, and now has over twelve years of established business behind it.

'The food style is distinctly Jamaican,' Michelle tells me. 'People tend to group the Caribbean or the West Indies together, but', she says, 'the islands may have the sun, sea and the coconut trees in common but the food is quite different.' Although now easing away from her hands-on approach to managing the restaurant—laughing as she remarks, 'It has taken the Head Chef more than a few years to get rid of me from the kitchen'—it is still very much in her style, and she sets the overall direction. Aiming not only to offer good food but also to educate her customers about Jamaican food, and in so doing give them a glimpse into its culture. Cottons seeks to provide a modern, though authentic, range of Jamaican dishes.

Although she spent her early schooldays in Jamaica, Michelle Bartlett moved with her family to Canada where, after high school, she went on to the University of Montreal to study fashion and fine arts. She left the university after only two years feeling lost and uncertain about the direction she was taking. She came alone on a one-way ticket to London in 1983 in search of a new direction. 'I wanted the challenge of doing something different with my life,' says Michelle. Of the prospect of life alone in a strange city, she says firmly, 'I am not, and have never been, afraid of challenges. I am a risk-taker.'

She says she found 'the right spiritual and cultural vibes' in London, but she missed her family greatly and returned to be with them once more in Jamaica. Shortly before her departure, she was driving through Camden with a friend, when she casually remarked on seeing a building she was immediately attracted to that it was going to be hers one day. Several years later, that same building houses Cottons Rum Bar and Restaurant.

After a period in Jamaica, Michelle Bartlett resolved to return to London because, she says, 'I knew I could succeed here.' On returning to the UK in 1987 she investigated the ownership of the building she had spotted earlier, only to discover that it was up for sale. Undeterred by a lack of funds, she approached the owner and convinced him that since he had premises she was looking for, and she had the know-how required to make a restaurant work— 'In reality I didn't have a clue at the time'—that they should become business partners. He agreed and remains her partner today.

The agreement with her new partner allowed Michelle a free hand in the use of the premises in return for a share of the profits, but she had to convert the building and outfit it on a shoestring budget. This she did by setting it up initially as a coffee bar with an upstairs gallery selling pieces of art produced by local college students. 'It was a nice place to be,' says Michelle, reminiscing on the early days. She recalls fondly that back then the coffee bar was frequented by lots of RADA students, some of whom worked part-time at the restaurant, and that a number of them have gone on to make names for themselves in acting. Marianne Jean-Baptiste, then a RADA student and now an acclaimed actress, was a regular customer and still is today.

Many people helped Michelle along the way, including her parents who instilled in her confidence and assurance, her business partner who gave her the break to get started, friends who gave support and encouragement, and local shopowner neighbours, one of whom invited a friend, the influential restaurant critic Fay Maschler, to the restaurant for a meal. Following her good review of Cottons, Michelle says, 'We have never looked back. I feel really blessed by the things that have happened for me.'

Feeling equally at home in London and Jamaica, Michelle Bartlett says, 'I love England and feel safe here, but I can never forget Jamaica, it is too deep within me.' Of her chosen business, Michelle says, 'It is very demanding and you need more than a desire to succeed. You have to be totally dedicated.' She believes that what makes the difference between a successful restaurant and those that come and go are high food standards, atmosphere, quality service and good music. 'It's the balance between these four factors. If we, or anyone else gets them right, we will succeed.' She is, she says, still looking forward with optimism, and adds, 'Who knows, perhaps there will be a chain of Cottons restaurants in the future. I have not fulfilled my dreams just yet and there is more to come from me.'

With the restaurant business booming in London, the millennium offers plenty of scope for Michelle Bartlett to weave her web of Cottons across the capital and, quite possibly, beyond.

Ozwald Boateng

Bespoke Couturier and Tailor

To many commentators and analysts, Ozwald Boateng's rise in the world of business and bespoke tailoring has been nothing short of meteoric. Still in his thirties, and without any formal training, he has created more than a splash in menswear fashion design. The first tailor to stage a catwalk show in Paris, Ozwald Boateng was soon named 'Menswear Designer of the Year', beating in the process all the bigger name designers. He became the youngest person, and certainly the first black person, to set up shop in London's Saville Row, the epicentre of traditional British tailoring. Ozwald believes himself to be the first person to establish a men's couture house anywhere in the world. This, and his many other 'firsts', were all achieved before he had reached the ripe old age of thirty!

And yet Ozwald Boateng tells me with much good humour and merriment that his father is far from satisfied since Ozwald is 'well behind schedule by his expectations'. Notwithstanding this wry aside, Ozwald speaks warmly of his father as a great mentor and big influence on his life— 'it was he who gave me the special regard for the suit'. From the time Ozwald was a young boy, his father had repeatedly told him that he was going to achieve something special with his life. Whether consciously responding to this encouragement or not, Ozwald Boateng is definitely a man in a hurry to succeed.

'I believe in the tradition of tailoring,' says Ozwald, 'and traditional tailoring can be made highly fashionable. I design very classic suits but with that "Ozwald Boateng" flair. I am seeking to revolutionize tailoring ... globally.' With outlets already established in Paris and Tokyo, and a mushrooming clientele, including celebrity names that other designers must view with some envy (Seal, Mick Jagger, Mick Hucknall, Samuel L. Jackson, George Michael, Lenny Henry, to name but a few), this is no idle boast. With regular clients being drawn from the offices of accountants, bankers, lawyers, City firms and the like —that is those who can afford to pay between £1,000 and £4,000 for a suit—Ozwald is already credited with educating a new generation in the pleasures of bespoke tailoring. Ozwald Boateng has a certain air about him. He exudes quiet, self-confident authority. Tall, slender and always immaculately dressed—forthrightly declaring that he only wears his own creations—he is the perfect model for his own cutting-edge designs and has buckets of likeable 'attitude' thrown in for good measure. I tried to capture some of that presence in my photographic shot of Ozwald at his newly opened couture house. The globe in the foreground adds, I feel, something of a prophetic touch.

Ozwald also talked about the other most significant influence on his career direction: a girl whom he fell in love with while studying computing at Southbank College in south London. It was his artistic and creative girlfriend who showed Ozwald how to cut and affirmed his talent for designing clothes. He says frankly, 'She changed the whole direction of my life.' Using his mother's sewing machine, to which he had hitherto paid scant attention, Ozwald was immediately able to sell clothes to fellow students at college and later to a wider market. He sold his first real collection, at sixteen, to a fashionable upmarket menswear shop in London's Covent Garden, and had set himself up full time in the business by the time he was twenty-three. Circumventing a more conventional apprenticeship, he was nevertheless keen to learn the best of traditional tailoring. Ozwald recalls how he would find out who best hand stitched buttonholes, who set sleeves the best way, who made the best linings, and so on, learning something from each of these skilled professionals as he went along, but at the same time accentuating the cut and giving it his own contemporary style and look. He mentions the late Tommy Nutter, a long-standing Saville Row proprietor, as being one of his personal heroes.

Ozwald Boateng coined the term 'bespoke couturier' to better describe what he felt he did, and initially earned a certain notoriety for doing so. 'To say I was a tailor was not enough, and to say I was a designer was also not sufficient, hence I combined the two concepts. In a nutshell, I am a creator, a creator of beautiful clothes.'

He is open and expansive about his future plans, aware that he and his clothes already have a certain name recognition. It is his intention to exploit that opportunity. Ozwald says quite simply, 'I want to develop a world brand. My vision is to create the biggest and most successful menswear business in the world.' A self-confessed workaholic, he admits that when he first started he was moving at '1000 mph'. Recognising that he could not continue at this pace indefinitely, he feels he has matured and slowed down somewhat, adding, 'I am probably moving now at just 500 mph!'

If Ozwald Boateng's approach is 'straight ahead and very forward looking', then his view of being black is just the same. He has always resolutely refused to see racism as 'a problem'. 'I have never taken the issue of my colour on board as a barrier stopping me from achieving anything. If I meet an obstacle I am more interested in getting around that hurdle than in being concerned with what might be going on in someone else's head, since it is ultimately irrelevant to me. Clearing that obstacle or barrier is what I am focused on.'

Given his drive and focus, it seems to me that some of the big name design houses like Versace, Armani and the like had better watch out because there is a new kid on the block. Black, bold and brilliant at what he does, Ozwald Boateng is making a mark for himself and for the British fashion industry.

A determined attitude

Jim Brathwaite

Entrepreneur

As we stroll though the streets of Brighton on the south coast of England, Jim Brathwaite's long connection and affinity with the town and the county of Sussex become apparent. A successful entrepreneur, Jim Brathwaite has the distinction of having been the first black Chief Executive Officer of a company quoted on the stock exchange. Having arrived in Worthing initially to take up a job, he stayed on in Sussex to make it his home and Brighton his eventual business base. He points with pride to various buildings where his companies began or are currently housed, and greets a number of townspeople with whom he has business links. It seemed fitting to take his portrait with one of Brighton's other landmarks—its famous pier—as a backdrop.

Jim Brathwaite, unlike his high-profile and rather more flamboyant role model, Richard Branson, comes across as a measured and self-effacing business person. Although he makes clear that he is not in Richard Branson's league in terms of wealth—Branson is, after all, the fourteenth richest person in Britain—it would appear that Jim Brathwaite does share his sharp entrepreneurial eye for a business opportunity. Like Branson, Jim Brathwaite also owns a clutch of both independent and interrelated businesses, and has a knack for bringing out the best in people who work for or with him. 'I am not a nuts and bolts person,' says Jim. 'I like to put teams together who are good at what they do and try to create the environment for them to thrive in.'

Clearly successful with this leadership style, Jim Brathwaite's various companies, all south coast based, operate in the television and film, IT, telecommunications and multimedia sectors. He started his first company with a friend— 'just the two of us in one room,' he says very matter of factly. Sixteen years later, that company. Epic Multimedia, employs over 200 people, and says Jim, gave him his claim to fame as the first black CEO of a public listed company.

Another of his companies, X-Tension, is one of the leading UK producers of software for the telecommunications industry, and he has high hopes that it too will be quoted on the stock exchange. He is also director of an electronic distribution company, and the CEO of XL Entertainment, his most recent enterprise, for which he proudly says he has very high hopes. XL, a television film production company, already has one much acclaimed children's television show in its fold—Jamboree—recently nominated for a BAFTA award (Britain's equivalent of an Oscar).

Besides his business empire, Jim Brathwaite is the Chairman of Sussex Business Link, a business information body which works in conjunction with the local Chamber of Commerce to assist local businesses, a director of the nearby University of Sussex and a governor of a local sixth form college.

How then did Jim Brathwaite, still in his early forties and raised for the early part of his life in the heart of inner city Liverpool, come to be responsible for creating businesses with a combined turnover of over £50m and employing several hundred people? 'Luck' and 'by accident' is the response from this modest man, although he later adds, 'I always have had, and still possess, a desire to do well, to achieve things and make money. I never wanted to be ordinary.'

Jim Brathwaite was born in Barbados and came to Britain just before his third birthday. He remembers vividly arriving by boat at Southampton in the cold of winter, and making the long journey by steam train to Liverpool. The family's first home was a top floor flat in a five-storey Victorian house in Liverpool's tough Toxteth district—all they could get at a time when many letting houses openly displayed signs declaring 'No Blacks, No Irish, No Dogs'. His parents struggled to get work in the city. His mother, a qualified nurse in the Caribbean, could only find work in a local factory in Liverpool, whilst his father had to travel each day to a factory job in another town—Warrington. In the end, his father's job situation worked to the family's advantage, Jim believes, and represented the first turning point in his career. The family settled down in the much smaller and less racially sensitive town of Warrington, where they were the first black family in the area. Jim went to the local grammar school and on to university to study zoology and physiology.

After university he joined Beechams as part of their graduate management programme, but the only position they could offer at the time was in accounting and was based at the company's plant in Worthing. Jim later moved into marketing and his career progressed well with Beechams. However, a pivotal point arose when he applied for a job as the head of one of the company's overseas bureaux. He was told that on account of his colour—which might be problematic for the locals—they could not appoint him to the position. In disgust, Jim Brathwaite left and moved to a competitor pharmaceutical company, Bayer, also based in

Sussex, as Marketing Manager. He would happily have remained with that company had it not decided to relocate. In an effort to remain in the county he had come to like so much, Jim got together with a friend to set up a company in the then new medium of video. It was this venture into the business world, with a company which would eventually become publicly listed, that launched Jim Brathwaite as an entrepreneur.

'I had no real notion of starting a business,' says Jim, asserting that it was only the unforeseen chain of events that led him down this path. Having decided, however, to take this route, he says with assurance, 'I worked out what I wanted to do and just got on with it.' Asked whether there were any issues he had to deal with along the way as a black business person, he says, 'If anything it's been to my advantage, because when you do well, you stand out and people tend to notice and remember you.' He implores other black people 'to give their ideas a go and not be deterred by perceived problems'.

Jim acknowledges the help and support he has received at various times. The unstinting support of his mother, the influence of an infant school teacher in Liverpool whom he describes as 'the first to really raise my horizons', the bank manager who gave him his first business loan despite his thinking, says Jim with a smile, 'that we and the hair-brained idea we had were crazy'. Jim also pays tribute to the continuing support he receives from a venture capitalist, John Davis, who has raised funds to invest in Jim's businesses from the financial markets in the City of London. Jim makes the point that what gives him most satisfaction from his various business ventures is knowing that he, too, has assisted others whilst pursuing his business goals. 'Seeing the people to whom I have given opportunities grow and develop, that is a great reward.'

Besides Richard Branson, whom Jim Brathwaite describes as 'extraordinary', he cites Bill Gates, the founder and majority shareowner of Microsoft, as 'a man of great vision,' and someone he finds particularly inspiring. Both, he says, are people who make things happen and do a lot of good in the process of developing their businesses. Jim, who regards Britain as his home, declares that one of his personal goals for the future is to set up and own a black television station in the UK. For a man of Jim Brathwaite's resourcefulness, it will come as no surprise if that goal is realised sooner rather than later in the new millennium.

Captain of industry

Sol Campbell

Footballer

Aged just twenty-four, Sol Campbell is already captain of his club side, Tottenham Hotspurs, and is as near as one can get to being an automatic choice for the England national football team. Sol's performances at the 1998 World Cup in France were so accomplished that they marked him out as one of Europe's most promising defenders and someone to watch on the world football stage. The 1998-99 season also saw him proudly and successfully leading his team out at Wembley in the League Cup Final, showcasing his immense talents once again at the highest level.

Fortunately, at a time when footballers are bathed in the media spotlight, can command huge fees, and are generally on the receiving end of unsatiated outpourings of public adulation, there is not a hint of flamboyance or flashiness about Sol Campbell. My interview with him reflected in many respects the way he plays the game of football—thoughtful, very considered, modest, but purposeful and incisive in his contributions and interventions. His quiet determination is predicated on confidence in his own abilities, but he is also humble enough to openly admit that he is still learning the game. 'Every game I play at Tottenham or with England, I am learning things.' This despite being regarded as the best young defender in the country.

Big, solid, but deceptively quick, he presents a daunting barrier that is consistently hard to beat whether in the air or on the ground. Sol Campbell defies the usual view held of British central defenders—that they are there to stop opponents and to win the ball for their team, but put a ball at their feet and ask them to run with it, they are more likely to fall over it than anything else! Put a ball at Sol Campbell's feet and he will, and often does, take off with a speed and style that some strikers would envy, as seen most vividly at the 1998 World Cup.

Such is Sol Campbell's all-round talent and skill that even though he plays as a central defender, at almost the halfway point of the 1998-99 season he was his club's leading goal scorer, scoring some absolutely decisive goals... an incredible feat for someone whose primary task is to marshal his team's defence. Captain Campbell clearly prefers to lead by example rather than bellow instructions to those on the field around him. One of Sol's most sterling qualities seems to be less about what he does with the ball than about his strength of character and temperament which are quite exceptional. As one sports commentator has remarked, 'Under pressure he is utterly unflappable.'

Sol Campbell, born and raised in the East End of London, revealed to me that it was only at the age of eighteen that he decided professional football really did offer him a genuine career possibility and that maybe he could and should try to make it in the game. 'It wasn't that I set out to be a professional footballer. I wanted to do other things,' he explained, 'but I loved playing football and fortunately other people saw the talent in me.' Clearly that talent was evident sufficiently early for Sol to be selected at the age of sixteen to attend the élite Football Association School of Excellence in Lilleshall, Shropshire, where the aim is to spot and nurture talented youngsters.

Sol looks back on his two years at Lilleshall as highly enjoyable, but feels that he was aware that early promise does not always blossom, and that there is a very high attrition rate amongst seemingly promising young players who for various reasons never make it either into the game or within the game. Indeed, of his fellow graduates from the school, who were all there because they had shown excellent early prospects, only two or three have made it along with Sol into professional football, and of these few, all except Sol presently earn their living in the lower divisions of English football.

I asked Sol about the celebrity status which accrues to many of today's football players and about his own experience of 'fame'. 'I enjoy certain aspects but certainly don't feed off it....I am essentially a very private person.' He cites the opportunities he gets to meet particular people and to visit places he otherwise might not, and mentions a recent audience he and the other England World Cup players had with HM the Queen. He also asserts that just as there are benefits there is also a downside to whatever celebrity status he and other footballers purportedly enjoy. 'Dealing with the press', Sol believes, 'is a big bugbear. Footballers are such easy targets, often the press simply make up stories about us. Sadly there is less coverage about the game and more focus on the tit bits surrounding it. Amazingly, it seems sometimes that is all people want to hear.' I am sure that Glen Hoddle, England's former manager, and a myriad of players and others involved in the game, who have so often received a rough ride from the press, would find little to disagree with Sol's sentiments.

Looking back, Sol Campbell pays credit to his parents who trusted him and gave him the freedom as a young man to go and play or watch football games across the country with his friends or sometimes by himself. This, Sol feels, greatly furthered his own development and love of the game. He also talked about the role of the football scout Len Cheesewright, who first brought him to the attention of Tottenham Hotspur football club, and to John Cartwright, one of the coaches at Lilleshall, who encouraged Sol to develop his skills and talents.

Sol also, quite touchingly, paid tribute to the black players who came before him in English football, stressing their importance as role models for him and for others. As a youngster. Sol supported Manchester United. 'One of the reasons for this was the fact that they had one of the few black players in the game at the time—Remi Moses—and this was so important to me.' Beyond football, the person whom Sol Campbell most admires is Nelson Mandela, a man whom he regards as a genuine living legend who, with his measured statesmanlike qualities, has achieved real change where others thought it improbable, if not impossible.

Of his future prospects. Sol admits that you cannot really predict or map out your future in football. Injury, the fortunes of your team, a change of team management, all exert an influence on a player's future prospects. That said, Sol adds, 'my goal is to keep my career going and to achieve my highest potential.' As for football in the new millennium, Sol speaks with a little more latitude. 'The last frontier in football is America, and despite hosting the 1994 World Cup football has still to take off there. It really would bring unbelievable changes if and when the game properly took off on the other side of the Atlantic!'

Whether Sol Campbell is destined to be one of those pioneers who will one day help to bridge this new frontier, we shall have to wait and see. In the meantime, Sol is providing youngsters coming up behind him—be they black or white—with a role model of technical finesse and growing personal stature.

Captain Campbell

Group Captain David Case

Senior Officer, Royal Air Force

Group Captain David Case is the highest ranking black officer in the Royal Air Force (RAF) and, one of the most senior black serving officers in the entire British military establishment. Yet one would struggle to find a more down-to-earth and unpretentious person.

With twenty-five years of service fast approaching, Group Captain Case is currently Director of the Department of Specialist Ground Training at the RAF College at Cranwell, the oldest military air academy in the world. Steeped in tradition, Cranwell is the RAF's equivalent of the Army's Sandhurst and, as such, is the entry point for all officers and aircrew joining the RAF. It was at RAF Cranwell that Sir Frank Whittle developed his ideas and wrote his thesis on what would later become the world's first jet-propelled engine. Group Captain Case's department provides the initial specialist training for all engineer and supply officers, as well as more advanced management and technical training.

David Case, who came to the UK from Guyana when he was five, was always interested in flying. He joined the school's cadet corps along with many of his friends precisely so that he would get the earliest opportunity to fly, and recalls—still with much enthusiasm—how he flew gliders and light aircraft as a young cadet. Jokingly, David views this early experience as effectively being the start of his long and ongoing RAF career.

When a medical examination revealed that David was long-sighted, thus ending his ambition to become a pilot, he decided that he so liked being involved with aircraft and enjoyed what he saw and knew of the RAF community, that he nevertheless still wanted to be in the Royal Air Force. Despite what must have been a major personal disappointment, he has never regretted this decision. On the contrary, he has gone on to build a highly distinguished and yet still developing career in the Royal Air Force.

After studying aeronautical engineering at Queens University, Belfast, David Case had his commission in the RAF confirmed in late 1975. Like the newly commissioned officers he now trains, he attended RAF Cranwell where he was awarded the distinguished 'Sword of Honour', which is bestowed on the top cadet officer of the year.

'I can still picture my mother's face at my passing out graduation parade, and more especially as I came down to collect my Sword of Honour,' says David, still with self-evident and well-deserved pride. It is not difficult to imagine how both he and his mother must have felt, particularly because David was the only black cadet officer at RAF Cranwell at that time. David readily acknowledges the pivotal role played by his mother in helping him to get a start in the RAF and pursue his career ambitions. With no prior military experience in the family, they nevertheless allowed him the freedom to make his own decision and supported his wish to join the Service. He also acknowledges the encouragement he received from various instructors who helped him along the way, and the spiritual support provided by ministers and congregations of the many churches he has attended over the years.

In response to my enquiry about people who have been role models or who have inspired him, David cites world figures like Mahatma Gandhi, Mother Theresa and Nelson Mandela. All are people, he feels, who have shown immense inner drive over a sustained period of time, compassion in the face of suffering, and have demonstrated exceptional leadership qualities.

Besides training the next generation of RAF officers, David's career has taken him to most of the RAF's UK bases and also overseas. He fondly recalls one posting in Germany where he was selected to be one of the RAF's representatives in an international team to procure the new Eurofighter aircraft for Britain's air defence system. He has also enjoyed a strong and long association with the Phantom aircraft.

Still brimming with enthusiasm after nearly twenty-five years in the Service, Group Captain David Case is something of a walking, talking advertisement for the RAF. He confidently proclaims, 'I positively enjoy what I do and I tell all my student officers to go and enjoy themselves, it's good for yourself, the people who work with you, and for the RAF.' Certainly, when I look at the picture of Group Captain Case alongside Major Eze Ugwuzor from the Army, both resplendent in their uniforms, I see pride and enthusiasm clearly expressed through his broad smile and upright posture.

Asked about the thorny issue of being black in the UK Armed Forces, his thoughtful and characteristic response was, 'I certainly encountered no barriers to joining. And I have reflected back over the period I have been in the Service on whether I have encountered discrimination and can honestly say I cannot identify any occasion when I thought this might have been a case in point. I try to educate people by simply being who I am.'

Although already the RAF's most senior black officer, Group Captain David Case's ambition burns as bright as ever. 'Having made a decision to go into the services, I wanted to do well in it. That remains an inner drive. In the armed services one cannot really predict where you will be in the future, but I would certainly like to get a star on my shoulder.'

Subsequent to our interview, I learnt that Group Captain David Case had been selected to attend the military's élite and highly distinguished senior officers' academy, the Royal College of Defence Studies, suggesting that his aspiration to one day become an Air Commodore (the RAF equivalent of an Army Brigadier), with that coveted star on his shoulder, may not be too far ahead.

David Case became Air Commodore Case in 2000.

and The Major

Major Ezenwa Ugwuzor

Army Major

Amongst the medals and emblems which adorn the uniformed chest of Major Ezenwa Ugwuzor are two which denote his tours of active service with the British Army. Major Ugwuzor is a veteran of the 1991 Gulf War and has also undertaken operational duties in Bosnia.

Major Ezenwa Ugwuzor—'Eze' to his friends and acquaintances—confides that amongst the various issues he had to seriously consider before he took the decision to join the Army, was the very real prospect of having to go to war and with it the possibility of losing his life. 'I had to be comfortable about this issue before joining,' says Eze. Of the experience of war, Eze is thoughtful and reflective. 'Being deployed on operations is a mixture of intensive work and protracted boredom. But,' he adds, 'you learn a great deal about yourself and the people around you. It is a very sobering experience. What particularly hits you is the enormity of it all.'

I met Major Ugwuzor for a joint interview and photo session with Group Captain David Case of the Royal Air Force (RAF) at the Imperial War Museum in London. It proved to be a highly enjoyable and fascinating session where I learnt and gained a great deal from two of the highest ranking black serving officers in the UK Armed Forces.

One enduring and somewhat unexpected mental image of our time together was the reaction these two black officers—impeccably turned out in their respective dress uniforms—elicited from passers-by observing the photo shoot. From sidelong glances, double takes, to wide open stares, these black British officers seemed to evoke a multitude of silent questions. Perhaps only those with military training could have known the seniority of the two officers, and fewer still would have guessed the extent of Major Eze Ugwuzor's active service duty.

After spending much of his early life not wanting to be in the military at all, although he was himself brought up in a military household (Eze's father had been an officer in the Nigerian Army), Eze only began to consider joining the Services on graduating from the University of East Anglia in economics and politics. 'I thought about the experience and adventure, about the excitement of training at Sandhurst, of being posted somewhere interesting, and just generally enjoying myself for two or three years,' is how Eze explains his decision to join the Army, which he did initially on a Short Service Commission.

Some ten years later, having attended the Royal Military Academy at Sandhurst, undertaken several tours of duty overseas, including the Gulf and Bosnia, and having achieved fairly rapid promotion through the officer corps, he confesses that he is still enjoying life in the Army. Although Eze does not see himself as a 'lifer', he feels he will stay in the Army for as long as he continues to enjoy it.

The Major is presently based with the Headquarters Land Command in Salisbury, where he forms part of the Army's Capital Project implementation team. Having been sent recently to the Royal Military College of Science at Shrivenham, where he gained a Master's degree in Defence Administration (the military equivalent of an MBA), Eze is now looking at strategic change management within the Army. Through the work of the Capital Project implementation team, the Army is seeking to introduce more commercial discipline in managing the resources under its command, ensuring that military capability is delivered whilst being mindful of the full resource implications of whatever action is taken.

Asked about his future prospects, Eze responds with a hint of his inner drive. 'I do not know where I want to be in five or ten years time, but whether it is in the Army or the commercial world, I want to be a success at it and to achieve whatever is within my potential.' His thoughts for the new millennium centre around his hope of seeing a Great Britain in which black people are featured and reflected more prominently across all areas and levels of society, and where—perhaps to sustain this ideal—the emerging black middle class will expand and develop.

Eze explains how he is motivated and inspired by various people without necessarily wanting or feeling the need to try and emulate them. He is especially moved by the power of music and musicians, and the ability of performers to touch people. One person for whom Eze expresses particular admiration is Muhammed Ali, although he confesses to having no real interest in boxing. Eze cites Ali's larger than life personality, his tremendous talent and drive, his undeniable achievements, but most of all his ability to have touched people profoundly through the art of boxing.

With regard to the experience of being black in the UK Armed Forces, Major Ugwuzor responds by acknowledging the negative view held by some people outside the service, but adds, 'There are many black people in the Army, RAF and Naval Service who are enjoying their careers and progressing. That does not mean that there may not be some people elsewhere in the force—maybe in the lower ranks—who are having a difficult time due to their colour, but this has not been my experience.'

I leave our session full of admiration for Major Eze Ugwuzor, respecting his professionalism, his calm and thoughtful nature, and feeling convinced that the British Army must be deeply satisfied to have officer material of the calibre of Major Eze Ugwuzor within its commission.

Pleased to meet you Officer

Strategy for success

René Carayol

Information Technology Director

When first meeting René Carayol, what is striking is his speed of movement, thought and, more especially, speech. Everything seems to be done in double-quick time and you feel as if you really need to be on your mark to keep up with him. This is a man who is unashamedly in a hurry to get things done and to arrive at where he wants to be!

As IT Director and Chief Information Officer of IPC Magazines, the largest consumer magazine publishing house in Europe, with some seventy titles in its list, René Carayol, at thirty-nine, is one of a rare breed of black British corporate board members. Not content, however, to be one of this select few, he is open and unabashed about his ultimate goal-to be the first black Chief Executive Officer of a major UK PLC. In his own words, 'Ambition burns brightly within me....I know I am a focused individual and I want to *get* there.'

Time spent in his company left me with no doubt that this is no idle ambition but one which he fully intends to realise. As if to emphasize his need to be constantly moving forward and to not waste a minute of his time, René laughs as he recounts how whenever they meet, on observing his pace, his mother usually enquires 'if anyone is chasing me'.

René Carayol is in many respects an exemplar of successful career management. His conversation is littered with expressions like 'I drive my career', 'I'm responsible for it, not anyone else', and 'ultimately, I am working for René Carayol Inc.' He personifies how one should not be afraid or reticent about changing career direction, about not being defeated by unexpected hurdles, about forward planning and about self-belief. He is also an exponent of the art of networking, believing that in order to succeed you must be visible and have the right contacts to help you along the way. And yet it has not always been that way. Raised in one of the tougher areas of London—Harlesdon—(he now lives in one of the more salubrious parts of the city—St John's Wood), René was the eldest of five children whose parents had come to the UK in 1961 from The Gambia specifically to further their children's education.

René's first career choice was accountancy. After establishing himself in the profession, he realised a lifelong career in accountancy was not for him. He felt insufficiently challenged or motivated by what he was doing and decided to look around for something different. He saw information technology as a major growth area. Calculating that companies were spending substantial sums developing new technology and enhancing the skills base of their staff, he decided that this was where his future lay. René Carayol has not looked back since making that decision. In the space of sixteen years, he has moved rapidly from being a trainee programmer, through middle and senior management positions, to where he is today— the youngest board member within the IPC group.

One of the companies for whom he worked was Marks and Spencer, a household name in British retailing. René readily credits 'M & S' for instilling in him much of his business, IT and management acumen, but most of all for nurturing his self-awareness and confidence. He says that he joined the organisation as a rather shy and reserved individual but left ten years later a much more knowledgeable, assertive and self-confident manager, 'positively hungry for success'. Sadly, he explains that he also learnt other less palatable lessons at Marks and Spencer. It was there that he was told that on account of his 'age and colour' he had gone as far as he could and that it was too 'risky' moving him any further up the managerial ladder. This put-down of the company's then most senior black executive served only to strengthen his resolve to make it to the top regardless of the hurdles he would have to jump along the way.

René Carayol has been a man on a mission ever since this experience, driven by his overriding ambition to make it onto the board of a major company. On leaving Marks and Spencer for a senior corporate position at Pizza Hut, it took him a mere eleven months to be promoted onto that company's main board as IT Director.

When he was head-hunted two years later by IPC, he was advised that it normally took several years for managers at his level to make it onto the board, and that he should be patient and wait his turn. In spite of such advice, René achieved the distinction of becoming a main board member in just under one year; in contrast, most of his colleagues on the board had been with the company an average of seventeen years. Responsible for the IT needs of the company and looking after the information aspects of the business, he has a staff of 125, largely hand-picked, whom he regards as 'the best in the UK IT field'.

Whilst usually taking a forward-looking approach, René is proud of his past achievements. He cites a touching experience when he was promoted to the main board position at Pizza Hut. A group of the company's black cleaners knocked on his door early one morning to say how proud they were of him. It is this kind of experience which makes René satisfied that by 'driving his own career' he can give something back to the community from which he has come: 'I would like to think that I am crashing down barriers and leaving the path open for others.'

René Carayol explains how he has ensured that IPC Magazines gets involved in local community projects. He personally mentors some nine individuals (he is guided by three mentors of his own, each one a captain of UK industry), and also spends a large amount of time outside work speaking at various community and public events.

René acknowledges that being a black board member is not without its trying and amusing moments. For example, when he and his fellow directors attend conferences or other business events, it is often assumed that he is an assistant to the delegation, and he recalls the looks of disbelief on the faces of business contacts who, perhaps judging by his name, are expecting to meet a white Frenchman!

It seemed somehow fitting to take René's portrait with London's Millennium Dome as the backdrop, since he embodies so much of the spirit of the new age of achievement, creative thinking and the 'can do' mentality. One suspects that as far as his ambition to become a black CEO of a major UK company is concerned, René Carayol is biding his time for the right opportunity.

Mutlti-media man

Blondel Cluff and Granville Hodge

Solicitors

Blondel Cluff and Granville Hodge own and manage what is probably the only black-established firm in the prestigious square mile of the City of London. They are partners in a firm of solicitors which specialises in commercial and banking law. These two high-powered solicitor partners are also brother and sister.

It seemed appropriate to present their profiles in combination given their close professional partnership as well as their blood relationship. When I interviewed and photographed the two partners the evident warmth, good humour and fascinating interchange which existed between them was a compelling reason to present them together in the book. The photograph of Blondel Cluff and Granville Hodge—taken in their offices looking towards St Paul's Cathedral—is a reflection of the highly enjoyable time I spent in their company and conveys something of the special relationship the sibling partners share.

Cluff, Hodge & Co. is no run-of-the-mill legal practice. While it is small in comparison to some of the big practices—the company has five lawyers and administrative support staff—its client list is distinctly 'blue chip'. Corporate clients include the Bank of England, the Stock Exchange, the Money Brokers Association, Barclays Bank and Abbey National, as well as various merchant banks.

Of their private clients, more than a sprinkling are 'names' in the fields of entertainment, media and fashion. As Blondel remarks, 'The City is a wonderful place to work. It's like a village but terribly international. It's quite an achievement and a challenge advising a billion pound money market knowing that you are drawing up legal documents which will be used throughout the world.' It is also evidently a lucrative business to be in judging by the firm's well-appointed offices and the siblings' occasional references to their prestige marque cars and other trappings of material success.

How, then, has this black brother and sister team got to where they are? What have been their experiences along the way, and have there been any issues that have impinged on them as black professionals in the legal field, and at the elevated level at which they operate?

Blondel and Granville's parents, both from the Caribbean island of Anguilla, migrated to Britain in the late 1950s. With their young family of four sons and one daughter—Blondel being the middle child and Granville the youngest—the key motive for emigrating to Britain was to enhance the educational prospects of the Hodge children. They chose to settle in Berkshire, away from the larger cities where most of the other new black emigrants found jobs and homes. This decision, and the personal sacrifices which were involved, were vindicated as all five children did well at school, went on to higher education and from there into a range of professional jobs.

Looking back on their school experiences, both Blondel and Granville admit that being the only two black children in their school produced its 'challenging and extremely difficult moments'. Blondel, for instance, still recalls how one teacher literally told her 'to get back on the banana boat'. She also ruefully remembers, despite passing twelve O levels and being the top-placed student in her year, receiving careers advice that she should either look for a factory job or train to become a nurse on the basis that 'she would feel more comfortable in those sorts of jobs'. Granville can also remember the name-calling he endured and similar discouraging careers advice, but both make the point that their late mother was more than a match for anyone who tried to hold back her children.

Mrs Hodge would not hesitate to present herself at the school to protect her children's interests, whilst at home she was a source of comforting advice, constantly instilling in all her children 'the need for them to be ten times better than anyone else to overcome the prejudice of others', says Blondel. Granville says forthrightly, 'All the nonsense we received at school was countered by our mother, and her advice was always for us to keep our eyes on the target.' That advice was heeded by Blondel, Granville and the other Hodge siblings, and that clear focus remains a feature in their professional and business lives today. In memory of their late mother, the two partners have recently launched a legal scholarship in her name—The Cora Hodge Memorial Scholarship—at Hull University.

Blondel vividly recalls the first meeting she attended as a legal consultant at the Stock Exchange, 'when there was that pregnant and embarrassed pause as I was introduced'. Falling back on her mother's constant training, Blondel explains. 'If you are switched on you don't crumble or cry oppression, you just open your briefcase and take out the work you have prepared.' Blondel admits that she and her team are always fully prepared, often to the point of being over-prepared, for any work they do for clients. Both brother and sister admit that in their professional lives, to varying degrees, they have had to deal with issues of being black virtually every day. 'But,' says Granville, 'we try to work out a strategy for dealing with it and moving on rather than being stumped by it.' Blondel adds proudly, 'Blue chip firms don't bat an eyelid about us now because they know our reputation.'

Having initially wanted to study medicine, Blondel decided instead on law, a decision helped in part by the opportunity she had to work in legal offices during her school and college summer vacations. She was particularly inspired by the experience of working for a black judge during one vacation spent with her parents in America. She has since spent all of her career in commercial practice, serving her apprenticeship with Gulf and Western before being head-hunted by the blue chip merchant bank Lazards, where she set up and managed their legal department. Having already established a considerable reputation for herself, when Blondel became pregnant the bank helped her to set up an office at home from where she continued to provide them with a consultancy service during and immediately after her maternity leave. It was this taste of working semi-independently that led Blondel to set up her own firm.

Meanwhile, Granville, after some years of government service, graduated in law from the University of Westminster. Serving an initial apprenticeship in shipping and maritime law, he too eventually took the decision to set up his own solicitor's practice. In 1995, brother and sister decided to merge their practices, thus creating Cluff, Hodge & Co.

Looking to the future, the practice is doing exceedingly well, although both declare that they have 'no

and Hodge

ambitions to conquer the world', but are aiming rather to build on what they have already achieved. 'It's a family firm, first and foremost,' asserts Granville. 'We may take on a few more partners but nothing beyond that as we will always want to retain control.' Besides work, they each want to find time for various other interests. Blondel was a Commissioner for the Commission for Racial Equality, a body about which she holds controversially strong views. She is also an active member of the National Art Collection Fund which works to raise funds to prevent pieces of art from being taken abroad and lost from the national art collection. Granville is an aficionado of the late great jazz musician John Coltrane, and aspires to write a book one day about the black contribution to Western civilisation.

Both lawyers happily see themselves as British and black. Granville makes the point: 'We are lawyers who are black and not black lawyers.' About the future position of black people in the UK, Blondel declares that 'education is the key to transforming black people's and anyone else's position.' Granville foresees 'the divergence of the black community, like it has in the United States, with the emergence of a black underclass', whom he sees as effectively 'the lost generation'. His concern is that there is a danger for black people in the UK that 'standards would then be set by and for the lowest common denominator and not the highest'. As if to counter this prospect single-handedly, our time together ends with Granville Hodge sharing with me his ambition for his son. 'We must aim for the top,' he says. 'I want my son to be the Prime Minister.'

Success is measured in many ways and the Cluff, Hodge & Co. partnership is clearly setting its own agenda for where it intends to be in the next millennium. I have no doubt that they will continue to be a successful law firm and to enjoy a harmonious working relationship, but it will all most certainly be achieved on their own terms.

City slickers

Pearls of wisdom

Karlene Davis

General Secretary, Royal College of Midwives

Karlene Davis is the head of a unique and powerful organisation which touches the lives of most people in the UK at some point or other. She is the General Secretary of the Royal College of Midwives (RCM), whose 37,000 members include virtually all practising midwives in the country who provide crucial clinical care to women in childbirth, who help bring most British-born infants into the world, and who generally provide ante- and post-natal support to new families.

It is an altogether impressive achievement that Karlene Davis, a black woman born in Jamaica, should have risen through the ranks of the nursing and midwifery professions to become the General Secretary of this august body which is steeped in British establishment history; founded in 1881, the RCM is the oldest professional organisation of midwives in the world and has HRH the Queen Mother as its distinguished patron. Karlene Davis fills this leadership role admirably, for she is a powerful and selfconfident black woman who combines the qualities of grace and good humour with a truly indomitable spirit.

Karlene explains that the Royal College of Midwives fulfils two interrelated but different functions. It is, first, a professional body, responsible for the education and training of midwives and, as such, for advancing the art and science of midwifery in order to improve the care of women in childbirth. It also acts as an independent trade union and general campaigning body for better employment conditions and recognition for midwives. Karlene admits that this dual role and twin focus does at times produce tensions and organisational challenges for the RCM. In addition to her duties as General Secretary (governed by trade union legislation), Karlene also acts as Company Secretary (the RCM is also a registered charity and a limited company) and as Chief Executive Officer, managing the body of staff directly employed by the RCM (sixty-six staff in total split between the head office and the country boards in Scotland, Wales and Northern Ireland). Despite her multiple roles, Karlene Davis is steadfastly focused on her key objectives. 'Essentially, if we want to deliver quality of care to women during pregnancy and childbirth, the midwives have to have a secure working environment, be well educated and trained, and have support in that environment. I see these two things working very much in tandem.'

To fulfil her roles, Karlene Davis has had to develop a high public profile. When I met her, midwives were campaigning through the RCM for improved recognition of their professional skills and responsibilities and for better remuneration, arguing for a separate pay structure from nurses, to be replaced with pay-parity with junior doctors. This campaign has brought Karlene and her colleagues into the media spotlight and resulted in regular and ongoing dialogue with the new Labour Government. Indeed, on the day we met, Karlene had just returned from a meeting with the Secretary of State for Health to discuss these very issues. Additionally, the RCM's acclaimed 'Safe Motherhood' initiative has also given Karlene and the RCM a strong international profile. Aimed at helping midwives in developing countries, the Safe Motherhood initiative is designed to enhance the overseas midwives' skills to try to reduce the high numbers of women and infants who still die each year in childbirth— some 600,000, mainly in developing countries.

Karlene Davis came to the UK from her native Jamaica in the 1960s to train as a nurse. She was happy to return home after completing her three years of training in Nottingham because, she says, 'coming to England was a massive shock to the system, an inhospitable environment for someone seen simply as "a little chocolate face".' Fate, however, intervened when her father died the year she returned to Jamaica, prompting Karlene to decide whether nursing was what she really wanted to do. She decided instead that she wanted to teach, and to pursue in more depth her professional interest as a family planning nurse. This pointed Karlene in the direction of midwifery. She returned to the UK to study for a teaching certificate and to train as a midwife (studying at the very College she now oversees), with the intention of combining the two skills back home in Jamaica. But like so many black Commonwealth migrants before and since, whilst Karlene was in the UK she gradually put down roots, got married and decided to stay.

Having attained her teaching and midwifery qualifications, Karlene says she was determined to be a good midwife. 'I wanted to succeed and make a difference. But I recognised that to do anything significant I would have to be at the level of decision-making and influence.' So began Karlene's steady progress towards the position she occupies today. Aware that other black midwives seemed somehow to remain stuck in the lower grades of clinical practice, never to become managers or educators, and therefore never adopting a leadership role in the profession, Karlene was determined to break the mould. After a number of years in clinical practice, she was appointed, in 1987, Director of Midwifery Education at Guy's and St Thomas's Hospitals in London. She later became Midwifery Advisor for the South East Thames Regional Health Authority before being headhunted, in 1994, for the post of Deputy General Secretary at the RCM. She was confirmed in the top post at the RCM—General Secretary—in 1996.

Reflecting on her career, she admits that she never imagined that she would achieve such a position of authority. 'I did not set tangible goals for myself but I did strive for recognition and I am ambitious—which is sometimes seen as a treatable condition,' jokingly adding, 'but I am not taking the medicine and haven't been cured yet!'

Karlene acknowledges the help and support she has received throughout her career. She recalls an early tutor and teaching mentor who helped sustain her sense of worth and self-confidence. This was underpinned by a loving and supportive home environment. Aware that being black and occupying such a visible position places added pressures on her, Karlene talks things through with a small group of trusted friends.

Not surprisingly, Karlene Davis draws inspiration from various female figures, historical and contemporary, whom she says 'have made a huge impression on me'. She cites amongst these Nanny, the Jamaican maroon woman who played an active part in the emancipation movement in Jamaica by organising female slaves; Maya Angelou, who as a single parent overcame many obstacles to become one of the most successful black writers in the USA; Winnie Mandela, for her strength and fortitude; and Gloria Knight and Beverley Manley, powerful and inspiring women in contemporary Jamaica.

Karlene expresses some concern for the millennium. Although she believes things in the UK are different from what they were twenty or thirty years ago, she feels there is not yet a sufficient critical mass of black role models and there is still a general problem of self-fulfilment amongst young black males in British society.

Karlene has lived the greater part of her life in Britain and I ask her which country she now regards as home. She laughingly but very pointedly responds: 'I feel this is where I ought to be, but home is more than where you live, it's where you feel you belong. I do not yet feel absolute recognition and a valuing of diversity sufficient to make me feel that I fully belong here.' A clear challenge, I felt, from Karlene Davis, herself a role model of immense stature, to Britain for the millennium.

Juliana Edwards

Principal Consultant, Korn Ferry International

In common parlance, Juliana Edwards is a professional head-hunter. Using somewhat more conventional terminology, she is a principal consultant in the executive search business, specialising in finding and recruiting senior-level managers and divisional or main board directors for major companies and organisations in the UK and overseas.

The nature of high-level corporate recruitment in today's business world dictates that few of these positions are ever advertised directly. Instead, companies prefer to use an executive search agency which will either do the head-hunting for them, that is, go out and find 'the players' who could do the required job—or, in many cases, also take on the next stage of setting up and running the selection interviews on the client's behalf. Typically, if a company is prepared to offer a starting salary of £100k, it wants someone who is going to make a fundamental impact on the organisation and its bottom line performance, and the belief is that such individuals are known quantities who have to be ferreted out of their current niches, preferably without the competition knowing what is going on and who is behind it. This is where Juliana Edwards and her colleagues in the executive search industry come into the picture.

Juliana Edwards is Principal Consultant with Korn Ferry International, a major American concern which is generally regarded as the world's top executive search agency. Based in central London, Juliana's role with Korn Ferry is to help build its portfolio in the UK and across Europe and the US in the public sector—a sector which, as a sign of the times, now also uses the services of search agencies. It's a huge sector,' says Juliana, 'encompassing central and local government, health care agencies, educational establishments, charities, international development agencies and the like.'

When I met Juliana for the *Millennium People* interview, she was only a few months into her new role at Korn Ferry and I was to learn from our discussion that she had been headhunted herself to join the firm. Prior to her move to Korn Ferry, in the preceding six years Juliana had owned and run the UK's first black-owned and managed executive search agency, Headfirst. Although a small company by the standards of some of the other agencies, employing at its height only five others besides Juliana, Headfirst had nonetheless succeeded in building a good reputation for itself in a relatively short period of time, and forging inroads into what is a highly competitive market.

Juliana recounted with evident pride and satisfaction how she had faced hurdles in getting her company off the ground. Although she had spent a number of years working for another big search company and had numerous contacts in the field and in the recruitment industry, Juliana explained how 'in the early period I was literally laughed at and patronised'. At twenty-eight, black and female, Juliana Edwards apparently did not fit the expected profile of someone likely to succeed in a business of this nature.

On the basis of her well-prepared business plan and promising telephone discussions, banks which at first seemed willing to advance the necessary capital would suddenly, and embarrassingly, backtrack on sight of Juliana. This did not deter her. She was spurred on by her firm belief that there was a significant gap in the market, precisely because many search agencies operated on the same stereotyped basis as the banks from which she was seeking her start-up loan. Juliana's experience and background told her she was more attuned and better able to spot talented people whom other agencies would either ignore or simply overlook: people with potential, people crossing industry sectors, but more especially, talented women and people of different ethnic backgrounds. Starting Headfirst, initially as a sole trader with simply a telephone, computer and bank overdraft, Juliana used her contacts to set up a database. She very quickly found that there was indeed a growing number of companies who were receptive to seeing a shortlist of such diverse but quality candidates who were in some way different from the norm.

Piggybacking fortuitously in the early 1990s on the launch of high-profile Government-backed initiatives such as 'Opportunity 2000'—aimed at increasing the profile of women in senior management across UK industry—Headfirst was soon competing with some of the big search companies and, most importantly, winning new client business. It was a tremendous experience,' says Juliana. 'We were involved with a number of key industry appointments,' and she cites among them some of the major companies who joined the client portfolio of Headfirst, such as EMI, American Express, Grand Metropolitan and Yardley, the cosmetic giant.

After six years in operation, Headfirst was at the stage where it would have to make the leap from being a small executive search company to a medium sized one when Juliana was herself unexpectedly headhunted by Korn Ferry. Juliana admits that 'there was more than a degree of sadness on closing the business I had built over the years. But you cannot dwell on the past too long, otherwise you will be unable to move forward.'

It is ironic and itself somewhat revealing to learn that for someone whose subsequent business and professional career has been to find and recruit leading players in industry at home and abroad, more than twenty years ago when she received her own careers advice at school, Juliana was discouraged from her interest in the field of personnel management and advised to consider nursing instead, because, it was explained, 'it did not require as many GCE O level qualifications'. Ignoring the advice she was given, and going on instead to achieve a degree in psychology, Juliana nonetheless forged a career in her chosen field and has followed an upward path ever since.

Juliana attributes the source of her drive to succeed partly to her mother, who not only instilled a high regard for education in all her children, but in raising five children virtually single-handed continues to provide Juliana with a strong role model. The separation and eventual divorce of her parents whilst Juliana was still at school also acted as a spur. She recalls 'wanting to rise above the stereotyping of the children of single parents and to become what people didn't expect me to become. The alternative,' she says, 'was to become a victim and for me that was totally unacceptable.'

This robust disposition throws light on the other dimension to her drive to succeed, that which comes from within. Juliana declares that 'I have always been motivated to be in a position where I can influence the direction of the organisation and make a real difference.' She adds ruefully. 'If I could not do that I would not be able to get myself out of bed in the morning!'

Born in London and raised in the Midlands town of Rugby, Juliana regards herself proudly as black British, and sees the millennium as potentially offering a milestone and pivotal turning point for black people in the UK. 'There is at last a recognition that we are here to stay.' She hopes that the new millennium will also bring with it a greater recognition and reflection of Britain's black talent in corprate boardrooms and senior management structures.

Hunting heads

Opening doors

Michael Fraser

Entrepreneur and Campaigner for Ex-Offenders

Michael Fraser is a highly successful entrepreneur who personifies all the old clichés about 'rags to riches', 'pulling yourself up by the bootstraps', 'succeeding against the odds', and so on. A modest man, Michael prefers to call himself simply 'an employer'.

Michael Fraser's life story is fascinating. Here is someone who spent much of his childhood in and out of the care of Social Services, was expelled from more than one school, eventually leaving with no qualifications to speak of, drifted into petty crime in his early adulthood, and generally looked to be heading down a steep and slippery slope. Yet today, at thirty-seven, Michael Fraser is the owner, chairman and managing director of a successful Midlands-based aluminium products company, MCF Services, which has an annual turnover of £8m and employs some fifty-five people.

Despite his position and the outward trappings of success—Michael's current stable of cars includes a Ferrari and a chauffeur-driven Bentley—he remains an exceedingly down-to-earth and unassuming man. During our time together, I was impressed by his disarming openness and honesty about his early life, including casually mentioning that even to this day he still has trouble with reading and writing. I feel that the photograph of Michael taken at his factory, amid stacks of aluminium strips, conveys something of his engaging charm.

Looking back, Michael records two factors which marked the turning-point in his fortunes and, indeed, his life. He recalls his sheer fright at the looming prospect of a jail sentence. Having been arrested for receiving stolen property at the age of sixteen, his social worker warned him that this time it could mean prison. The shock of what could lie ahead made him resolve 'to get a job, work hard, and try to get my life in order!'

The next pivotal point was getting started in a job. Despite his criminal record and tearaway past, the owner of a small aluminium company was somehow prepared to take a risk with Michael and employed him as a junior or, more accurately, a general factotum. However humble the start, this willingness to see beyond the record sheet and give people a chance to make up for their early mistakes has not been lost on Michael. It has become his personal mission and emblematic of how he conducts his own business. More than twenty years later, Michael is still in touch with his former 'mentor' and boss, whose company is now a much smaller client company of his own business.

Michael relates his story and explains his rise from the shop floor to manager's office and boardroom. He quickly progressed from sweeping the factory floor to becoming a cutter working a milling machine. Once there, although boring and monotonous, he found he had a knack for the work, and was able to cut aluminium door frames two or three times faster than anyone else. If he really applied himself—by setting targets to relieve the boredom, and often working seven days a week to achieve them—Michael found he could bring in a tidy wage at sixty pence a frame. Later, as the fortunes of the company dipped and his earnings diminished, Michael was approached by one of the customer companies aware of his prodigious output as a cutter. He was told that, should he think of going into business for himself, they would be willing to purchase his aluminium frames at £6.50 each!

Although Michael had never seen himself as anything but, at best, a jobber and a wage earner, given the lure of the contrasting figures (60 pence versus £6.50 per frame), and encouragement from his wife, he somewhat apprehensively decided to give it a go. He set himself up as a sole trader, took a small bank loan, found basic premises and, for the next two years, proceeded 'to work all the hours I could making frames and building the company towards what it is today'. After two years, Michael took on his first employee (who is still with him today), and has seen his turnover grow steadily from £80k a year to the present figure of £8m, over the last ten years.

In response to questions about how being black may have had an impact on his life and on his business, Michael cites the fact that he is still more at ease conducting most of his business over the telephone, precisely because of his colour. In his view, 'potential business contacts are less likely to make judgements based on my colour or any other superficial criteria if they do not know the colour of the person they are speaking to'. Furthermore, when he drives his cars, one of his great pleasures in life, he is sometimes stopped by the police to prove ownership of the vehicles, and he also finds himself putting up with the odd racist calls from passing white motorists. Michael chuckles as he recounts how he often responds to shouts of 'Nigger!' from passing motorists with his own retort, 'No, it's a Ferrari ...!'

His experiences as a black businessman notwithstanding, Michael Fraser feels that the biggest barrier he has had to overcome is that of being an ex-offender, and that is why he now channels much of his energy into helping other ex-offenders get back on track. In acknowledgement of what 'being given a chance' meant for him, Michael makes a point of employing ex-offenders in his own company, helping them to re-establish their self-esteem and providing them with a stepping stone back into society. He is also a national board member of the Apex Trust—an organisation which works on behalf of ex-offenders—through which he regularly gives talks to schools and youth groups, as well as visiting prisons. Michael Fraser is trying, as he puts it, 'to get others to believe in themselves and to feel that they too can achieve their goals, whatever their start in life'. Perhaps without fully appreciating it himself, Michael Fraser is in his own right an impressive example and role model for the very cause he espouses.

Angie Greaves

Radio and Television Broadcaster

For several years on my daily commute to work, I would tune in to London's Choice FM radio station to listen to Angie Greaves on her early morning programme. As I mulled over the idea of *Millennium People* on those long drives, I was captivated by the deeply soulful and touching voice of the first black woman to hold a prime-time anchor position on a London breakfast radio show. It was clear to me even then that this was a woman of great talent and enormous depth and someone who should surely be included in any future *Millennium People* project. Several years later, my interview with Angie Greaves confirmed my initial impressions and provided many more insights into this gifted broadcaster.

With over fifteen years experience in radio, eight of them as a broadcaster, Angie Greaves has, in the last few years, also begun to make her mark in television. After some initial work on cable stations, she made her national TV debut when she was selected to present the black light entertainment show 'Get it On' as part of the BBC 2's 'A Force' series. More recently she was one of the presenters on the acclaimed 'Windrush' series aired by BBC 1. She is nonetheless more regularly to be found presenting her radio programme on London's GLR radio, which is where I managed to interview and photograph her shortly before she went on air.

Angie is open and honest enough to admit that she is still learning the ropes of television, and that radio remains her first love. 'I still feel more at home on radio. What I love about it is that you can actually become somebody's friend through the speaker. I could broadcast in jeans and a sweatshirt and nobody would know. As long as I am feeling good inside and can put that across, that is all that matters.'

Whether clad in jeans and sweatshirt—or dressed more sartorially—Angie Greaves has been touching people with her radio broadcasts for many years. At Choice FM, a local black radio station, she achieved an almost cult following. Whilst there she earned the distinction of being the only broadcaster in any medium whom Jesse Jackson, US Special Envoy and former presidential candidate, would give an interview to on a whistle-stop visit of Britain in 1997, at a time when US policy in Africa was hot news. 'I still get the odd letter even now from people who remember the interview,' says Angie, clearly touched by the recollection.

Her daily readings on the show from *Acts of Faith* by Iyanla Vanzant and *Black Pearls for Parents* by Eric V. Coppage—two books which provide inspiration and philosophies of life—were so moving that they led to the radio station being inundated with calls. Bookshops across London were also swamped with orders. Such was the interest she generated that the national press quickly followed up wanting to know who this broadcaster was who had created such an impression.

Although playing 'first cut records' and getting exclusive interviews with prominent bands and stars—of which Angie Greaves has done many—the real thrill and challenge as a broadcaster, she believes, is in making a more profound impact on people's lives. This is the direction in which she hopes to move in the future. 'There is something inside of me just itching to get out from light entertainment and to get into more serious radio and television.'

With her talent and drive for broadcasting, it came as a surprise to learn that initially Angie Greaves had no aspiration to be a broadcaster. If anything,' she says, 'it was the most frightening thing I could ever envisage.' Her first career ambition was to become a teacher. Taking a temporary secretarial position with the BBC as a means of earning money to attend teacher training college, led instead to Angie remaining in the industry for the next six years as an administrator. It was whilst working at Capital Radio as a radio archivist, that the door to broadcasting was unlocked for her.

In setting up an archive of all the celebrity interviews broadcast by Capital Radio, Angie's job brought her into contact with the station's presenters. It also required her to spend hours in the studios listening to and editing tapes in order to catalogue them. One day in the studio Angie found herself on the receiving end of some good-humoured teasing and she responded off the cuff in a mock-American gospel accent. The exchange was overheard by one of the station's presenters, David Jensen, who immediately asked her to put it on tape. This inadvertent exchange led to Angie making voice 'jingles' for David Jensen's programme and, subsequently, for many of the station's other disc jockeys. Angie recalls, 'There came a point when my voice was heard on the radio virtually every hour.'

The door of opportunity opened further during a holiday visit to her native Barbados in 1987. Unbeknown to

Angie, her eldest brother had leaked the news to the local press that a 'Capital Radio presenter' was visiting the island and was hoping to broadcast on Barbados's Liberty radio station. Although in reality Angie was still a production assistant, albeit also a maker of jingles, the local press coverage given to her resulted in an invitation to present on the radio station. 'In the end I had no alternative but to do it,' says Angie, 'but that programme made me realise that the fear of being behind the mic was only as big as I made it, and in truth it was not frightening at all.'

Returning to Capital Radio motivated by her experience, Angie put in countless hours after work and during breaks making tapes and practising the art of radio broadcasting. She would often ask presenters like David Jensen, Tony Blackburn, David Hamilton, Lynn Parsons, and Charlie Gillick to listen to her tapes and give their honest feedback, which they readily did. Recalling their insightful advice and constant encouragement, Angie is effusive in her praise for the help she received. 'Had it not been for Capital Radio I would not be where I am now. Everyone I asked for help stuck their necks out for me.'

Her thoughts and reflections about the millennium range from optimism about the continued penetration and rise of black people in corporate Britain to feeling troubled by the difficult position she still sees for black youths. 'Black youths need to be nurtured and encouraged to believe they can achieve,' she says. 'It only takes one small apple to start an orchard.' Angie is equally reflective about radio broadcasting: 'Black people do more than go to clubs and listen to music,' she asserts. 'Radio stations need to reflect the broad spectrum of interests that black people have rather than just the narrow stereotypical ones.'

Amongst people whom Angie most admires are Oprah Winfrey— 'as a black woman who started out way behind others and came through as she has, I admire her strength'— and Jesse Jackson— 'one of the few black men whose personal standing allows him to call the US President and say I need to see you. I long for the day when a black man or woman can do that in Britain,' says Angie. She adds, 'I have never hidden my Bajan roots. I am proud of them and don't want to lose that connection. I am a black British woman of Bajan descent.' To my mind, Britain is enriched by the likes of Angie Greaves. I believe the millennium holds many things for this truly soulful broadcaster.

On the right wavelength

Paul Greene

Journalist and Television News Presenter

'I believe we have a duty to ourselves to explore our own potential and to pursue that potential wherever it may lead us,' says Paul Greene unequivocally. One could be forgiven for thinking that here is a person who has found his niche and is actively pursuing his potential at the highest professional level. Yet my interview with Paul Greene revealed that besides being a well-known and talented journalist, he is also someone with other, less known creative skills, to which he is positively yearning to give full expression.

Paul Greene is of that select group of journalists whose talents enable them to straddle concurrently all the main news mediums. He is familiar as a news presenter on Carlton television, and before that as a reporter and presenter of a variety of other television news and current affairs programmes, such as 'Thames Report' and 'Reporting London'. Paul Greene also has his own live current affairs radio programme, which is broadcast twice a week on the BBC's GLR radio station. In the field of print, he has a regular column in the weekly black features magazine, *Pride.*

Paul describes his television work as 'paying the rent', whilst the other mediums, more especially his column in *Pride,* offer an opportunity to express his own views on issues of the day. Paul confides that whilst he is in the main happy with this basket of journalistic outlets, he would still like to explore and do other things unrelated to his present profession. ' I would like to think that I am more than the sum of my journalistic parts, and I certainly believe I have other things to offer.'

Sitting in his stylish London loft apartment—which I discovered reflects its owner's artistic talents—Paul Greene shared with me the other side of his creative aspirations. He is a painter and graphic designer, has a mean eye for interior design and, more recently, has begun exploring furniture design. Indeed, when asked what had given him greatest satisfaction, Paul cites an item of furniture which he designed and which he is currently having made up as a piece for his home. So interested is he in this potential parallel—or possibly new—career avenue, that he has a web site displaying his various furniture designs. 'I have always been interested in the visual arts, and sooner or later that expressive need will come out and possibly offer me a new career direction,' he declares. 'I am already in that transitional stage. My ultimate ambition is to design things for sale.'

Lest others be surprised by such a complete change of career, Paul explains that in his view an individual's creative energy and talents are transportable across boundaries, and that to some extent it is often quite arbitrary where those talents are ultimately directed.

His career in journalism was, he believes, a natural progression from his love of literature and desire to use words creatively. At school, English was his favourite subject and he particularly enjoyed writing essays. 'I was a complete bookworm as a child,' he laughingly declares. And although he attended a rather tough comprehensive school where, despite being the only black pupil, he became head boy, he succeeded in pursuing his passion for literature at university level where he read English and philosophy.

After university he initially tried a career in publishing before opting for journalism. His experience of getting into journalism demonstrates that one's creative talents need to be backed by determination and self-belief. Paul recounts how after making numerous unsuccessful applications for journalist positions, he concluded that the only way he could break into the field was to do a post-graduate course in journalism at Cardiff University. This made all the difference. On graduating, he succeeded in gaining a trainee journalist position with the *Birmingham Evening Post,* part of the biggest local newspaper group in the country.

Reflecting on the three years he spent with the group, Paul says it gave him an excellent grounding upon which he has gone on to build his career. He describes each of his subsequent journalism jobs—reporter and producer with GLR radio, researcher with the award-winning 'London Programme' on LWT, reporter with Thames Television—as providing the career stepping stones and experience vital in preparing him for his present position. Amongst the elements of his journalism career that give him most satisfaction, he again highlights not his work presenting prime-time television news programmes, as one might have expected, but his column in *Pride.*

'As a black man in Britain, I feel I have something to say on a variety of issues affecting black people. I focus on the most difficult issues and try to get my head round them—for instance, what it means to be black and British, mixed relationships, etc. Even if people disagree with what I say, I hope they think the pieces are well argued and thought-provoking.'

In response to whether he regards himself as black British, Paul is quite clear: 'My home is Britain, no question about that.' He elaborates that his parents are from Jamaica, and although he has visited the island several times and feels a great affinity with it, such that he would be keen to help the country's development in whatever way he can, he views himself as being of Jamaican origin rather than being Jamaican. 'This issue of identity', he says—jovially imploring me to read his column on the subject in *Pride*—'is of major importance to black people in the UK.' Paul adds, 'Once black people come to terms with the issue, it can become tremendously empowering because we can take the best from both worlds.'

Asserting that racism and discrimination have not disappeared but instead become more subtle, Paul Greene offers further views on the future for black people in Britain in the new millennium. He sees trends already under way as continuing into the third millennium, such as the increasing incidence of mixed relationships and intermarriage across ethnic boundaries, and the general blurring of cultures as styles, music, language, food and the like interchange and are adopted across cultures.

Paul Green is in the enviable position of having identified at least two forms which give expression to his creative talents and energies. Which one he chooses to pursue into the new millennium—should a choice be necessary—remains to be seen, but whichever it is he will no doubt bring to it the thoughtful and considered application and commitment he has always given to whatever he does. Who knows, he may even surprise us with yet further strings to his talented how.

From where I see it...

Lenny Henry

Entertainer

Variously described as 'a master of comedy' and 'one of Britain's best loved personalities', Lenny Henry is also arguably the best known black British person across any field in Britain, today. Show a picture of his genial features to a broad spectrum of people in the UK — regardless of ethnicity or age—and besides the ready recognition, another typical response might be an appreciative grin, such is the popularity and public persona of Lenworth Henry, more affectionately known as 'Lenny'.

Still in his early forties, Lenny Henry in his various guises, has been a regular on British television screens for well over twenty-five years. Although, perhaps, best known as an infectious stand-up comedian and front person for the hugely successful Comic Relief charity—which with Lenny's help raises millions of pounds in humanitarian aid for Africa —Lenny Henry possesses an impressive portfolio of creative skills and talents.

He is also an actor of growing accomplishment, has authored a series of children's story books and writes for television. He has presented a variety of serious documentary programmes and was until recently the chairman of his own television production company, 'Crucial Films'. And not to be overlooked, he is a father, husband and a would-be 'funkateer' (as his entry in *Who's Who* amusingly reveals).

Such a range of talents and responsibilities inevitably brings with it great demands. 'Success can be a double bind', says Lenny, 'when what I mainly want to do is be with my family. It's the most important thing of all.' As if to confirm Lenny's standing as well as the untold demands placed upon him, my own experience in securing this interview gave perhaps a brief glimpse of this.

His was among the first names penned in the planning and deliberation of *Millennium People*. And yet, although he was incredibly the first subject, without exception, to respond affirmatively to the dozens of letters sent to potential subjects —a huge fillip to a project still at the time in its infancy—it was, literally, some years later before we were able to conduct the interview. It was, nevertheless, well worth the wait. Despite interviewing him whilst he was on the set, and between takes, for the television drama series *Hope and Glory*, Lenny was gracious with his time and expansive in his responses, and all with great humour—such that I felt at times as if I had been granted my very own *Lenny Henry Show*.

Born in the West Midlands town of Dudley, the sixth of seven children to Jamaican factory worker parents, Lenny Henry first burst onto our screens in 1975, as the high-octane, sixteen year old winner of the then highly popular television talent show *New Faces*. With his zany impressions and jokes he became an overnight sensation and was immediately sought after as a stand-up comic in clubs across the country. Giving up his job in a local engineering factory on the strength of these early bookings, but with no prior entertainment experience behind him, Lenny readily admits to having a bruising apprenticeship as a comic entertainer. Says Lenny, with typical honesty and humour, 'After a successful three minute act on *New Faces*, I was suddenly in great demand and paid a lot of money to do a forty minute headline act… but I really didn't have an act to speak of, just a few gags and impressions.' Wanting to give up his fledgling career on numerous occasions during this immensely difficult period, Lenny stuck it out. Encouraged by his stalwart mother, Lenny Henry learnt his craft, and has grown into the all round entertainer he is today.

If his early career started off hesitantly and somewhat less than 'politically correct'—he spent five of his early showbiz years on the *Black and White Minstrel Show*, which although he admits helped hone his stagecraft, for a young black man of the time it was decidedly dodgy for his image –it is evident he has since matured into a very savvy and astute entertainer. He developed over the years a strong repertoire of black comic characters and themes in his material, which confidently and hilariously depict aspects of black British life. This not only endeared him hugely to black viewers, but with his primetime airing and amiable persona, he engaged and enlightened his majority white audience in equal measure.

His acting career has followed a similar upward progression. From early appearances in the seventies black situation comedy, *The Fosters*, he has appeared in various feature films—including a foray as the comic lead in the Hollywood production, *True Identity*—through to his lead role in the BBC production of *Chef*, and more latterly as the headteacher (Ian George) in the acclaimed television series *Hope and Glory*. With its setting and story lines about the British education system, Lenny is particularly proud of *Hope and Glory*, which he sees as an inspirational drama. 'When the script came through I leapt up and down and said, "This is it!" I really wanted to be involved. Hopefully,' he adds, 'the message and issues we touch on will have some kind of positive effect.'

Lenny is effusive in expressing his indebtedness to those whom he feels helped lay the foundations to his success. 'My childhood friends, who encouraged me to be funny and inspired me with their encouragement…various DJ's in and around Dudley, who would let me get up in front of the disco crowd and do my act…the Dudley comedian, Don McLean, who saw I was struggling and basically taught me how to be a comedian…Chris Tarrant, the television presenter, who was like the school head boy whose approval I sought, and from who—as such a fearless broadcaster—I learnt not to be scared of the camera.' He reserves particular praise, however, for two special people: his wife Dawn, herself a renowned comedy actress, whom he says glowingly, 'has been an incredible influence on my work from the beginning'; and his late mother, Winnie, whom he adds touchingly, 'made huge sacrifices for her family and gave up so much to bring us all up. She was just such an inspiration.'

Prominent amongst historical and contemporary figures Lenny Henry admires is the Revd. Martin Luther King – 'his "I Have a Dream" speech still makes me tingle,' says Lenny. Influenced perhaps in part by his own musical and 'funkateer' interests, Lenny also proclaims his admiration for 'the incredible talent and work ethic of Stevie Wonder and Prince.' On changes he has witnessed in the entertainment industry, Lenny observes, 'there are more black people around in the business today, but as far as mainstream British television is concerned, it is still sparsely populated by black people…very few mainstream shows have a black lead. It's a real slow process, like water dripping on a stone, but will have an effect one day.'

Strongly proud to be both black and British, Lenny adds that being of West Indian extraction and growing up in the West Midlands has given him a particular sense of humour, with a rich frame of reference to draw on. For Lenny, 'the high ground to capture in this country is helping people understand each other.' Clearly, with his unique brand of humour and multi-faceted talents, Lenny Henry has been doing just that to admirable effect for the best part of a quarter of a century and given his still driving ambition—'I think this will be the most creative period of my life' says Lenny—his reign as the king of comedy looks set to continue for a good time yet.

Seriously funny

Philip Henry

Assistant Director, Serious Fraud Office

As an Assistant Director of the Serious Fraud Office (SFO), Philip Henry has the distinction of being one of Britain's most senior black civil servants. In civil service parlance, he is a member of the 'First Division', which is the staff association for the most senior grades within the civil service. What defines Philip Henry perhaps more than his senior civil servant status, however, is the fact that he is a barrister by profession— 'I am a lawyer first and foremost, who happens to be a civil servant,' says Philip—and with it a senior Crown Prosecutor in the Serious Fraud Office.

The SFO was established in 1988 to investigate and prosecute serious and complex fraud. Based on the recommendation of a Royal Commission, the Government recognised that given the increasingly complex and intricate nature of crimes of fraud, which often involve spectacularly huge sums of money dispersed and hidden through an elaborate and international web, it required an agency with a specialist range of skills to properly investigate and prosecute these crimes. The inauguration of the SFO, with its teams of lawyers, accountants and other specialist staff working in conjunction with police officers (who form part of the investigation team), was the Government's response to this issue.

Joining the SFO virtually at its outset, Philip Henry leads a divisional team of about twenty-two staff. For cases to be assigned to the SFO they have to involve alleged fraud in excess of £1m, while cases below this figure are dealt with by the respective police constabulary in which the alleged fraud occurred. 'Everyone in the team is a skilled professional. Even the administrative staff and our law clerks have fantastic skills to interrogate systems, search and follow accounts all over the world,' says Philip with evident pride and confidence in the team he leads. More complex cases will often see additional external expertise from the big accounting practices being brought in where necessary, and some cases can take two to three years to investigate.

'It's not a question of looking for a thumbprint on a window,' Philip explains in response to a query about the media perception that the SFO can be slow and ponderous in prosecuting cases. 'A tremendous amount of information has to be tracked down and sifted. One case alone produced over three million documents.' He also points out that with assets purposely hidden overseas to prevent their recovery, his job and that of his team regularly takes on a diplomatic dimension. Approaches and requests have to be made in accordance with international law, and with much sensitivity, through a variety of overseas governmental agencies. 'It takes time to flush out such information,' says Philip.

A recent Parliamentary Answer provided by the Solicitor General revealed that in the year to the end of February 1999, the SFO had secured convictions in nineteen of the twenty cases it had prosecuted. 'We cannot do much better than that,' says Philip. He is meticulous in making clear that as a Crown Prosecutor—appointed to investigate and present the facts to Court—he is not, and should not be, triumphalist, but he adds, 'We are rightly proud when we do a job well.'

Prior to joining the SFO—initially as a Case Controller before being promoted to his current position—Philip Henry spent a number of years in practice in the UK and at the Bar in his native Antigua. I was to learn, however, that Philip Henry's career path was not always the straight, upward progression that one might assume from his status today.

Born in Antigua, Philip left with his family when he was two to live for a period elsewhere in the Caribbean prior to coming to the UK. He admits to not doing particularly well at school in England and leaving with 'limited qualifications'. Unsure of what to do career-wise, he drifted into accountancy, 'simply because they gave me exemptions from certain examinations', he says. He had part-qualified in accountancy before realising just how bored and unchallenged he felt, and decided to do something constructive about it. At the age of twenty-three he went back to college—Kingston Polytechnic—to study law. 'But', he says, 'once I decided to become a barrister, I was single-minded about it and intent on doing the best I possibly could.'

Winning his law school prize and qualifying as a lawyer, given his faltering career start, still provides Philip Henry with a great sense of satisfaction. Philip also fondly remembers his first case at the Bar, jokingly recalling being up against a senior lawyer and 'being completely useless', but winning nevertheless. He laughs as he says, 'I think the jury felt more sympathy for me than for my client!'

From an early stage in his legal career Philip took a liking to prosecuting rather than defending—although he has experience of both. The cases he has prosecuted include conspiracy and murder trials in Antigua, where he says rather matter of factly, 'I was prosecuting defendants who were sentenced to hang.'

Philip's uncle, himself a QC in Antigua, was particularly influential in his career. He also acknowledges his father's support and advice when he struggled to gain a place in chambers in the UK. On his father's advice, he successfully applied for a position with the Antiguan Prosecution Service and gained valuable experience during the three years he spent there. 'I was taking cases far beyond what I would have had the opportunity to do in the UK.' In answer to whether he regards himself as black British or Antiguan, Philip explains, 'After three years away I was ready to come "home" to England.' With his parents and brother and sister still living in Antigua, he says, 'I anticipate spending some time there, perhaps even buying property, but Britain is definitely home.'

Although enjoying his work at the SFO, Philip is unsure how long he will remain a civil servant and ponders whether he may return to the Bar owing to his strong interest in advocacy. He shares his one regret at leaving the Bar when he did, which meant he could not explore the possibilities of becoming a judge, but declares that wherever his career takes him in future, 'I do not feel my ceiling has been reached and would like to think I have the potential to go a lot higher.'

Fighting fraud

Jazzie B

Recording Artist, Producer and Entrepreneur

Jazzie B is variously described as front man, artistic figurehead, chief architect or, more simply, leader of the Soul II Soul band and its wider business organisation. These are not titles that sit easily with Jazzie B, who stresses that Soul II Soul is a collective organisation and group of musicians. It's not about "I and I" but about "we",' says Jazzie. There is little doubt, however, that when Soul II Soul burst onto the music scene in the late 1980s and early 1990s, becoming the biggest and most successful purveyors of black British music worldwide, it was in Jazzie B himself that most people were interested. He not only symbolised the group, with his trademark 'locks', and stood as its media spokesperson, but he was its creative driving force. As a result, Jazzie B became, and remains something of, a cult figure within Britain's black community as well as further afield.

I was especially pleased that Jazzie B (otherwise known as Beresford Romeo) agreed to be featured in *Millennium People.* Not only am I an admirer of Soul II Soul's music, but I also admire the way in which Jazzie B and friends have handled their huge success and celebrity status. Notwithstanding the trappings of wealth (which has sometimes brought Jazzie and company unfair criticism), they have in the main stayed together since their dizzy rise to fame over a decade ago. They have also very astutely created a Soul II Soul business empire in which the band and their music remain at the centre, but which extends to a record label, a string of music studios, property, publishing and the ubiquitous Soul II Soul fashion line.

I asked Jazzie how he describes himself professionally. He laughs loudly as he says, 'Musician, managing director and cleaner. Cleaner', he elaborates, 'is when I am having a bit of fun. I have been known to put that down on visa or immigration forms whilst travelling first class. But then that is what I was at one stage!'

Soul II Soul started essentially as a sound system— a mobile disco, for want of a better description—put together and owned by Jazzie and a group of his school and neighbourhood friends during their schooldays in north London. They began by playing their music at community centres, youth clubs, local dances, street parties or wherever else they could get bookings. So focused on music systems was he that Jazzie admits it interfered with his schooling. In his physics classes, for instance, whilst the other pupils

experimented with circuits, he built amplifiers and turntables; in design, he made speaker boxes, and in drama lessons, he tried to bring his music into the scene.

Although Jazzie's dedication to music earned him a certain reputation at school and in his neighbourhood, it did not enhance his job prospects. Thus, when the teenage Jazzie B left school, one of his first jobs was, he says, 'nothing more than a glorified cleaner'. He then moved on to other jobs which brought him into contact with his beloved music. For example, while working for a public address sound company, he built speakers. He also had a job with the Royal National Institute for the Blind making recordings for talking books. At the same time, he and his group of friends continued with their sound system, then a major part of black youth culture in Britain.

As they got older, Jazzie's team got into the warehouse party scene—when warehouses or other large venues would be commandeered and turned into pro-tem music venues attracting hundreds or even thousands of young people for a night of musical entertainment. In this way Jazzie and his friends garnered a large following. Says Jazzie, 'We were one of the most organised outfits on the warehouse scene, with estate agents who found us venues, facilities firms who provided crash barriers, and cash and carry companies who gave us drinks on sale or return. We even had smoke machines for special effects.' Through Jazzie's contacts in the sound companies he worked for, the group always had the very best audio equipment.

Jazzie explains that what was also part of the attraction was that unlike DJs at discos, in black music culture the sound system person sings their own tunes over the records and effectively creates their own music—sometimes known as dub plates or specials. 'We became popular,' says Jazzie, 'because we were the only ones at the time playing that style of music.' With Jazzie B and some of the others wearing their hair in trademark 'locks', and with their particular sense of style and fashion, an aura developed around them and they acquired the nickname of the 'Funki Dreds'.

It was not a big jump to the group becoming recording artistes. However, it helped that through Jazzie's work they had access to recording studios. They recorded a song that had become their trademark in the warehouses, called 'Fair Play', and it very quickly became a cult record and eventually a major commercial success. A string of

other hits followed, not least of which was 'Keep on Movin', written by Jazzie B, which became a massive international best seller. Soul II Soul went on to win two Grammy's—the music industry's equivalent of the Oscars—and a host of other awards, catapulting the band and black British music in general onto the world stage.

Reflecting on their rise from relative obscurity to celebrity status, Jazzie remarks, 'We really did not want to work in mundane jobs, so we needed to create something for ourselves that would give us a certain lifestyle, but just as importantly, we wanted to be something that our friends and families would be proud of. It was also about believing in ourselves.' He is especially proud, he says, that the group stuck together. 'We are still the same people who used to travel all those years ago in the back of vans, hanging onto our equipment. Away from all the money, the success, the rock and roll, we still have each other to share the glory with, and that is the greatest satisfaction.'

Another source of pride for Jazzie B is the award he won from the famous American civil rights organisation —the National Association for the Advancement of Colored People—for being an outstanding role model. Despite his success, Jazzie has remained a DJ playing music on London's Kiss FM radio station. He holds some very outspoken views about the position of black people in the British music industry. 'Despite the growing number of black artistes, very few black people in the music business are in positions where they can make major decisions.' He also believes that many record companies are only willing to commit money and effort to promoting bands which are white fronted because they believe it is not commercially advantageous to have too many black faces selling their products. Asked what he hopes for the next millennium, he replies, with a broad smile, the Soul II Soul trademark line: 'A happy face, a thumping base for a loving race.'

Jazzie views being black British as having the best of both worlds. 'I feel equally at home in the Caribbean and Africa as I do in England.' He says that his ambition is 'just to achieve'. 'Knowing I have already achieved a little in my time and that it helps those coming through now gives me a big buzz.' Whilst the industry and the public may be waiting to see if Jazzie B and Soul II Soul regain the musical heights they had previously attained, Jazzie says, 'I still have so many things I want to do,' and, adds intriguingly, 'There is much more to come.'

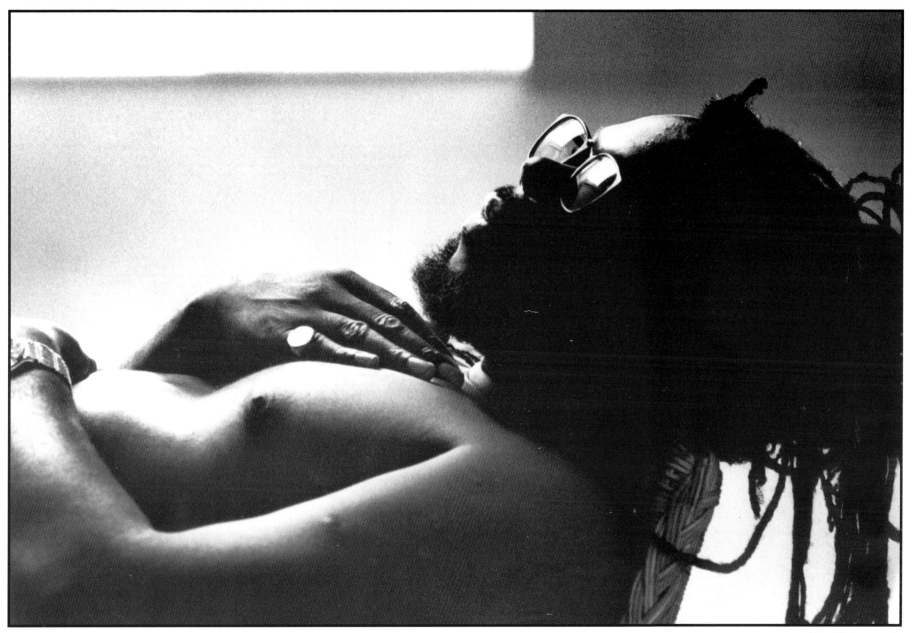

Soulful sounds

The right ingredients

Malcolm John

Head Chef

In the 1990s, London's reputation moved from fairly low down the culinary scale to a point where the city was widely hailed as one of the culinary capitals of the world. When London, with its large, cosmopolitan population emerged from the recession of the late 1980s, it experienced a burgeoning of restaurants of all types, offering a broad range of cuisines and catering to all styles and wallets. One of the by-products of this trend has been the growth of the celebrity or 'named' chef. Diners are sometimes attracted to a particular restaurant as much to engage the larger-than-life personality or witness the zany antics of their preferred chef as they are to sample the restaurant's food.

Someone who very much bucks the trend of the celebrity is Malcolm John, the highly experienced and well-travelled Head Chef of Brasserie St Quentin in Knightsbridge, London. In his late thirties, with over twenty years' experience in some of the finest restaurants in London and elsewhere, he remains decidedly unpretentious regarding his accomplishments. Histrionics and showboating are not his style. He refers to his staff as 'colleagues' and does not stand for any form of bullying in his kitchens. Diners are instead attracted to the establishment for the seemingly old-fashioned reason of its high-quality food and creative French - Italian cuisine.

Malcolm John, who came to the UK from St Vincent in the Caribbean when he was four, loves food, loves cooking and believes that it is his dishes which should do the talking. He says rather forthrightly for such a modest man, 'My food speaks volumes!'

'To work in this industry', says Malcolm John, 'you need more than to like food or to like cooking. You need to love it because it is also very hard work. I even love to cook at home for my wife and children.' In Malcolm's view, people are sometimes attracted to a career as a chef by its supposed glamour, but despite his management position—and he has fifteen staff working with him at his current restaurant—he spends as much time as possible on the kitchen floor, where it counts most, he contends. This means working in hot, often crowded and pressurised conditions. 'I want to see what my chefs are doing and what the customers are receiving,' he explains, and adds that the day before our interview he arrived at the restaurant at eight in the morning and was there until after midnight. It is an aspect of being a chef that is often overlooked by those who focus on the glamourous side of the business.

Malcolm started in the industry direct from school in the late 1970s as a 'kitchen assistant', a euphemism, he says, for 'general dogsbody'. He had learnt to cook whilst growing up at home, regarding this as effectively his 'informal apprenticeship'. 'Coming from a large West Indian family, with four sisters and one brother, we all had to do our share in the kitchen,' he jokes. He served his formal apprenticeship in a hotel in Coventry where he grew up, before moving to London to work at the prestigious Berkely Hotel, one of the Savoy Group of hotels.

Malcolm looks back on the five years he spent at the Berkely, including stints at the Savoy, as an excellent foundation for his developing career. 'For any young chef who wants good, solid experience in the industry, you have to work in a big hotel,' he says, 'and the Berkely and the Savoy have world-class reputations.' It was the era of the big kitchen, and there were more than ninety chefs at the Berkely. Despite this, Malcolm nevertheless rapidly moved through the ranks to become Sous Chef at the relatively young age of twenty-one.

With a deep interest in and love for Italian cuisine, Malcolm John went to work for a period in Florence and later on the Italian south coast, in order to gain greater insight into that cuisine. Returning to England, and after spells running the kitchens of one or two smaller but well-placed restaurants, he moved as the Executive Sous Chef to London's Michelin-starred Café Royal Grill Room. Owing to its star rating and its reputation as one of London's top restaurants, the Grill Room is frequently commissioned to also provide catering at prestigious outside events. Malcolm and the other chefs were often called upon to prepare meals at events such as Royal Ascot, and on cruise liners. 'It was a tremendous experience', says Malcolm, 'working at the very top end of the market.' Now Head Chef of a top Knightsbridge restaurant, Malcolm John particularly enjoys creating new and interesting menus and testing the skills and experience he has gained over the years.

Malcolm confides that a future career move for him is to buy and run his own restaurant, which would then allow him to give full expression to his creative talents. That, he declares is his definite goal, 'to own and run a restaurant which attracts customers prepared to pay for quality'.

Malcolm explains that being a black Head Chef has its trying moments. Not least because his preferred style of cooking is French - Italian, 'cuisines that are not too obviously associated with black people', he jokes. He recounts applying for a job at one of the more famous London restaurants. 'The advert for the job emphasised the need for Italian cuisine background, but when I walked in, I could see the stunned look on the owner's face. It was soon evident, however, that I knew what I was talking about and my track record was pretty indisputable. I got the job though, as in all my jobs, I then had to win over the staff and the customers. But', says Malcolm, 'after they have eaten my food all doubts are gone.'

Malcolm John laments what he sees as the virtual passing of the one-off stylish restaurant. To survive in the business today, he believes, restaurateurs need to own two or three restaurants to enjoy the benefits of economies of scale. Hence, most of London's well-known restaurants are now part of large groups. Looking to the future, there are some aspects of the business which Malcolm John will not be sad to see the end of, for example, some of the more excessive and poorer employment practices and working conditions that are still to be found in the industry. Says Malcolm, a chef very much involved with the industry's new Chef Apprenticeship Scheme, 'The removal of such practices would improve the quality of the working life of all kitchen staff and ultimately give customers a better all-round standard of service.'

It is clear that besides his creative culinary offerings, Head Chef Malcolm John's thoughts and views about the restaurant business in general could equally benefit from being savoured and digested by an ever-growing clientele.

Dr Terry John

Principal General Practitioner

As Dr Terry John approaches his twenty-fifth anniversary of qualifying as a doctor, it is hard to imagine that even in his younger days he could have been much more enthusiastic and forward-thinking about his work and issues related to the medical profession, than he is today. Graduating from the University of Birmingham's medical school in 1975, somewhat unsure of which medical specialism to pursue, Dr Terry John is now a Principal General Practitioner, at his practice in Waltham Forest, north east London, and a highly respected figure in the medical field. Indeed, his very inclusion in *Millennium People* is owed to the fact that he was personally recommended by the British Medical Association (BMA) as an ideal candidate for this book. Time spent in his company left me in no doubt why he is held in such high regard.

Dr John, a warm, jovial and unassuming man, struck me as a doctor with a great passion for his subject, and whose deep involvement and concern for the future training and development of new doctors, especially in the field of primary care, is akin to a mission. As he generously took time to explain the nature of his work and with it something of the structure and organisation of medical practice, I could not but be impressed by his knowledge of, and commitment to, the wider medical field.

As a Principal General Practitioner (GP), Dr John's status is equivalent to that of a senior consultant in any of the medical specialisms provided in hospitals. He explains that it is only since the early 1970s that 'general practice' and the work of those providing 'primary care', has come to be seen as a medical specialism in its own right. Hitherto, hospitals had been seen as all important, so that doctors in the main only turned to general practice if they had not progressed sufficiently in their careers within hospital practice. Today, Dr John adds, doctors cannot just walk into general practice, but can only become GPs once they have been properly trained, and prepared for work in the primary care field. This includes having spent time covering a number of hospital specialisms to a reasonably senior level, and having spent a year as a trainee GP or Registrar with an accredited GP

trainer. This is a subject I discovered that is clearly close to Dr John's heart, as he is the accredited GP trainer for his practice and also an undergraduate medical tutor for the London hospitals, St Bartholomew's and the Royal Free.

Beyond his interests and involvement in matters of medical education, Dr Terry John is an elected member of the General Practitioners Committee, a national committee within the BMA which represents GPs nationwide and which, amongst other things, negotiates directly with the Department of Health on behalf of doctors. He also sits on various of its sub-committees at both local and national levels. Another position he holds with great pride is that of Vice-President of the African Caribbean Medical Society (and was the former Chairman of the Society for a number of years). Established in 1981 by the late Lord David Pitt, the Society has over 100 black African Caribbean doctors in its membership and works both to educate the public about medical issues of interest and importance to black people—such as the incidence of diabetes, hypertension and sickle cell anaemia amongst black people—and to highlight issues of concern within the medical profession affecting black doctors.

Terry admits that growing up in his native Trinidad, although his parents wanted him to be a doctor, he rather took a liking to modern languages. It was only after having taken A levels in languages, and uncertain about which career route to take that he finally made the decision to switch to medicine. He chuckles as he recalls the price he paid at pre-medical school for having concentrated on languages to the exclusion of science subjects at A level: 'it really was intense hell catching up with the science I had not previously studied'. He stuck with it, however, and again it was only after qualifying and doing a spell at a small cottage hospital in Clacton-on-Sea—where he remembers for the first time engaging with a number of GPs, and observing the breadth of their work—that he decided general practice and primary care was the field in which he wished to specialise. Apart from a brief period when he returned to practice in Trinidad, Dr Terry John has

devoted himself to working in general practice in the National Health Service (NHS).

Whilst acknowledging the importance of parental influence in his career aspirations, and the support of some particularly encouraging teachers from his period at school in the Caribbean, Terry John is of the view that 'once one gets to a certain age it is more your own interest and personal drive that determines your future career direction and development.' Terry declares that he is particularly inspired by people such as Nelson Mandela— 'it's something to do with his indominability, strength and charm,' he says. 'Here is someone who has gone through so much yet has rolled with the punches and is able to give, as he does, with such grace and humility'—the Revd. Martin Luther King Jr. — 'his speeches still bowl me over'—and also mentions figures like Franz Fanon and Marcus Garvey.

Asked where he regards as home, Dr Terry John laughs as he points out that despite having spent his formative years in Trinidad, 'whenever I have been abroad, including even returning to the Caribbean, as I am flying back to London I always see it as "coming home". 'I have made my home here', he says laughingly, 'and I ain't moving!'

Looking to the millennium, Terry highlights the further, and what he sees as more far-reaching, changes that will affect the National Health Service under the new Labour Government, with the formation of 'Primary Care Groups'. The new structure will, he believes, impact even more on GPs and primary care provision than did the previous Government's changes to NHS practice. 'But', says Terry John in typical fashion, 'I am optimistic, it's in my personality. No change is not an option, you have to learn to roll with the changes. I believe you should get in there and try to make things work to your perspective. I see it as a challenge and it's quite exciting.'

Dr Terry John, with his enthusiasm, drive and vision, clearly has much he still wants to contribute to the medical profession into the new millennium, and the British National Health Service can only but benefit from the presence of this engaging doctor.

Finger on the pulse

Diane Louise Jordan

Television and Radio Presenter

The notion of giving '200 per cent effort to whatever you are doing, whether it is cleaning the country or running it', is something of a watchword in Diane Louise Jordan's family and one which she believes has helped her to get to where she is today.

Despite her diminutive figure, Diane Louise Jordan undoubtedly has stature in the broadcasting arena, where she makes an impact on whatever she does. This she seems to achieve almost effortlessly, even with an audience of one—me! After just two sessions together, her charm, warmth and good nature were so evident that it felt as if we were old friends meeting after a long absence.

Diane is perhaps best remembered amongst younger television viewers as a presenter of the BBC's flagship children's programme, 'Blue Peter', and more recently from another children's programme, 'Bright Sparks'. Indeed, her television career began in 1989 when she became the first black presenter of the high-profile Blue Peter programme. Such was Diane's popularity and impact that when she decided six years later it was time to move on, the BBC's Blue Peter office was deluged with calls, letters and presents from viewers whom she had clearly touched in some way. Over 90,000 people called during two days of voting to have their favourite film of her screened.

As Diane recalls, 'To receive such recognition and contact from the audience was an overwhelming and incredibly humbling experience.' It also confirmed that she was well on course to realise her guiding professional ambition: 'to reach out through my work to as many, and as wide a range of people as possible'. I witnessed at first hand Diane's enduring popularity and continued links with a programme she had left a few years previously; she was spotted as soon as she arrived for our photo session by crowds of schoolchildren who followed her every movement.

To other television viewers, she is known and admired for the presentations she makes on the BBC's 'Songs of Praise' programme. Diane's first 'Songs of Praise'—a special from Lourdes—must have made a huge impact as the BBC's switchboard recorded a fivefold increase in the normal volume of calls, each complimenting Diane's contribution and calling for her continued presence on the programme.

As well as her regular involvement with 'Songs of Praise', Diane has presented up to four different series in a season and makes frequent guest appearances on other television and radio programmes. She also does occasional stage work.

For someone who has established herself so firmly in the upper echelons of the broadcasting world, it might come as a surprise to learn that she only got into the profession as 'a dare' and in response to a challenge, having had no real ambition of becoming an actress or entertainer. When Diane's school friends dared her to complete an application form for a place at the Rose Bruford College of Speech & Drama because she 'was seen as the most unlikely person to be accepted', she decided to take them on.

Adopting her grandfather's philosophy of 'doing everything to the very best of your ability', Diane spent time putting together an application which secured her an audition. Furthermore, in readiness for the audition, and with the help of her school drama teacher, she prepared herself as thoroughly as she could, practising and rehearsing her pieces over and over again. Such was Diane's impact on the day that she achieved the unusual distinction of being offered a place at the college on the spot.

However, what really propelled Diane into the acting profession were the words of a well-meaning course director at the drama college. His advice to Diane was that although she had talent she would not be able to make a career of acting. Her colour, together with her small size and youthful appearance, would conspire against her getting many lead or strong roles and she would spend a lot of time 'resting'! Affronted by such comments, Diane determined that she had to rise to the challenge and prove to others as well as to herself that 'talent should not be overridden by purely superficial criteria'. Thus, leaving aside her previous thoughts of becoming an English teacher, she once again set about applying her grandfather's philosophy to her new goal.

Not only did Diane succeed in leaving college with an immediate long-term acting contract—the only student in her year to achieve this—but more than fifteen years later she has never been out of work in her chosen profession. Her achievements in theatre, film and broadcasting have proven without doubt that talent and ability cannot be thwarted by mere superficial considerations.

Diane extends this philosophy across life in general. 'You do not need to be exceptionally talented in order to achieve,' she asserts, 'but you do need to believe in yourself...If you can instill hope and ambition into someone when they are young, chances are that person will go on to achieve.'

Given the guiding influence provided by her family, it is not altogether surprising that Diane Louise Jordan cites her father and grandfather as being particularly inspiring role models. 'Ordinary people,' she says, 'but for whom I have the utmost respect.' She also greatly admires Nelson Mandela, 'a giver who was blessed with truly special qualities of leadership and vision but also humility and tolerance.'

In addition to her broadcasting career, Diane is immensely proud of, and committed to, her work as a member of the 'Diana, Princess of Wales Memorial Committee', a body chaired by the Chancellor of the Exchequer and set up to advise the Government on how the life of Diana, Princess of Wales, should best be commemorated. The fact that she was the only television personality asked to sit on the Memorial Committee is testimony to her wide-ranging appeal and a glowing endorsement by the nation at large.

With her kind words of encouragement, her genuine good grace and her expressions of practical support, it was a pleasure to have had the opportunity to meet someone as refreshing and as nice as Diane Louise Jordan.

Presenting Diane

Julian Joseph

Jazz Musician and Composer

Julian Joseph is forthright in proclaiming his passion for music. Although classically trained and at ease with all musical forms, it is jazz which very much defines Julian Joseph. As he eloquently puts it, 'Jazz is what I am. It's like my house, where I grew up and where I feel most comfortable and most creative. It's my roots and my foundations. And it offers me the power and grounding to work in any field, and that is jazz's great strength.'

Whilst still in his teens, Julian Joseph was already playing with many of the big names in British jazz and was one of the generation of brilliant young black British jazz musicians who helped to revive an interest in jazz in the UK during the latter part of the 1980s. Now in his early thirties, he is an acclaimed and highly accomplished jazz pianist and composer, and is a leading member of the British jazz firmament. Internationally, Julian Joseph has managed to carve out a niche for himself as a gifted musician with impeccable credentials. Such is his reputation that Julian's musical talents have taken him around the world. He has made concert tours of Japan, Australia, India, America and Europe, and it is fair to say that if jazz music had a higher level of exposure in the UK, akin to that of pop or rock music, Julian Joseph would be a household name with the British public in general.

Julian admits that although Britain is his home and where he would like jazz to have a stronger impact and presence on the music scene, 'Britain is not a deeply jazz friendly country. But', he adds self-assuredly, 'we can do so much more for jazz here. The potential for growth is huge, and that is the great challenge!' His further observation on this point reveals much about the man and his music. 'Besides', he says, 'whenever you have a real passion for something—and I am passionate about jazz—it's about fulfilling your passion, rather than about seeking fame or adulation. You might hope that fame and fortune follow, but that is not the driver.'

I met Julian Joseph for our *Millennium People* interview and photo session at Steinway Hall in central London. The stunning array of beautiful grand pianos made it a great location for photographing Julian at his craft. What particularly struck me in meeting and talking to this talented musician, is how gentle and genial this giant of a man is. Cutting an imposing physical presence, he is at the same time articulate, softly spoken, and very respectful and measured in his responses.

It is also evident that Julian's sense of artistic integrity, and his strong desire for acknowledgement and recognition by his musical peers—both objectives he already successfully achieves—matter more to him than simply attaining commercial fame alone. His conversation, for example, is littered with expressions and sentiments such as, 'I would like my music to have some kind of profound impact on the people whom I respect, and for me to inspire the people of my own and the younger generation.... Once your peers notice that you are setting goals and musical expectations that go beyond the norm and with a style that is uniquely yours—more so if they actually start to adopt your style—then to my mind you have really accomplished something....Essentially I am trying to harness and use my ability to make a great impact on the soul of the people who listen to my music.'

Julian Joseph, who variously leads, or performs with, his own trio, quartet, eight-piece band, big band and world-renowned orchestras, acknowledges his mother as being the primary influence behind his success. Born and raised in Wandsworth, south London, where he still lives, his mother saw to it that Julian and his two brothers were given early and continuing exposure to all forms of musical and creative expression, for example, by 'getting us piano lessons and encouraging us to watch musicians like Oscar Peterson when they were on television, taking us to concerts, galleries, museums, the ballet or anything artistic. Those things completely shaped my interests and my ideas,' says Julian.

Although all three brothers received piano lessons, it was Julian's talent which emerged earliest and strongest. Whether falling back on his family's musical tradition—Julian's architect father from Grenada was an R 'n' B singer in the 1960s and early 1970s, and his grandfather, legend has it, played the trumpet with Duke Ellington—or words of encouragement from his mother and his various piano teachers, or simply his own innate ability, Julian continued to progress rapidly. At eighteen, he was awarded a scholarship to attend a four-year degree course at the Berklee School of Music in Boston, Massachusetts. Although finding it a great wrench to leave home at the time, Julian's musical education was even further enhanced whilst at Berklee by the close friendship he developed there with the acclaimed Marsalis brothers—Wynton, Branford and Delfeayo. This association would lead to his early introduction to the American jazz scene when he toured across the United States with the brothers whilst still a student.

Julian Joseph could have elected to remain on in the much more jazz friendly America and develop his career there, but owing in part to the closeness of the Joseph family—his younger brother is today his manager and his mother is his accountant—as well as Julian's wish to make a contribution and give something back to the younger UK talent, he chose to return to Britain. Julian calls Britain his home. 'Whether or not black people go back several generations in the UK, our foreparents contributed to the growth and development of Britain, and if we want to fight for equality here then we must regard it as home,' he asserts.

Amongst those whom Julian Joseph finds most inspiring is the late Duke Ellington: 'A monsterous talent with incredible drive and focus who was constantly creative,' says Julian. Of contemporary figures, he cites Herbie Hancock and Wynton Marsalis, whom he says, 'really made me want to become a jazz musician'.

For the future, Julian's sense of mission about jazz has created a desire within him to see a 'jazz forum' established in Britain, through television, radio, education and important venues, 'somewhere young people can go, see, hear and learn about jazz'. For himself, he says modestly and much in keeping with his gentle personality, 'I would just like to continue to be creative and become a better musician and better composer, and be somebody who can reach out to more people and have a greater influence through my music.'

Jazzman

Kanya King

Chief Executive Officer, Music Of Black Origin

For many years Kanya King held a personal wish that one day the richness and depth of Britain's black musical talent would be properly recognised and celebrated. Quite simply, she longed to see a major musical award event which showcased the talent she felt had long made its mark on the contemporary British and, indeed, world music scene, but which more often than not was marginalised. Her vision was for a music award event which she could relate to and which, in giving due acknowledgement to black artistes and to black music, she would find personally uplifting and inspiring.

Although music award shows continued to proliferate and become more sophisticated and higher profile, nothing emerged over the years that coincided with Kanya King's vision. That is, until Kanya came to the conclusion that if no-one else was going to take up the idea, then she would have to herself. Today, a few short years since the MOBO awards—Music of Black Origin—were first launched (with Kanya King at the helm of the organising company), they have become an established part of the British music scene and are much coveted by those artistes fortunate enough to receive them.

'I had the idea for years,' says Kanya King, 'but never dreamt of putting on the event myself. All I wanted was the joy of seeing an event like this as a member of the viewing public.' As she began to give more serious thought to the idea, her first impulse was to try and convince other companies in the music industry to take it up. Not finding any success with this approach, Kanya describes coming to the view in early 1996 'that if she really believed in the idea and wanted to see these artistes being recognised in a show of this nature, then she would have to be prepared to put her hand in her own pocket and do something about it herself.

Starting on her quest in January 1996 as a complete outsider to the music business—although she had a few musician friends—she recalls working initially from a bedroom at her home with just a computer and fax machine. Desperate to raise sponsorship, she eventually found help in the form of the BIG Group, a PR and music promotions company, who liked Kanya's idea and gave her initial support. This, however, did not stop Kanya from having to dig deeper and deeper into her own pockets as the concept progressed. In order to meet the costs of the first MOBO launch event of that year, Kanya King re-mortgaged her house to raise £50k. Looking back at this decision, she candidly remarks. 'It probably made little or no sense from a financial investment point of view, but it was my dream.'

It was only after obtaining a definite television slot some seven weeks before the first MOBO awards, held in November 1996, that Kanya says, 'We suddenly realised we now had a real event to stage.' In an enormous effort, she and her team—in the last week working virtually round the clock—pulled all the organisational and PR threads together and staged the first MOBO awards. Held at the New Connaught Rooms, London, 500 invited guests and artistes were in attendance, including prominent politicians such as the Prime Minister to be—Tony Blair—and the then leader of the Opposition—William Hague—as well as some of the biggest names in black music. Highlights of the event were broadcast on television in London and in one or two other regions.

The event has grown rapidly in its short history, and has established a reputation as a premier music award event. The most recent event, held in 1998, took place at London's Royal Albert Hall. Not only was it was shown nationwide on British television, but was transmitted to a further 57 countries worldwide. Kanya King's rather modest initial vision had become a reality in a very big way. 'There are lots of people now involved. It's a real team effort,' says Kanya, but she adds with a sparkle, 'I still see MOBO as my baby. It's very hard work but I really enjoy it.'

Kanya King is the youngest of nine children. Her father Ghanaian and her mother Irish, but Kanya was born and raised in London. She refers to the difficult times the family had following the death of her father when Kanya was still young. She pays touching tribute to her mother. 'Not only did she marry a black man when it was not the done thing, but she brought up nine children in a strange city and under very difficult circumstances, It's amazing how she kept the family together, working so hard doing several jobs. I really admire her and she has certainly inspired me a great deal.' Her father, too, instilled values which Kanya remembers warmly, and which she feels still guide her today, especially his view that there are no short cuts to success, and that it is only arrived at through education, hard work and preparation.

Kanya describes herself as having done a range of weird and wonderful jobs, from working in a bakery to running her own promotional company supplying people to do market research. Prior to establishing MOBO, she was a senior researcher for Carlton Television, where she was a founding member and part of the production team on the Chrystal Rose Show. She talks about the impact of working for Chrystal Rose, whom she views as a confident, assertive, determined and energetic black woman and whom she describes as a role model. Having had the privilege of interviewing both Chrystal and Kanya for inclusion in *Millennium People*, I cannot but see the similarities between these two equally impressive women.

What is especially apparent about Kanya King is her focus and resolve. While acknowledging the moral support she received from family and friends in establishing MOBO, and the practical support from the BIG Group, she shares her general philosophy and approach to life. 'We had a lot of doors closed on us in the initial stages, not least because we had no track record in the industry.' She was not deterred by such obstacles, however and adds, 'You must be determined and just not take no for an answer. You also need to be prepared, and if and when you get your chance, to then deliver. Above all, you must be willing to take risks. I am not frightened of taking risks. If it doesn't work, I still won't give up, I'll just try something else.'

Kanya King describes herself as black British, but adds, 'I have Ghana in my heart and see it as my home, too.' It was her father's wish that his children should one day see his homeland, and Kanya shares with me the fact that she is due to visit the country for the first time in the coming months. 'It will be an emotional journey,' she says, 'made partly for myself and partly for my father.' Of the millennium, she says confidently, 'I feel it is an exciting time for black people. We have been held back for so long but I really feel our time has come and that the possibilities are there.'

With her plans to develop the already successful MOBO into a major communications company, with the awards event at its business core, but with many other related activities and ventures in the music field, Kanya King is quite literally living out her dream, and is one person whose time has definitely come by virtue of her own vision, resolve and single - minded determination.

Kanya do it too?

Oona King

Member of Parliament

The 'New' Labour Party's landslide victory in the May 1997 general election brought into Parliament a tranche of new MPs, among them Oona King. What is different about Oona King MP is that, for someone so new to Westminster, who admits to still be adjusting to her position as a backbench MP, and who is amongst the youngest of the 659 MPs in the House of Commons, she has already been tipped by sections of the media and by other parliamentarians and commentators to hold high ministerial office because of her considerable political potential.

When one then takes into account that Oona King is a young, rather chic black woman of Jewish origin, who has only just turned thirty, one can even more appreciate just how talented and able she is to have got to the position she occupies today—a mould-breaking woman MP.

When we finally managed to meet for our session it was late one evening at the House of Commons in between her Committee meetings and other commitments. Despite her busy schedule, and the late hour, she was fresh, charming and open. I tried hard in the short time we had to portray in her photograph something of her vitality and wide-eyed optimism.

'Becoming an MP', she jokingly explains, 'is like having a baby. You never sleep anymore and you start to speak a simple language—sometimes called soundbites!' She talks about the constant late nights at the House ('home by midnight if you are lucky, but more usually one or two a.m.'), the massive daily in-tray of letters from constituents and others she has to deal with (up to 1,000 a week), and the sometimes bewildering array of parliamentary protocols, practices and rituals which, as a new MP, she has to get to grips with and put to good effect.

Yet it was obvious to me how much Oona King enjoys and thrives on being a Member of Parliament. 'It is a great honour and privilege to be able to channel people into Westminster and give them access to government and the process of politics, especially people who would otherwise not have gone there or had the opportunity to experience it. I want to use the avenues that I have open to me, to open them

up to other people. That is what I believe is the role of an MP.' She tells me how heartened she recently felt in escorting a coach load of Bangladeshi women, dressed resplendently in their saris, through the House of Commons, much to the stares of some of the older, more conservative MPs who are still unused to seeing such groups in 'their' hallowed chambers.

Oona King is well aware of her place in political history. She is only the second black woman MP (Diane Abbot being the first in 1987), and one of only 239 women MPs to have ever been elected to the British Parliament (of which 120 are currently sitting MPs). She knows that she is up against years of ingrained tradition, but she believes that in trying to counter this she has the advantage of age on her side. In being elected while so young, not only can she give better expression in Parliament to the views and experiences of younger people, but she feels she has more time to learn how to make the parliamentary system work for her and the issues she believes in—in particular the twin issues of poverty and racism.

'Both sides of my family escaped poverty of the most grinding kind. One side endured slavery and the other side survived the holocaust,' says Oona. She has spent the early part of her parliamentary career grappling with the challenges of representing a tough inner city constituency (Bethnal Green and Bow in east London) with its high ethnic population mix alongside its high unemployment and other indices of social deprivation, as well as trying to maintain a more global perspective through UNICEF fact-finding missions to Sudan and Rwanda.

Intrigued by my enquiries into what drives a 'twenty-something' year-old to want to become an MP, Oona takes great delight in telling me that she had wanted to be an MP, indeed prime minister, from the age of five! So burning was this ambition throughout her formative years, that at one stage she thought herself a failure for not becoming an MP by the time she was twenty-four!

She credits both her parents—her black American father from Georgia, USA, and her white Jewish mother of Scottish, Irish and Hungarian extraction—but especially

her mother, for helping her attain her lifelong ambition. Oona's mother's response to her craving as a child to be an MP was always, she says, one of reassurance and encouragement that this ambition was well within the realms of possibility even for 'a black Jew girl'. This endorsement contrasted sharply with the careers advice she received at fifteen when she told her school careers teacher that she wanted to become an MP. The careers teacher advised her to set her sights on something more realistic, and perhaps think about becoming a librarian!

After graduating from York University with a first class degree in politics, Oona's ambition still burned brightly. She wrote to every Labour MP in the UK asking for a job before eventually landing a position in Brussels as a political assistant to the European Parliament. She spent five years there working for Labour MEPs, which gave her a good insight into the world of politics, before leaving to become more involved 'at the grass-roots level' as a race equality officer with the General and Municipal Boilermakers (GMB) trade union.

She also fondly remembers the helpful advice she was given by Labour MEP, Mel Read, on some of the practical steps she would need to take in order to become either an MEP or MP, and informed me that this nine point list has since been made generally available from the Labour Party Women's Network.

Oona King cites her mother as her biggest source of personal inspiration, but acknowledges that the great liberation leaders from around the world, like Dr. Martin Luther King, Mahatma Gandhi and Salvador Allende, have also left their mark on her.

'Britain is my home,' she proclaims. 'Although I was born in Sheffield, and Africa is also dear to my heart as I went to nursery school in Nairobi, I am a Londoner.' She describes herself as black Jewish because, she says, she was brought up culturally Jewish, though adds that she is not religious in any way.

As Oona King MP was called away to her next meeting, I left Parliament having met 'the new kid on the block', convinced that I had glimpsed something of the future.

The eyes have it

Nigel Kirby-Green

Management Consultant

There has been a great deal of media coverage on the so-called 'millennium bug' and the 'Y2K fallout', the consequences of which, we are told, could spell potential disaster in just about every aspect of our modern computer-driven society. While many are worried about a possible doomsday scenario in which aeroplanes plunge from the sky and a total meltdown occurs in our communications systems, one person who is on top of the millennium bug issue is Nigel Kirby-Green whose professional responsibilities as Senior Management Consultant with the leading accounting firm of Ernst & Young include advising major UK businesses and organisations of the potential business implications.

As one might expect from a high-powered and highly skilled management consultant, and in keeping with his personal style, which I have come to know and respect over the last fifteen years, Nigel Kirby-Green's stance on the millennium bug issue is decidedly more measured and considered. He talks less of a doomsday scenario—although quick to add that the implications are all too real for aeroplanes, trains, hospitals, electricity and water companies and the like whose critical operational systems are heavily dependent on microchips—than on the significant management and business implications of failure to be Y2K-compliant. In Nigel Kirby-Green's view, those key businesses and organisations in which a failure of systems would be life threatening, have been actively addressing the potential Y2K scenario for some time. What has attracted less attention are the much more numerous business systems which are less life threatening in the event of Y2K problems, but which are no less dependent on microchips for their operation.

A qualified accountant, Nigel gives an example from his own professional discipline. 'If accounting systems are not made Y2K-compliant, the world will not stop, but it could cost businesses substantial sums of money to deal with the problem after the event. Moreover, the time spent rectifying the problem would most likely interfere with the running of the business and cause further impact on the bottom line. All told Y2K and the existence and effectiveness of strategies for coping with it, is essentially an issue about mangement competence.'

As a senior executive management consultant, Nigel Kirby-Green is just one rung away in the consultancy hierarchy from the role of Partner—to which he aspires. Meanwhile, as part of his current role, and that of the team he leads, in selling technology and support services to business organisations—focusing on central government, the utility companies, and the transportation industry—he is responsible for briefing such organisations on the need to align their business systems to cope with Y2K. Nigel Kirby-Green is eminently suited to the role he performs. Leaving aside his impeccable management skills and experience, he takes great care to be precise in his communications and delivery, is utterly unflappable under pressure, and looks every bit the part of a sharp and sophisticated management consultant. I think that this comes across well in his photograph, in which Nigel's attire, bearing and posture clearly reflect the prestigious position he occupies.

In our meeting, Nigel provides a brief overview of the world of management consultancy, and it is evident that the financial sums concerned are not inconsiderable. Given the rates at which senior consultants like Nigel Kirby-Green are charged out to client companies—usually in the region of £2,000 per day—management consultancy at the level at which Nigel Kirby-Green operates is strictly big business. Nigel informs me that the level of contractual work with client companies at which he would typically be engaged would start from around £500k to £1m.

Nigel Kirby-Green, born in Jamaica of mixed parentage—his mother is black and his father of Middle East origin—spent the early years of his life in America, but from the age of five was schooled and raised in the UK. He admits that on graduating from university he had no definite career plan and could have pursued any number of possible career directions. However, he took a job in finance at the Greater London Council because it offered training leading to a qualification in accountancy. Although initially uncertain of his preferred career direction, he was driven by a wish to be successful, 'Once I get into something I want to succeed at it, to show what I can do and to achieve.' Within a short period, Nigel was doing just that, and the progress of his career has continued on an upward plane ever since.

He spent a further four years working with some very good people and learning a great deal at the Inner London Education Authority, where our professional paths first crossed. Later, looking for new challenges, Nigel thought he would try his hand at management consulting, and in marketing himself to the industry received no fewer than four offers from consultancies eager to use his services. He opted for Price Waterhouse, where he gained invaluable experience, before moving on to the BBC as a senior management accountant, and where we would once again be professional colleagues. Nigel highlights his four years at the BBC—an organisation undergoing then, as now, great organisational change—as immensely satisfying and valuable to his personal development. He then joined Ernst & Young, his present company.

Asked if, on his climb through the various organisations for whom he has worked he has ever encountered issues related to his ethnic origin, Nigel replies, 'If anything, people have sometimes been confused by my appearance and unsure how to categorise me.' He shares with me the rather more perverse situation that has sometimes arisen: he has more had the occasional racist remark made in his presence about other black people than been the subject of such remarks himself.

Amongst the many people Nigel Kirby-Green admires, he mentions two in particular for whom he has the highest regard: Viv Richards, the acclaimed West Indian cricketer ('an inspiring genius, not only of superb cricketing skill but with great nobility') and the late writer and historian, C. L. R. James ('he used the beauty of the English language with a sensibility which was distinctly Caribbean').

Looking to the new millennium, Nigel—while seeing himself as British though 'in synergy with Jamaica'—is decidedly optimistic. 'There is a lot to look forward to and with the right conditions—those which allow everyone to realise their own potential—we could be even more successful in the new millennium. Although racism and discrimination still prevail, Britain has made more progress in addressing these issues than any other Western country.' The greater uncertainty, he sees, relates to the bigger global perspective, such as the unpredictability of the global economy, on-going regional turbulence and war.

For Nigel Kirby-Green, the future looks bright as he continues his steady climb up the corporate ladder on his way to becoming, I am confident, one of the first black British Partners in the top bracket of management consultancies in the UK.

Accounting for the future

Driving the music machine

Dej Mahoney

Vice-President, Sony Music UK

Dej Mahoney laughs as he makes the self-deprecating comment that in his opinion there is often an inverse correlation between the length of one's job title and how much work one actually does. His full title, he explains, is Vice-President, Business Affairs and New Media Development, Sony Music (UK). What I sense, however, is that this is someone with much self-assuredness and whose understated self-confidence allows him rather endearingly to turn his humour on himself.

Still in his early thirties, and having already served four years in his present post with Sony Music, Dej Mahoney is one of the most senior black executives in the British music industry. Based at the corporate centre, Dej's job involves providing two key functions to the company. As a barrister by profession, Dej's primary responsibility is to manage and oversee the company's contractual relationships with talent across all its music labels in the UK. The chances are, that if you are a budding musical talent about to be signed by Columbia Records, Epic, S2, INCredible, or any of the other UK labels in the Sony Music stable, or an artist with an on-going contractual relationship with the company, Dej Mahoney will have had either direct or indirect input into the commercial deal offered to you. 'There needs to be a balance struck between ensuring the artist is acquired and the cost of the acquisition balanced against the likely return for the company. I help define the terms under which the talent is contracted to Sony Music,' says Dej.

The secondary aspect of his job is to oversee, from a legal and business perspective, the company's expansion into on-line development and sales of its music products. He points to the success of Amazon as a shining example in the book industry, and explains that it is also the way the music industry is heading in the longer term. Since Sony is a technologically orientated company, it needs to be at the forefront of this new media field coming onstream, and Dej's role is to assist in establishing the business practices and commercial parameters required to achieve this objective. 'Taken together', Dej says, 'I am involved in determining a lot of the ways in which we do business.'

As Head of Department, Dej Mahoney has Business Affairs Executives working to him on each of the company's music labels. Underscoring his seniority in the hierarchy, he reports directly to the Chairman. Whilst in his office awaiting the start of our interview, I could not help but overhear his telephone discussion with an agent or manager of an artiste over what appeared to be a contractual negotiation of sorts. Dej is warm, friendly, very measured and accommodating, but razor sharp in establishing his and the company's position. I acquired something of a feel from this exchange of what has taken Dej Mahoney to the impressive height he has already reached in his career.

Dej Mahoney comes from The Gambia and has lived in Britain since he was nine, when he was sent to a Surrey boarding school by his parents, both of whom had studied in the UK many years earlier. Dej recounts the key role played by his parents in his career progression. Not only did they influence his education and career direction at critical points, but he says very warmly, 'From a very early stage they planted the idea in our heads (he has two equally high-achieving older brothers) that we would be successful. It was just expected of us.'

Dej's parents and a fondly remembered teacher-mentor at school— 'I was blessed with some fantastic teachers,' says Dej—advised him to go on to college when he wanted to leave school after A levels to get a job. They also steered him towards reading law at Cambridge, when he initially considered modern languages, and he confesses they suggested he qualify at the Bar when his career thoughts lay elsewhere.

On completing his pupillage at a leading, general common law set, it was, ironically, his failure to secure tenancy that led to his move to the commercial arena. Dej says he does not know where his career would have taken him had he been offered tenancy in Chambers. Instead, at twenty-three, he landed a legal position with CBS Records, now Sony Music (UK), and within six years of joining the company had climbed the corporate ladder to the executive ranks. 'I did not set out to be a corporate climber,' says Dej, 'but I did want to be successful. I set very high standards for myself and have to feel personally satisfied with whatever it is that I do. I don't like the idea of trying to busk my way through, but rather I prefer to move from a position of strength.' He continues, 'I am one of those people who would rather play well and lose than perform poorly and win.'

Asked of the issues of being a black senior executive, Dej Mahoney makes the point that he was the only black pupil at his preparatory school and one of only a few black pupils at his subsequent public school, and yet at both schools he went on to become Head of School. 'My experience has on the whole been very positive. I have always felt that if you reach a certain standard, to some extent your colour is to your advantage because people are not necessarily expecting you to be at that standard.' He adds, however, 'I've always been surprised and felt it odd when people say things like "my colour is not an issue". Racism and prejudice are everywhere. To say that there is none, even in my privileged position, is crazy.' For Dej Mahoney, both The Gambia—where his parents still live—and London, where he feels rooted, are places he sees equally as 'home'.

As Dej Mahoney reflects on his future, he shares one of his long-term ambitions. Interestingly, it is not about rising further up the corporate ladder but about how he would like to be more directly involved with the success of artists and their music. A future possibility is for Dej to set up a record label, or imprint, and to use the experience he has gained in the industry to help bring on new talent, which he feels is still out there in large quantities. Alternatively, he would like to explore various ideas he has for television.

This assured and modest high flyer is most definitely a corporate asset which Sony Music will do well to maintain and utilise to the maximum. With many more career years ahead of him, Dej Mahoney will no doubt evolve and grow with the changing business environment. What is certain is that he will be a prominent figure on the British corporate scene well into the next millennium.

Val McCalla

Publisher and Chairman of the Voice Group

From my research and interviews with other subjects for *Millennium People,* I learnt that Val McCalla was held in high regard by many people in Britain's black community. Owner and chairman of the Voice Group, Val McCalla is also the founder and publisher of Britain's most successful black-owned newspaper—*The Voice*— which for the last eighteen years has enjoyed the largest black readership of any newspaper in Britain and been the champion of numerous causes and issues close to the heart of Britain's black community. Although no longer directly involved in the day-to-day running of *The Voice,* Val McCalla remains very much the driving force behind his newspaper and the wider publishing group.

I was honoured that Val McCalla was willing to be featured in *Millennium People,* especially as he rarely gives interviews. There are also very few photographs of him on file or in any picture library. He is in every sense of the word a deeply private man who now lives a somewhat reclusive though prosperous life on the south coast of England, where he maintains his racehorses. He keeps in touch daily with his business empire, and convenes meetings with his senior staff at his lovely home overlooking the South Downs. I met Val twice for his *Millennium People* interview and photography session, and found him warm, gracious and exceedingly encouraging towards the project. I selected this image of Val McCalla taken in the studio at *The Voice* newspaper offices because I believe it reflects his personality well—a thoughtful and engaging man who is, at the same time, deeply guarded and reserved and something of an enigma to anyone who has not had the chance to meet and talk with him.

Val McCalla arrived in the UK from Jamaica in May 1959, at the age of fifteen. He laughingly recalls how 'it was springtime in London and yet the minute I stepped off the plane dressed in my new rayon suit I started to freeze!' Within a year of his arrival, Val had joined the Royal Air Force (RAF). Although his parents wanted him to become a doctor or take up some other profession, he had always longed to be a pilot. Sadly, a perforated eardrum ruined his chances of flying, and he trained instead to become an accountant bookkeeper, working in the Supplies section for the five years in which he served. Looking back on his RAF career, he appreciates the opportunity it gave him to acquire a professional skill—in later years his accounts and bookkeeping skills proved to be invaluable in helping him to establish his newspaper group—as well as to explore other parts of Britain and to travel overseas.

When he left the RAF in the mid-1960s, he initially found it difficult to get a job. He then held a variety of administrative, accounts and bookkeeping positions, and was generally drifting along until he reached what he describes as a pivotal point in his life—the break-up of his marriage when he was thirty-four. He began to reappraise his life, thinking about what he had achieved and what he still wanted to do, and how he was going to fulfil his responsibilities towards his children. He was in this frame of mind when a circular dropped through the door of his East End of London home canvassing for volunteers to help start a new community-based newspaper. After offering his services to the newspaper—*The East End News*—in his spare time, Val soon found himself on its management committee as well as the writer of one of its regular features— 'Black Voices'—which was aimed at the local Bengali and other ethnic minority communities who made up a good proportion of the readership of the newspaper.

'This was effectively the birth of *The Voice*,' says Val McCalla jokingly but with evident pride, since from this beginning he has gone on to build a successful publishing enterprise. He was particularly inspired by the fact that much of the feedback received by the paper came from its black and ethnic minority readers about issues raised in the 'Black Voices' section of the paper. When *The East End News* (which survived largely on local authority grants) ran into serious financial difficulties and ceased publication, Val and a couple of his colleagues tried to pick up the pieces of the defunct newspaper, but when this did not prove possible, Val resolved to set up his own newspaper.

His aim was to establish an independent newspaper targeted explicitly at the black community. Mainstream newspapers, he felt, gave scant coverage of black issues or perspectives, and the black newspapers already in circulation were aimed more at the older generation of migrants. They focused more on issues 'back home', rather than on the interests and aspirations of black people either born or living in Britain today.

Perhaps inevitably, Val's thoughts, philosophy and general approach towards establishing his embryonic newspaper changed direction a number of times. He thought initially that it might only be an east London newspaper, existing more as a community service than a commercial venture, and that he could get it off the ground in his spare time whilst continuing his freelance accountancy work in the City. Instead, *The Voice* was launched commercially in 1982 at London's Notting Hill Carnival as a national newspaper aimed at 'giving a voice to black people in Britain'. Operating in its early period on a shoestring budget and from 'a little hut in Hackney', says Val, with many of its staff (including fresh young black graduates) eager to give their services and working only for the reward of a Chinese restaurant meal at the end of the week. *The Voice's* first lead story, about the firebombing of an East End Asian family, set the tone for future issues.

After a shaky start—150,000 copies were given away free at its launch but in the following week only 4,000 copies were sold of the 50,000 printed—the paper gradually found its feet and secured a niche. Today's weekly sales figures stand at around 50,000 copies, and although competitors have come and gone *The Voice* remains Britain's best known and most widely read black newspaper.

In recounting these early times, Val McCalla says 'it was an exciting period although it was a struggle. I look back on those days with affection. People were so energised.' Over the years, the newspaper has gone on to spawn a variety of other titles to complement *The Voice.* One or two have since folded whilst other successful titles have been sold off. Operating now from large, well-equipped offices in the heart of London's Brixton, the Voice Group currently has two other publications besides *The Voice* on its list—*The Journal,* a broadsheet newspaper, and *Woman to Woman* magazine—and is also a book publishing house. The group's turnover is in the region of £5m a year.

For the future Val says enthusiastically, 'I would like to see a black television channel in the UK.' He feels this would complement his newspaper. In his view, the growth and development of Britain's black and ethnic minority population could sustain such an enterprise, and it is one that the Voice Group continues to seriously consider. The interview draws to a close with Val acknowledging that whilst his 'spiritual home' is Jamaica, his real home and that of his children is in Britain. He adds somewhat poignantly, 'I am not interested in personal glory, I am more interested in seeing *The Voice* read by the next generation and for it to become a British institution.'

Val McCalla —deceased, 2002.

Publishing pioneer

Chief Inspector Dalton McConney

Senior Officer, Metropolitan Police Service

'**B**lack police officers were so few on the ground that when I walked down Battersea High Street in my uniform, there were plenty of near accidents as drivers turned their heads because they were so unused to seeing a black policeman,' recalls Chief Inspector Dalton McConney of the Metropolitan Police Service, with great amusement. 'Mind you', he says, 'heads still turn now, though much less than before, and maybe', he suspects, 'because of the pips on my uniform.'

Chief Inspector Dalton McConney—Mac to his friends and acquaintances—joined the police service in 1975 and is today among the most senior black officers in all the British police forces. He is also one of the most respected, having been awarded an MBE in 1994 in recognition of his standing and for his services to the wider community. Listening to his story one cannot but ponder how much further up the chain of command this able and likeable man might have risen if circumstances had been different at various points in his career.

As a former police operations manager and, prior to that, an instructor at the Police College, Chief Inspector McConney and the team of police officers and civilian staff he now leads, work across the three police divisions which together cover the London Borough of Lambeth. He reports to the divisional commanders of Brixton, Streatham and Vauxhall on a wide range of strategic community policing responsibilities, and some operational duties.

On behalf of the divisional commanders, he and his team co-ordinate all partnership issues where the police either work, or liaise, with the local authority and other statutory agencies in their area. He also heads a youth and community section which deals with all matters related to juvenile crime, and undertakes crime preventative project work with young people.

'It's a wide and varied role,' says Mac, 'and when the need arises I still put on my uniform and get out there.' Wearing his uniform has long been a source of immense pride to Dalton McConney. He remarks firmly, 'I am very proud to wear my uniform because it was a choice I made about my career and I have no regrets about making that choice.'

Dalton McConney admits that when he arrived in the UK in the early 1960s from his native Barbados, he had no thoughts of joining the British police force. Rather, looking for something of a similar nature to the civil service for whom he worked in Barbados, he worked initially for London

Transport and then in industry. Frustrated, however, by his lack of progress in those fields and seeing job advertisements for the Metropolitan Police, he recalls applying on two separate occasions in the early 1960s to join the service. Whether the product of any formal policy to debar black people from joining—as is alleged existed at the time—or not, the result was the same; his first application did not even receive a response and his second fared little better, but at least elicited a rejection letter.

It was several years later, in 1975, when he once again felt his career had reached a plateau that Dalton McConney saw the then Commissioner of the Metropolitan Police, Sir Robert Marks, on a television news programme talking about the police services' recruitment campaign specifically aimed at attracting black and ethnic minority applicants. By then aged thirty-six, and believing that he would in any case be too old to join the police service, it was his wife who persuaded Mac to apply for a third time. 'This time the response was totally different.' Within three weeks of submitting his application, he had been called for an interview, sat a selection test, undergone a medical, and was appointed to the Metropolitan Police Service.

During Mac's training at Hendon Police College, not only was he the oldest police recruit on the course, but he was also older than some of his instructors. His maturity worked to his advantage, he believes, as he was made Class Captain and was generally looked up to by recruits and instructors alike. He finished first in his group every month for the two year training period and topped off this achievement with a final examination score of ninety-eight per cent—one of the highest scores achieved by any one at the time. To complement this, his supervising officers commended his on-the-job performance as 'outstanding'.

Indeed, so impressed was his Commanding Officer that he gave immediate permission for the then PC McConney to sit for the Sergeant's examination, when regulations ordinarily required five years prior service except under exceptional circumstances. Mac was placed sixth out of 1,200 officers taking the Sergeant's examination. Although he scored above the required level for automatic promotion to Sergeant, and was well within the top one hundred group usually considered for fast-track promotion to the higher ranks, he was denied promotion on the grounds of his age. This constraint on his progress in the Service would occur at other points in

his career, for different reasons. Although he subsequently climbed the ranks to become a Chief Inspector, Mac does wonder how far he might otherwise have risen had these impediments not occurred, and especially had he been allowed to join the service when he first applied.

Mac cites the six years he spent at Brixton division, when he first became an Inspector, as the most enjoyable years of his police service, despite the fact that he was posted there in the period immediately following the street riots and disturbances of the late 1980s. He arrived amid much suspicion, distrust and even animosity towards the police. Being a black officer in such a volatile environment was not easy. 'I wanted people to see I was different,' says Mac, 'that I was professional. I had no truck with people who committed crimes but I insisted people be treated properly and in accordance with the law.' He quickly gained a reputation within the local community and amongst his officers as someone of integrity and high standards. On receiving his MBE in 1994, he discovered that the recommendation for the award had come from the people of Lambeth. 'It was a very proud moment for me—such a positive and tangible expression of support from the community after all the distrust and hostility only a few years earlier.'

Asked whether he has ever encountered racism or discrimination during his years of police service, Mac answers forthrightly, 'I can honestly say that no-one has ever challenged me to my face or committed any racist act or comment that I was aware of. There have been questionable things, such as my earlier applications, but nothing overt.'

Chief Inspector McConney recalls his old school motto: 'Nothing is too difficult for me', adding that his personal approach is 'to see things as battles to be fought and won'. He warmly acknowledges the help and support he has received along the way from various senior officers, such as his first superintendent, Colin Coles, who backed Mac by giving him a permanent Acting Sergeant's position when he was not appointed Sergeant because of his age, and his former Chief Superintendent at Brixton, Roger Street.

Chief Inspector McConney expresses both hopes and concerns with respect to the future of the police service. One hope which is particularly heartfelt is his wish to one day see 'a black face wearing the Police Commissioner's regalia'. He adds, 'The police service is a vital part of our society and I would like to see more black people becoming part of it. If they want to change it, join it and change it from within.'

Hands-on policing

The mentor

Norman McLean

Director, National Mentoring Consortium

The mentor scheme which Norman McLean first established in 1992 for African, Caribbean and Asian undergraduates at the University of East London has developed from a relatively modest idea into a highly acclaimed and nationally noted project. Such has been its impact and success that in 1996 Norman McLean was awarded an MBE in recognition of his services to Britain's ethnic minority community. Whilst justly proud of his award, Norman regards it as official recognition and acknowledgement of the work and achievements of all the contributors to the project, rather than simply a personal accolade.

Norman McLean is the Director of the National Mentoring Consortium, an organisation which runs, advises and oversees mentoring schemes for black and ethnic minorities and other disadvantaged communities across the UK. Yet, when Norman McLean was first appointed as a Careers Adviser at the University of East London, with special responsibility for its African, Asian and Caribbean students, and came up with the idea of setting up a pilot mentoring scheme, his aim was merely to provide a service to the university's own students.

The University of East London enjoys the distinction of having the largest number of black students in higher education in Britain. In line with its declared commitment to ensuring equal opportunities—it is the first university to have a designated Dean of equal opportunities—it was concerned with how its black and ethnic minority students were faring in the job market on graduation. Concerned that these students were having far greater difficulty securing positions than their white counterparts, Norman proposed to the university that a mentoring scheme be set up to help them.

The idea was to link individual students to professionals, managers or executives in companies and organisations, in order to facilitate the students' developing one-to-one relationships with their professional mentors, thereby enhancing their self-confidence and personal development. In its first year of operation, in 1992, the University of East London's mentoring scheme, initiated by Norman McLean, had some twenty-five students linked to a similar number of mentors from industry. Within two years, the considerable interest expressed by other educational institutions wanting advice and information about the mentoring scheme—who even requested for their students to participate in the University of East London scheme—was so great that it led Norman to put

a further proposal to the university that they set up a National Mentoring Consortium to lead and co-ordinate the work across the country.

The University of East London had the foresight to back Norman McLean's proposal. Today, the Consortium which Norman manages still provides a mentoring service aimed at black and ethnic minority undergraduates but this is now run collectively for twenty universities across the UK. Over 3,000 participants have benefited from the programme, and the number of companies affiliated to it and offering their managers as mentors has reached 140 and is rising. Many are well-known market leader companies.

Norman cites amongst the achievements of the mentoring scheme the fact that both the black students and the industry mentors report in high numbers the great value and personal satisfaction they have derived from participating; the regular feedback from students who have said that their career horizons and ambitions had been very much broadened by their experience; the number of student mentees who have subsequently succeeded in securing jobs either with their mentor's company or elsewhere; and, more generally, the changed climate within companies towards black undergraduates who are now seen far more as talented assets and potentially desirable recruits than they ever were previously.

Having succeeded in establishing the value of mentoring as a social and economic tool, the National Mentoring Consortium has in recent years been invited to extend its pioneering work. Parallel to the main scheme for black and ethnic minority undergraduates, the Consortium now works with an impressive list of government agencies and bodies to establish mentoring schemes aimed at different target groups. For example, there are mentoring schemes run on behalf of the Teacher Training Agency to attract more black people into the teaching profession, a mentoring scheme for the unemployed in east London and another set up in conjunction with the Home Office targeted at young black offenders about to be released from prison.

Norman McLean recounts that in his own early career he experienced some of the difficulties and frustrations encountered by the black students which his project seeks to help. 'After graduating', he explains, 'I went in to a deep depression. It was the worst period of my life.' Armed with his degree and all his hopes and expectations about establishing

a career, he was unable to secure anything approaching a career job for well over two years. 'Race may have played a part,' he says, 'but it was probably just as much due to my lack of career awareness and preparation for the job market.' Whilst it was a very painful experience, with hindsight he learnt a lot from the period and feels it gave him the insight to do what he has since gone on to achieve. Indeed, one of his frequent catchphrases to the students on his schemes today is, 'If you want the rainbow, you have to put up with the rain.'

As a result of his work and reputation earned from the success of the National Mentoring Consortium, not only has Norman McLean been awarded an MBE but he now sits on a number of national committees and other distinguished bodies. Included amongst these are the Home Secretary's Race Relations Advisory Forum, the board of Investors in People (UK), and the national committees for both the Association of Graduate Recruiters and the Teacher Training Agency. More recently he has been invited to sit on the Prime Minister's Giving Age Working Group, set up to advise the Government on the promotion of volunteering in the community.

Of the people who helped him along the way, Norman particularly remembers friends and family members who, in effect, 'mentored' him at the low point of his unemployment. He also recalls his economics lecturer at college, 'whose sheer love and enthusiasm for his subject was so overwhelming that it virtually carried me through the course'. But Norman pays special tribute to his father—'my main influence'—and the person he most wanted to impress by doing well. Those whom Norman finds inspiring as role models include both historical and contemporary figures, such as Martin Luther King, Malcolm X, Mohammed Ali and Oprah Winfrey.

Looking to the new millennium, Norman acknowledges that having established and managed the National Mentoring Consortium from its outset, it has come to be regarded as 'his baby'. 'But', he adds, 'if that is the case, my plan for the future is to see that the baby grows and matures into a well-rounded adult.' Of the future, more generally, he believes that the report card shows both good indicators and issues which still remain to be addressed. 'The position for black graduates is definitely improving, slowly but surely.' he says. 'but the goal now is to get more black people into the corporate boardrooms of British industry.'

Reverend Bazil Meade

Director, London Community Gospel Choir

The Reverend Bazil Meade is the founder, musical director and inspiration behind the London Community Gospel Choir. Under his leadership, the London Community Gospel Choir has not only established itself as a world-class gospel choir—with concert tours and advance bookings coming in from around the world—but it has raised the whole profile of gospel music in the UK. Most of those who tune in to listen to black gospel music associate the genre with the US, and indeed many people believe that there is no such thing as British black gospel music. The London Community Gospel Choir, with the Revd. Bazil Meade at its helm, has probably done more than any other group to challenge this view, and to achieve a growing recognition of, and regard for, black gospel music in Britain.

I had the good fortune and privilege to be invited to interview the Revd. Bazil Meade—or 'Baz' or 'Rev' as he is affectionately known—on an evening when the choir was rehearsing for a forthcoming television appearance, one of many they have had over the years. As I sat observing and listening to the choir being taken through some of the songs in its repertoire, I was spellbound by the powerful harmonies of the combined voices of the London Community Gospel Choir. 'Out of many, one voice' is their motto, one which they certainly live up to. Here were five or six dozen young people, predominantly black, but not exclusively so, who had journeyed from all corners of London and beyond, dressed in their workday clothes—including baseball caps and the like—whose voices, even in rehearsal, had a heavenly ring to them.

With Bazil at the keyboard gently coaxing the company, and adding his own sublime vocal contribution, the voices interchanged and dovetailed, rose and strengthened, fell to a soft whisper, sometimes moving between these ranges with amazing speed, but always with precision and energy. It was also evident that the group members singing their hearts out, were at the same time, enjoying the fellowship and camaraderie of one another. My photograph of the Revd. Bazil Meade was taken rather hurriedly between songs and I was heartened to find that I had managed to capture his charisma and joie de vivre.

The London Community Gospel Choir was established in 1982 by Bazil Meade and two other church leaders, Lawrence Johnson and Delroy Powell. They shared an ambition and a vision to create a mass choir wtlich would unite Christian youth from across the different denominations, bringing together the best musicians and singers from London's many churches. This was a period in the aftermath of the street riots which had erupted in Brixton, south London, during the preceding year, and which had thrown issues of race into the spotlight, especially the position of black youth. Thus, Bazil explains, apart from wanting to bring gospel music to the wider community, in establishing the choir he and his colleagues also wanted 'to redress the popular and often negative image of black youth, and to project something of the depth of talent which we knew was abundant in the black community'.

Two early events in the embryonic choir's history gave it impetus and set it well on its future course to international success. Bazil admits that they were initially unsure whether there was a long-term future for the choir and indeed its first concert was organised on the basis that it would very probably be a one-off event. However, an appearance on the London Weekend Television programme 'Black on Black', at Christmas 1982, and the response to its debut concert at Kensington Temple in May 1983, led to a massive surge of interest in the choir. 'We were inundated with calls and letters from people either wanting to join us or wishing to book the choir,' says the Revd. Meade, at which point he decided he would personally put all his energies into seeing that the choir continue, and he has been true to his word.

In its first year, the London Community Gospel Choir grew from sixty to 110 members, representing over forty Christian churches. Over fifty performances were given in that year at venues ranging from churches, concert halls and theatres to schools, clubs and prisons. Seventeen years later, the Revd. Meade and the choir have had several overseas tours, including destinations in Eastern Europe and Japan, and have performed with many well-known artistes, such as Paul McCartney, Stevie Wonder, Elton John, George Michael, Celine Dion and Sting, to name a few.

The Revd. Meade is particularly proud of the fact that the London Community Gospel Choir has spawned a number of singers and musicians who have gone on to establish their own successful recording careers in the music field, using their experience in the choir as a launching pad. 'Over the years we have assembled the cream of gospel vocalists and gospel musicians,' says Bazil with immense pride. The Revd. cites several highly memorable events, but recalls one particularly touching and emotional concert when the choir sang in Morocco. Although the choir was performing in a Muslim country to an audience who could barely speak English, the venue—a beautiful cathedral—was nevertheless filled to capacity, such that some of the younger members of the audience had to sit on the stage. 'They were literally sitting under my arms as I directed the choir,' recounted Bazil, 'but the emotion that swept through the place was incredible. It was a powerful experience, showing that God's message can be communicated across cultures and language barriers through music.'

Bazil Meade came to the UK in 1961, aged nine, from the Caribbean island of Montserrat. 'I thank God for giving me the opportunity to proclaim my faith and spread his word through music.' He adds, 'The choir is very much united by faith, and the content of what we sing is of fundamental importance to us. It's what stimulates our artistic expression and gives us that uplifting quality.' That said, he also acknowledges the more temporal and spiritual support and guidance he received from the Revd. Olive Parris, with whom he lived for several of his early adult years. After leaving school without any formal qualifications, and unsure of his true career direction, it was the Revd. Olive Parris who taught Bazil to play the keyboards and whose 'evangelical crusades' afforded him the opportunity to cut his musical teeth through organising the music for these events.

The Revd. Meade is pleased with what the London Community Gospel Choir has already achieved, not only, he says, in terms of communicating God's message through the medium of music to a wider audience outside the more traditional places of worship, but also in promoting positive images and setting positive behavioural examples for other young people. Although gospel music's profile in the UK has undoubtedly been enhanced by the talents and endeavours of Bazil Meade and the London Community Gospel Choir, Bazil still has further hopes for the future growth and development of gospel music in Britain. For example, he hopes that the new millennium will see the establishment of a national gospel radio station, and has ambitions to one day set up an academy of gospel music—similar to the schools of other creative art forms—where children can be taught to write, create and play gospel music. He also feels that Britain and gospel music generally would benefit from the creation of an annual televised gospel music award event, showcasing all the best gospel choirs from across the country. With so much energy and vision for his gospel music ministry, there will surely be many more 'Happy Days' to come for the Revd. Bazil Meade.

Heavenly voices

Chi-Chi Nwanoku

Classical Musician

'As classical musicians we have to express ourselves with our mouths closed. It all has to come out through our instruments, and I have a great passion for mine,' Chi-Chi Nwanoku proudly declares. And she certainly does express herself through her bow with a style and verve which has gained her an international reputation as a classical double bass player.

People not only get the note when Chi-Chi Nwanoku performs, they also get 'the works', the total all-round performance, the full repertoire along with the visual and dramatic effects, coupled with raw energy and emotion. As she says, 'they get fire and brimstone'.

Chi-Chi Nwanoku is a principal bass player who currently performs with the Orchestra of the Age of Enlightenment. She is someone who, by her very nature, seems to challenge many of the preconceptions that abound about classical music, for example, that it is staid and rather controlled music lacking emotion, that it is highbrow and élitist, played by and for the white middle class with a clear gender divide on which instruments can be played by whom.

Chi-Chi Nwanoku is a charming and diminutive black female classical musician who plays the towering double bass with such talent and gusto that she seems to stand out in any orchestra with which she plays, even if placed at the rear as double bass players so often are. Such is her stature and accomplishments in the classical music field that she was recently made a Distinguished Fellow of the Royal Academy of Music (a coveted honour held by only 100 musicians at any one time). In addition to being a performer, she is also Professor of Double Bass Studies at Trinity College of Music, London.

It therefore came as a surprise to learn that music was, in fact, Chi-Chi Nwanoku's second love and that until tragedy struck she had never even conceived of a career in music. Chi-Chi's story is characterised not just by tremendous musical talent but also by self-motivation and steely determination to make the most of the opportunities which came her way, and to not let herself be bowed by adversity.

At age eight, Chi-Chi was spotted by an athletics coach who saw in her the makings of a top-class sprinter. With her parents' and school's approval, she was given intensive personal after-school coaching three days a week and soon progressed to national level as a teenager, only just missing out on a place in the British sprinting team for the Munich Olympics. Tragedy struck Chi-Chi, however, at seventeen when she was in her last year at school. With the prospect of the Montreal Olympics looming, she was invited to play in a women's charity football match and so badly injured her knee that not only was she hospitalised for two weeks, but it brought her budding athletics career to an immediate end. 'Even today, I have never really laid to rest my first passion for sport...it was at the time akin to a bereavement,' Chi-Chi poignantly admits.

From about the same age that she was discovered as an athlete of the future, she had been diligently learning to play the piano. When the church organist retired and left the local family church without an organist, it was to Chi-Chi, aged nine and barely able to reach the pedals, to whom they turned. The one pound per term pocket money she earned from this was wisely invested by her parents in further piano lessons. Her interest in the piano developed alongside her main love of sprinting and went as far as to enable her to study A-level music at school.

Chi-Chi remembers the occasion very well and recalls with still evident fondness and appreciation how on her very first day back at school after her hospitalisation through her knee injury, and with her broken athletic dreams still very much on her mind, she was approached by her head teacher and the head of music. They proceeded to tell Chi-Chi what a wonderful musician she was and that she could make an alternative career in music if she thought about playing an orchestral instrument, whereupon they suggested she try the double bass.

As Chi-Chi Nwanoku acknowledges herself, literally as one door closed another opened. 'Luck' is how she modestly describes this. But if her unexpected injury also opened a door of opportunity, it took courage and determination to enter and make the most of what she found.

She fell back, she believes, on her parents' teachings and influence. Her parents' marriage (her father a traditional Ibo Nigerian and her mother from Tipperary, Southern Ireland) in the 1950s was so frowned upon that her mother was forever cast out from her family. No doubt as a result of their own experiences, they had instilled in their children a belief that they should never do anything half-heartedly, but rather should make the very best of whatever lay before them. With this inbuilt focus and determination, Chi-Chi threw herself headlong into first learning, and then mastering, her new instrument which she took to instantly, helped she says because 'I was suddenly and for the first time playing in a social environment, the orchestra'.

In just a few short months she had won a place and scholarship to attend Cambridge Technical College to study music, and from there went on to the Royal Academy of Music, finally gaining a rare and coveted opportunity to study with a double bass master virtuoso—Franco Petracchi—in Italy. Today, with a burgeoning and still unfolding career to her credit, Chi-Chi Nwanoku is herself a master of her art, and has the distinction of having accomplished musicians travelling halfway around the globe for the privilege of studying the double bass under her tutelage.

Many more women now play the double bass than when Chi-Chi took up what was then a most unpopular instrument, and certainly one rarely played by women. She takes great pride and comfort from the feedback she has received from various female bass players and teachers around the world, who have told her how much she inspired them and gave them hope that they too could be bass players.

Perhaps the greatest compliment paid to Chi-Chi Nwanoku was when a retiring British virtuoso bass player—Francis Baines—offered her his rare and highly treasured near 400-year-old double bass (made by Nicholas Amati, the teacher of Stradivarius), because she was 'the only one he wanted to have it', turning down in the process huge sums of money offered by dealers for this classic masterpiece. I was privileged to have Chi-Chi play some pieces for me on this magnificent instrument whilst I took some photographic shots of her in her lovely home, and could at once see why and what she meant about having 'a great passion for the double bass'.

Touching bass

Bruce Oldfield

Fashion Designer

Ask a group of people on the proverbial Clapham Omnibus to name a famous contemporary British fashion designer and chances are the name which will come up most often will be that of Bruce Oldfield. Just as he is arguably Britain's most famous name in the fashion world, he is also quite possibly its most popular.

Probe the Omnibus travellers more deeply about their impressions of Bruce Oldfield and a variety of images and opinions are likely to emerge, none of them in any way negative or uncomplimentary, since he enjoys an excellent media profile. He is seen as a designer to the rich and famous. With this goes a perception that he is very much an establishment figure; that he was a designer to, and close friend of, the late Diana, Princess of Wales, and, Bruce Oldfield's most well-known tag, that he is an example of a Barnardo boy made good. While there is more than a modicum of truth to all of these, there is also of course much more to Bruce Oldfield. What is rarely acknowledged is that he is also a member of Britain's black population, and one of the earliest examples of a successful black British entrepreneur.

Bruce Oldfield has been carving his niche in the fashion business for over twenty-five years. Like other businesses, his has had its ups and downs. Bruce has weathered the cold winds of the late 1980s recession—coming close to bankruptcy at the time—but in an industry renowned for its fickleness, where even big names come and go like the seasons, his has stood the test of time.

Bruce's trademark is couture women's fashion, although in recent years he has re-entered the field of ready-to-wear clothes with a new shop in the heart of London's West End. His custom-made, soft, sexy, slinky clothes carry a price tag of anything from £2,500 to £50,000 which inevitably means that his clients hail from the élite and well-heeled end of the social spectrum. Certainly, his most famous client was the Princess of Wales, but many of his other clients are no less well known. They include, for example, Queen Noor of Jordan, glamorous stars and models such as Liza Minnelli, Joan Collins and Jerry Hall, a clutch of society names, high-profile businesswomen and the wives and daughters of the rich and well to do.

Bruce laughingly admits of his public image, 'I am seen as a very funny little establishment figure,' and is bemused by it given that he never tries to hide his rather more humble origins. He also acknowledges that his name is not synonymous with cutting-edge fashion. Not for him catwalk fashion shows. 'I am too pragmatic for that,' he says. 'I have seen too many people come and go in the business.'

What distinguishes, and to some extent defines, Bruce Oldfield's style are his classic designs, made to the highest quality. 'I'm not interested in the slightest in volume production or having a huge empire around the world. I only want to make good clothes that sell. It's the pursuit of excellence that drives me—well-made garments, in a beautiful fabric and made to last,' he declares. He makes the light-hearted, but one suspects equally serious point, 'I have always liked the notion that someone could go into a thrift shop in say twenty or thirty years' time and find a few still wearable Bruce Oldfield dresses.'

Another ingredient of Bruce's success is his legendary laid-back charm, which was much in evidence during our brief time together. Clients come back time and again, and in some cases bring along older and younger generations of the family, in part because he has a way with people. He is also, one suspects, an incredibly hard and focused worker and a keen taskmaster who readily admits to being 'driven'. On the day of our interview he had been at his desk since 6 a.m. and, despite his celebrity status, working days of sixteen hours are not unusual.

What then is Bruce Oldfield's background and how did he start in the business? His father, it is reputed, was a Jamaican boxer, although he never knew his natural parents. Bruce Oldfield was just a day and a half old when he became a Barnardo baby, and was fostered a little later by a dressmaker in solidly working-class County Durham in the north east of England. He learnt to sew and cut cloth from an early age, and although his foster mother apparently spotted the signs of his potential at age eight, Bruce never really gave fashion much thought as a possible career until he was in his early twenties.

Sadly, at thirteen, Bruce Oldfield was on the slippery slope to juvenile delinquency and was sent back to the children's home. He himself regards this as a turning point in his life. In returning to Barnardo's in Ripon, he got the unexpected opportunity to attend Ripon Grammar School, ironically a much better school than he would have attended had he stayed in the north east. Bruce Oldfield knuckled down and acquired two A levels. Initially, he considered becoming a teacher and, in fact, attended teacher training college, but after completing the course decided to switch to an art college in London, with the help of a Barnardo's educational grant (they would later also provide him with a start-up loan for his fledgling business).

The circumstances related to his gaining a place at St Martin's School of Art speak volumes about Bruce Oldfield's character. The course he sought to join was already at its mid-point and it was also mid-academic term. Not surprisingly, the Head of St Martin's School of Art declined Bruce's application for a place at the college, but Bruce delights in explaining, 'I stood on her doorstep for three days with my portfolio until she agreed to look at it and to let me in.' Bruce Oldfield to this day still says, 'I thank God for Muriel Pemberton' (the late Head of St Martin's), because faced with such determination she did relent and look at his portfolio, and must have seen his talent, as Bruce was offered a place at the college.

She did not regret her decision. Within nine months, Bruce Oldfield had won a major design competition and was chosen by Revlon to design a collection in conjunction with the launch of one of their new perfumes. Such was Bruce's drive and ambition that he decided to leave St Martin's at twenty-three after less than an academic year, feeling that he had learnt all he needed and that he was ready to make his way in the business!

'I was always very ambitious,' says Bruce. 'I did not imagine for one minute that I was not going to succeed. I was not just looking to earn a living, I wanted to be the best at what I did and to be acknowledged for it.' Today, besides being the sole owner of a highly successful couture house and women's fashion business, he also has several other design consultancies, and, interestingly, is Vice-President of the Barnardo's charity.

Asked whether his ethnic background had ever presented challenges, Bruce is forthright in explaining that where he lived in the north east and in Ripon there were very few other black children or black people generally. 'I was different. I got attention because of it. It was what I wanted. My colour has not been to my disadvantage at all.'

The owner of a fashion label, yet one who himself defies labelling, this is a man who uses the sheer force of his talent and the strength of his personality to render potential barriers irrelevant to him. Like his gowns, Bruce Oldfield looks set to become a British classic, remaining stylishly in vogue and in demand as we move into the new millennium.

Success by design

Wayne Otto

World Karate Champion

If I asked even the most ardent sports aficionados to name the sport in which England has a truly enviable track record at team level, and to name a British sports person who holds nine world titles, few would identify karate as the sport and most would not have heard of Wayne Otto.

Originating in Japan as an ancient martial art, karate was only introduced to the UK in the late 1960s and early 1970s. But Britain has virtually dominated the world karate team championships, which are held every two years, since the country's emergence as a karate power in the 1980s. And there is no more successful exponent of this sport than Wayne Otto who, on the basis of world titles held, is arguably the most successful British athlete today. Since winning his first world title in 1988, he has won either the World Championship, the World Cup or the World Games titles at each outing, holding all three titles concurrently in 1992-3.

Regrettably for Wayne Otto, however, karate is not only an amateur sport still awaiting Olympic recognition (it is to be introduced at the 2004 Olympic Games), but it also languishes as a rather low-profile, amateur sport. Quite simply, karate has not been seriously marketed to the British public and therefore attracts little or no media coverage.

This situation, Wayne explains, is somewhat different in neighbouring countries, and certainly elsewhere in the world, where even allowing for its amateur status, karate is a much higher profile sport. 'In some countries when I arrive for championships, there is a lot of media interest, including national press coverage, and we regularly perform in packed stadiums, but as soon as I return to the UK ... nothing!'

In response to my observations about the contrast between the profiles of karate and other sports, notably boxing, Wayne Otto gives me a glimpse of his positive and focused approach to his sport. This became increasingly apparent as I talked to him, and is what no doubt has made him the champion that he is. 'Sometimes I do feel down about the lack of recognition and about the rewards enjoyed in other sports, but I cannot be preoccupied with negatives. I use them instead as a positive challenge to enhance my own performance and to make me even better, and to try to make things different for the next generation of karate exponents.'

Wayne's vision for the future includes a 'shop window' for karate. 'I would eventually like to be the Don King of karate, running a professional karate circuit which enables other fighters to get their just rewards and for karate to take its rightful place as a top sport alongside all the other main sports in the UK.'

I met Wayne Otto on a dark, wintry night at a training session where he and other members of the England karate squad were being put through their paces ahead of a forthcoming Open Championship in the Netherlands. Privileged to see a good part of the session, I was impressed by the demonstration of skill and power, but also by the sheer hard work, discipline and dedication which Wayne and his colleagues put into their training.

Amateur sport it may be, but karate's exponents definitely train just as hard as any other professional athletes. Wayne Otto trains up to five hours a day, six days a week, and he has to fit this in around his 'day job'. Although he holds a degree in communications engineering, Wayne works as a karate teacher with young children—a job from which he derives a lot of pleasure as his students progress, and which also helps him pay the bills.

Wayne feels that his winning edge is partly due to the fact that he trains harder and longer than any of his opponents. He recalled that in his younger days he would routinely go out for runs in the still of the night, and would make a point of running in the snow or during any other inclement weather, knowing that his opponents would probably not be training at that time. As he proudly points out, 'I have sacrificed everything to be where I am. I have trained harder than anyone else I know, and I have put in the time to reap the rewards I have enjoyed.'

Even allowing for his own sacrifices, Wayne acknowledges that 'I could never have got to where I am on my own. Countless people have helped along the way, from the support of my family, to my instructor who took me under his wing, the various other coaches who have guided me, as well as help from other squad members.'

What came across powerfully as I talked to Wayne, and what is probably the hallmark of champions the world over, is his strong sense of self-belief. He is not overly brash or arrogant, but direct and purposeful, as witnessed by

some of the remarks he made during the course of our interview. 'I approach every tournament as positively as I can. I always believe that if I perform to my best I will win. I never consider losing but always reserve two per cent doubt about the possibility of losing. It's my mark of respect for my opponent and necessary so that I do not take it for granted that I'll always win. But my opponent must be willing to go to hell and back if he really does want to win!'

One has a sense that Wayne Otto has been on a mission to get where he is and that his mission is far from complete. He got into karate, as he puts it, 'out of pure jealousy'. A friend had come to school one day with a trophy he had won in a karate competition. Wayne so envied the symbol of success that he decided there and then that he too would take up karate in order to get a trophy to be similarly admired. For the first six months of training, Wayne recalls being beaten time and again by the other club members, but from the moment he entered his first tournament and won a silver medal, he was so overjoyed with his sense of accomplishment—and with his trophy—that he has been in relentless puisuit of others ever since.

'Despite my many titles I am never satisfied with my achievements. I have the same burning desire to win world titles as when I first started, maybe even more so. I want to dominate the records, to be remembered for something nobody can take away. I want to be so far ahead in winning that others will feel unable to match my achievements. I want to be a legend in the sport.' Wayne is equally direct about his black Britishness. 'I have no confusion about where my home is. My home is in the UK. I have never even been to the Caribbean. I am black British and proud of that fact.'

The photograph was taken of Wayne immediately following his gruelling training session with other members of the England national squad, and shows him looking as calm and self-composed as at the outset of the training session. The image also reflects the steely glint in his eyes. One imagines being an opponent fixed in his glare. The trophies which have been Wayne's motivation and focus in his relentless pursuit to dominate the world of karate are a fitting symbol in the background of his portrait.

The champion

Reflecting on equality

Sir Herman Ouseley

Chairman, Commission for Racial Equality

Sir Herman Ouseley enjoys a reputation as someone of high personal standing, and as an unstinting worker for those organisations and causes for whom he has given loyal service. But he is perhaps most of all seen as a remarkable leader, one who leads by the sheer force of example.

As someone who has had the opportunity and privilege to work for Sir Herman in the past, and to observe at close quarters some of these attributes and qualities being applied to considerable effect, I have long regarded him as a personal role model—immensely inspiring and yet, to be honest, just that little bit daunting. He is inspiring because his style is to lead from the front, instilling in those around him added focus and assuredness. Any small doubt arises simply because he sets such a pace and standard that invariably one feels left in his wake.

I was very pleased that Sir Herman agreed to be featured in *Millennium People,* but was, once again, slightly daunted at the prospect of interviewing someone of his calibre. I need not have worried. He was as warm and accommodating as ever, and I came away having gained new and even amusing insights into the man deservedly knighted in the 1997 New Year's Honours List for his services to the community.

Sir Herman Ouseley is the present Chairman of the Commission for Racial Equality (CRE), the statutory body which oversees the operation of the UK's race relations legislation. He is the first black person to hold this office having been appointed by the Conservative Home Secretary in 1993, and re-appointed by the new Labour Home Secretary in 1998—itself something of an accomplishment. He is widely credited with having restored the CRE's flagging credibility. Indeed, Sir Herman's professional career is littered with many such firsts, confirming his reputation as a trailblazer and mould-breaker.

Prior to becoming Chairman of the CRE, Herman was the first black Chief Executive Officer in British local government where he occupied the top management position firstly at the Inner London Education Authority (ILEA), and then at the London Borough of Lambeth. He earned plaudits at Lambeth for his determined effort to turn around an ailing local council that had become riven with poor administration and even malpractices. Similarly, as the first black Director of Education and Chief Executive Officer, he led the ILEA in the late 1980s when it was the largest education authority in Western Europe, responsible for well over a thousand schools and colleges across the capital city. It was whilst at the ILEA that I had the pleasure of working with him as my line manager and it was clear to me even then what a talented and hard-working leader he was. Stories about his prodigious work rate were legendary.

Earlier in his career he had been appointed the first principal race relations adviser in local government—again with Lambeth Council—and his subsequent achievements as the Head of the Greater London Council's (GLC's) Ethnic Minorities Unit through its campaigns and interventionist strategies on racism and discrimination were such that their impact will probably never be matched.

With such a creditable track record, it is not surprising that when Sir Herman Ouseley speaks, especially on matters of race equality, people tend to listen. Yet Herman (as he prefers to be known) remains down to earth despite the title and position he holds. He still lives, for example, in inner city Peckham, south London, as he has for the past thirty years, well before his steady climb up the organisational ladder.

From my interview with Sir Herman, I learnt that, in contrast to his more serious and measured persona, he once harbored ambitions of finding success in the sporting and entertainment fields. He had aspired at one time to be a professional footballer, and reached the not insignificant level of semi-professional status. He was also a budding disk jockey and singer. These talents he exploited in the evenings on a part-time basis whilst maintaining his regular day job. 'They were dreams along the way,' he laughingly recalls, 'but I got a thrill from doing them.' In each case, he realised that he either did not have sufficient talent to take him to the top, or that they were simply not for him. 'But,' he adds, 'I learnt something from each.'

For instance, and again in stark contrast to his reputation and image, he readily admits that during his brief foray into football, he was 'a reluctant trainer'. He would routinely cut corners on training runs, and if asked to do five circuits he would conspire to do four! 'One of the telling lessons I learnt from football' Herman declares, 'is that if you do not put in enough effort and fail as a result, you have ultimately only cheated on yourself.'

The theme of 'cheating on yourself' or 'letting yourself and others down' is one Herman returns to time and again. In elaborating on what motivates him today, Herman makes a revealing point: 'When I hit the pillow at night I want to be able to rest easily knowing that I did not short-change anyone, and that I could not have given more effort or done any more than I had.'

Herman's first job as an administrative clerk with Middlesex County Council in the early 1960s was instrumental in setting him on the right path. He feels he was fortunate to learn many good business and organisational practices which he has used as a foundation to build his career. He also credits his mother and stepfather— who had come to the UK from Guyana in the 1950s and 'had to struggle to make ends meet'— for instilling in him from an early age an appreciation that things do not come easily but through hard work.

Not decrying official accolades such as his knighthood, especially since it has given a lot of pleasure to his family, friend's and other black people, what gives Sir Herman Ouseley most satisfaction, he adds, 'is seeing so many people I have worked with develop and grow, and move into more senior levels themselves. And there is a feeling of immense pleasure,' he warmly declares, 'when one hears them say that they learnt something from me along the way or that I may have helped them at some point.'

Amongst those Herman Ouseley particularly admires is Nelson Mandela, 'an inspirational figure to so many people and whom I have had the privilege of meeting.' He also refers to individuals whom he feels have 'made a difference' to the position of black people in the UK. Here be cites people such as Paul Boateng MP, the late Rudy Narayan, barrister, the late Lord David Pitt and Claudia Jones, campaigners, and the political theorist and intellectual, A. Sivanandan

Given Herman's unique position as Chairman of the CRE, I am intrigued by his view of the path ahead. 'Looking to the next millennium,' Herman says, 'I am cautiously optimistic. As black people, we are moving forward on a continuum, but progress is slow.' He sums this up somewhat lightheartedly as 'same problems, different times'. Of his own future, he is looking, he says, 'simply to try and have a less frenetic life' .

From my perspective, even in less frenetic mode, Sir Herman Ouseley has a great deal more to contribute to help shape the Britain of the third millennium. His knighthood is but a fitting tribute to the struggle he has led so admirably for racial equality in British society.

Sir Herman Ouseley became Lord Ouseley in 2001.

Elsie Owusu

Architect

Housed in a quaint period building along London's busy Euston Road, the original Victorian gatehouse to the station, is an architectural practice with a difference. Here are the offices of Elsie Owusu Architects, one of just a handful of female owned and run architectural practices in the UK.

Although it is a small practice compared to some of the big City companies, employing just five other architect-ural and administrative staff besides Elsie Owusu herself (all of whom are women), it is not a firm short on ambition. This is evidenced by the fact that Elsie Owusu Architects have recently been selected as the architects on what Elsie enthusiastically describes as 'a huge project', to design and build a Multicultural Centre for Performing Arts located in north London. Budgeted to cost over £100m, the Centre will house a multimedia studio, art galleries, workshops, cinemas and restaurants. Elsie is understandably proud of the achievement and recognition that a project of this scale and significance represents, although she is candid enough to admit that she does lose the occasional moment of sleep musing over the details and progress of the project.

Elsie Owusu's architectural practice grew out of considerably more humble beginnings. After qualifying in 1986, Elsie worked for the first few years initially from an office at home, but as the work steadily came in and the traffic through her home became too disruptive, she set up outside offices, recruited staff and established the practice she runs today. Prestigious projects notwithstanding (such as the Multicultural Centre for Performing Arts), it is social housing that is the architectural field and area of specialisation with which Elsie Owusu has long been associated and to which she remains passionately committed. 'One of the nice things about being an architect is going back to buildings that you have designed and talking to people who are living in them and getting feedback that they are enjoying living there. That is a real joy,' says Elsie.

Elsie elaborates on her professional development choices: 'If I were white and male I probably would have joined an architectural company and by now would very likely have worked my way up to Associate or Partner level.' But, she adds, she and a newly qualified fellow female Ghanaian architect were so concerned with the general level of service which they saw being provided by the big architectural companies to black people—and to women—that they decided they would form a partnership to cater to this poorly served market. Although her partner eventually moved on to run a fashion design company with the actress Dawn French, Elsie has chosen to remain close to her love of architecture.

Elsie Owusu was schooled and brought up in the UK from the age of nine, after her parents moved to Britain with their daughter and her two younger brothers. She recalls that she was always drawing and sketching things while she was growing up, and that she was probably about eleven years old when she first voiced an interest in becoming an architect. Although other career ambitions surfaced from time to time, none remained as firmly embedded as architecture in the dreams of the young Elsie Owusu.

In probing about how easy or difficult it was, as a young black woman, to enter and follow such a career path in a field still largely seen as a male preserve, Elsie replies very matter of factly that 'It never occurred to me that I couldn't be an architect or anything else that I wanted to be.' It was, she says, only when she actually started her architectural course that she noticed that virtually all the other students were white and male. But even this, she adds, worked for rather than against her in that 'it helped to galvanise and push me forward all the more'.

A factor which I believe sheds light on Elsie Owusu's approach to life and on her laudable struggles to establish the career which she so successfully manages today, is that she had a daughter at the age of eighteen. All through Elsie's architectural studies she had to fulfil both the demands of her course and the needs of her young daughter. Indeed, she chose to study at the Architectural Association in London's Bedford Square precisely because its course structure and system allowed her to attend classes but to do most of her course work from home. After the difficulties of managing competing demands of home and work, Elsie tells me with great pride that 'one of the most satisfying things for me is to see my grown-up daughter developing a similar interest in architecture. Now that is really gratifying.'

She acknowledges that many people have helped her along her chosen path. She mentions her parents and, following her father's death, her mother's dogged determination as a source of inspiration and example to her. Particular tutors have also, she feels, encouraged and nurtured her progress, and more latterly she reserves special praise for the late Bemie Grant MP whom, she believes, as chairperson of the committee which commissioned her firm to carry out the Arts Centre project, showed great faith and trust in the Elsie Owusu practice.

Those whom Elsie most admires and finds inspiring are 'people in my everyday life'. She gives the example of an eighty-year-old black woman who lives in one of the housing projects Elsie has designed in Oxford. Having brought up eight children, mostly on her own, this lady still has a strength of character and spirit which Elsie finds quite remarkable. 'It makes me think that in comparison my life has been an absolute doddle.'

Her empathy and solidarity with others makes me admire all the more her own indomitable spirit which seems to be characterised by her almost permanently smiling face. Besides her struggles to build her architectural practice, Elsie Owusu was one of the founders and, for two years, chairperson of the Society for Black Architects, a body set up in 1992 to provide networking opportunities, self-help and political support for black architects in the UK. Elsie speaks enthusiastically about the work of the group and is greatly heartened by its achievements to date.

Looking to the millennium, Elsie is very optimistic about what lies ahead. Not only does she see the architectural profession finally showing signs of embracing diversity within its body, but she also sees a changed picture across UK PLC. 'When people talk about "the English" or "the British" they have a different picture of what this is today than they might have had twenty years ago. This has not happened as a result of government action but more because people have come together and made the changes themselves. This gives me good reason for opti-mism for our future.' I would suggest that people like Elsie Owusu are themselves key contributors to that optimism. In her case, Elsie is quite literally helping to put the building blocks in place for the Britain of tomorrow.

Spiralling to success

Star light

Andi Peters

Television Presenter, Producer and Commissioning Editor

From the earliest days of his television career, Audi Peters was regarded as someone with immense potential. Before he was twenty-five, he was already considered likely to rise to the very top in British television. This was being said not only in respect to his prodigious on-screen talents as a television presenter, but also, and perhaps even more significantly, with respect to his potential as a top television executive.

Andi Peters has not disappointed anyone. Still under thirty, he is today one of the hottest names in broadcasting. He is a much sought-after presenter and a budding producer. He has also recently been appointed Commisioning Editor, Children's Programmes for Channel 4—making him one of the youngest senior executives, and one of the few black senior executives, in the broadcasting industry. He is well on schedule to gain the even bigger executive posts for which he has been tipped and to which he is self-assured enough to admit that he aspires. I was fortunate enough to interview Andi only a week after he had taken up his new post as Commissioning Editor at Channel 4 where he is responsible for determining and scheduling the station's programme output for children and younger people.

Asked how he manages to juggle both artistic and management functions, Andi's response is modest and unassuming. 'Where I am so lucky is that the roles have a direct synergy with each other. I get to see things from multiple angles. But I am at pains to ensure I actually only perform one role at a time. When I am in the studio as a presenter, I am a presenter. Likewise, when I work as a producer or look at a proposal as a commissioning editor, I only perform that role or view the project from that perspective. Besides, I enjoy being busy and I thrive on new challenges.'

After more than ten years in the business, Andi Peters is still a youthful looking and fresh-faced personality, who seems to be constantly radiating vitality and good humour. Described previously by one commentator as 'the little ray of sunshine that greets and revives you when you turn on the television on Saturday morning', he was an ideal candidate for children's television, which is where he first gained attention in broadcasting. After a short period in the late 1980s and early 1990s cutting his teeth in a variety of presenting roles, Andi became a link man for Children's BBC He was so popular with the younger viewers that when the BBC launched a new Saturday morning children's show, 'Live and Kicking', in 1993, Andi was chosen as co-host with Emma Forbes. The programme proved to be an instant hit with its target audience and has never been matched in popularity since. With Andi and Emma at the helm, the success of the programme had the effect of catapulting their respective television careers, and making them sought-after for guest appearances on other television shows and at events like Royal Variety Performances and Children in Need. Andi looks back on his time at 'Live and Kicking' as one of his career highlights. 'It was a unique and brilliant experience.' he says proudly.

Given Andi Peters' broad television appeal, not just to children but to viewers across the spectrum, it is not surprising that after several years of unbridled success at the BBC, he was poached by a rival ITV television company in a deal which was reputed to make him one of Britain's highest paid television presenters. The move gave Andi the opportunity to present and produce a wide range of programmes, some aimed at children but others at mainstream television audiences. These included his own music show, 'The Noise', 'Train 2 Win', a junior version of 'Gladiators' and 'Showbiz UK', a live light entertainment show with celebrity interviews. His rapid rate of career progress culminated in 1998 when he was appointed Commissioning Editor at Channel 4.

In addition to his enduring popularity with viewers, Andi Peters has an enviable reputation within the television business itself and amongst his fellow professionals. Described as 'television's Mr Nice Guy', he is seen as a consumate professional and an accomplished performer. Although he has been in the business a relatively short time, he has packed a lot into his career, combining considerable live television and front-of-camera performances with solid behind-camera experience. Andi's view of himself is of a 'hardworking perfectionist', adding that he has been fortunate in being able to take on jobs which he liked doing and therefore wanted to do well.

Born and raised in south London, Andi Peters is very matter of fact about how he got his first break in television. 'Luck,' he openly asserts. 'You have to have that element of luck—we all need it, no matter how talented.' At seventeen, when he was working at his Saturday job as the resident disk jockey at the Top Shop clothing store in London's Oxford Circus, Andi received great encouragement for his talents from a good friend and fellow employee (whom he fondly calls 'Julie Cash Only'). He decided to write a letter to the producer of a Thames Television children's show he had seen, asking for a job as a presenter. Luck must indeed have played a part because the station was on the lockout for new presenters for a forthcoming show, and Andi was invited to audition. Thus, on the back of a single letter, he managed to get his foot firmly in the door of what is a notoriously difficult, competitive and fickle industry to penetrate. The initial offer was only for a short-term contract and Andi is quick to acknowledge the support his parents gave him during this critical time. He believes it was a pivotal decision to take up the short-term job rather than go to university as he had previously intended. 'My parents allowed me to make my own decision, and frankly the opportunity may never have arisen again.' He remains very close to his parents and points out how important his family members are to him and to his career.

Andi is philosophical about his celebrity status. 'You have to take the rough with the smooth,' he says, acknowledging that whilst it has many advantages, it also has its downside. Amongst the disadvantages he cites 'the loss of anonymity and sometimes privacy, and the fact that people's attitudes about you have very often already been formed well before they even meet you'. He also feels that because there are relatively few black celebrities, other black people do not realise how they sometimes place unacceptable demands on black performers like him. That said. one of Andi's wishes for the millennium is to see more black people on the screen and he hopes that more black people will indeed give it a go.

As regards his own future, Andi is endearingly open about his intention not to allow his rapid rise to success to plateau in any way. 'Channel Controller, preferably for BBC 1,' he jokingly declares to be a future target post, adding, more seriously, 'I would love to perform this role ahead of almost anything else.' Given his multifarious talents and focused ambition, and with age firmly on his side, I for one would not wager against him achieving his goal to get to the very top of British broadcasting.

Mike Phillips

Writer and Broadcaster

'The millennium is not just an historical date but a moment in time when you can stand like a high mountain and survey the terrain behind you, as well as assess the landscape ahead,' says Mike Phillips in his typically elegant and eloquent way. Talking to Mike Phillips one is aware of being engaged with a genuine wordsmith. Moreover, his deep. mellifluous tones sugges 'broadcaster' with almost every syllable he speaks. Mike Phillips is, of course, an accomplished exponent of both arts, and as I was to learn from this jovial and interesting man, a veteran of many more careers as well.

One gets the clear sense that of all the career roles he has fulfilled, writing is at the very core of Mike Phillips. Indeed, as his younger brother Trevor (also a broadcaster and journalist) says, 'For Mike, being a writer isn't just a task, it's an identity.' Although Mike Phillips has been writing short stories since he was a teenager, and was fascinated by literature from an even earlier age—he says he always knew deep down that he wanted to be a writer— it took many years before he achieved his long-held ambition and to be able to call himself a writer. Mike takes a philosophical view about this. 'My writing career emerged from my age,' he says, 'I think of the time spent before that as a preparation for my becoming a writer.'

To date, Mike Phillips has published eight novels, including one written under a pseudonym, 'just for the money', he laughingly declares, and has another book on the way entitled *A Shadow of Myself.* Two of his novels have been turned into screenplays, with one televised and the other made into a feature film.

Although Mike Phillips is predominantly a crime and thriller writer, critics quite correctly deduce that his writing seems as much to be a vehicle for making his sharp and astute social and political comment through this popular medium, than strict adherence to the genre. This sub-agenda has not prevented him from winning several literary awards, including the Crime Writers Association's Silver Dagger for his second novel, *The Late Candidate,* and the Arts Foundation Fellowship for thriller writing in 1997. More recently he co-wrote with his brother, Trevor, the highly acclaimed social history, *Windrush: The Irresistible Rise of Multi-Racial Britain,* to accompany the BBC television series of the same name. He was also Writer in Residence at London's South Bank Centre, Royal Festival Hall.

But to understand and gain a proper perspective of Mike Phillips' achievements, one has to have an appreciation of his long and often arduous path to become a writer. Mike Phillips came to Britain from Guyana in the 1950s with his parents when he was a young child. He admits that after graduating from the University of London with a degree in English and Philosophy in the late 1960s, what he really wanted to do at that stage was get a management or executive position in industry like many of his peers. The reality, however, was that 1960s Britain— before the enactment of race discrimination legislation— was a very different place for a black graduate than it is today. Thus, despite numerous applications for professional jobs, nothing commensurate with his degree qualification came along. Instead, the only work he could secure of any description were a variety of manual jobs such as hospital porter, petrol pump attendant and mechanic's mate.

Mike Phillips returned time and again to full-time education as a safe haven from the humiliations of the job market, and is able to joke today about the array of qualifications he amassed as a result: a Bachelor's degree, two Masters degrees, and a teaching certificate. 'After completing each course I applied for various jobs, and after a year or so, as my heart sank, I drifted back to education.'

His break came whilst doing a youth and community work job, 'the one field in those days', he says self-mockingly, 'where being black and educated was actually desirable'. A BBC producer named Harry Levington came to Mike's youth project in Paddington, west London to interview some of the black youths there for a television documentary on the theme of 'In Search of an Identity'. Noticing Mike's easy rapport with the youngsters and his knowledge of the subject matter, the producer asked Mike if he would like to prepare the script and commentary for the interviews.

Impressed with Mike's effort, and thinking that Mike's voice actually fitted the piece rather better than his own, the producer generously invited him to go one stage further and present the piece to camera. This Mike did, and as a result of the programme being aired, he received an offer to be involved with another being put together about black teachers. This, in turn, led to other broadcasting opportunities, and so began Mike Phillips' foray into the world of broadcasting. He eventually became a regular contributor and, indeed, producer on BBC World Service, as well as a freelance journalist with various Fleet Street newspapers and the black press.

After several years of freelancing, Mike Phillips applied for, and was appointed to, the first professional job he had managed to secure through the conventional recruitment route. He became a senior lecturer in Media Studies and Journalism at the Polytechnic of Central London, a position he held for over a decade. During this period, Mike wrote his first two books between 5.30 and 7a.m. in the morning before going to work! He is now a full-time novelist.

If Mike Phillips' route to becoming a writer was somewhat circuitous, it is evident that he did eventually find his calling, and that he still takes much pride and pleasure in having done so. 'Being a writer is something special,' he says. 'There are writers who make me shiver with admiration—Charles Dickens, Joseph Conrad, Vaclav Havel, to name but a few—and the thought that I am in the same game as them really pulls me up and makes me aspire to be the best writer that I can.' He cites the Italian writer Umberto Eco, who used the genre of the thriller to incorporate historical, social and political ideas, as his reason for also choosing the same medium.

Given Mike Phillips' long and varied experience of life as a black man in Britain, his views are interesting and enlightening. Happy to regard himself as black British, Mike explains, 'When I walk the streets of Britain now, I do not feel that I do not belong, I feel very much that I do belong, and that is entirely different from how I felt thirty years ago.' There are still issues and problems, he emphasises, but overall things have moved on for black people. Just as importantly, he asserts, 'black people have also changed Britain. We have left our imprint on society in a multitude of different ways.'

Viewing the millennium as much more than just a brief, historical occurrence, but rather a time for reflection and projection, Mike Phillips casts a philosophical eye to the future and observes, 'I am optimistic about the new millennium because if we do not kill ourselves or ruin the earth totally, we have an opportunity to finally appreciate that life is beautiful and that human beings are wonderful creatures.'

The wordsmith

In the news

Trevor Phillips

Broadcaster and Chairman, London Arts Board

Trying to sum up Trevor Phillips' career and professional involvements is rather like attempting to put into words a journey from Ealing to Ongar, stopping off for lunch at Covent Garden, travelling by a combination of tube, taxi, train and a bright red London double-decker bus.

Trevor Phillips is one of those quintessential multitalented individuals whose professional interests and involvements fan out like a spider's web across a range of interrelated but yet disparate fields.

For some, he might be regarded as something akin to television's voice and the face of contemporary London. Trevor Phillips has, after all, presented television's award winning weekly current affairs show, 'The London Programme', for the past thirteen or so years, and it is in this role, which he has made so much his own, that he is perhaps best known. As Trevor readily admits, 'I have made my living in the main from reporting about London,' and the theme of London and the medium of television continue to provide the central themes of his ever-burgeoning career.

Trevor is not only the presenter of this popular programme but has also been the executive producer of the series, and the head of the current affairs department at London Weekend Television (LWT) where 'The London Programme' is made. As head of current affairs at LWT, Trevor Phillips was one of the small number of black senior executives of major British broadcasting organisations. Trevor does not seek to hold such positions closely to himself, and he is not slow to use the other platforms open to him to berate the broadcasting industry about its poor performance in putting more black faces onto their executive floors, or to cajole them into trying to improve this situation.

As a journalist, he has the distinction of working concurrently in all three mediums—print, radio and television. In addition to television. Trevor writes regularly for The Evening Standard and The Times Educational Supplement as well as providing articles for other British newspapers, including from time to time for Britain's black press. Trevor also presents his own current affairs show for the BBC's Radio 4.

Trevor Phillips' involvement in the world of broadcasting also extends to part ownership of an independent production company, 'Pepper Productions'. It was one of his company's recent productions—the 'Windrush' series —aired nationwide in 1998 by the BBC to mark the fiftieth anniversary of the arrival of the Empire Windrush which brought the early Caribbean settlers to Britain's shores, for which Trevor feels a special sense of pride. 'It was', he explains, 'so much more than just a television series.' He believes it has given Britain's black population more pride in itself and helped affirm their place in the wider community.

Still in the pipeline at Pepper Productions is a period feature film, a drama production and an historical documentary, each based on the company's central theme and mission which, Trevor explains, is 'to reflect the rich tradition of black British life and help establish its reintegration into the wider British story'. As if his multi-faceted involvement in the media were not enough, Trevor Phillips manages to don other caps and perform other professional roles and activities, all of them demanding in terms of time and commitment.

Over the last five years, for instance, he has been the chairman of the Runnymede Trust, an independent race relations think-tank and campaigning body. More recently, in 1997, having been a board member for the preceding two years, he was appointed chairman of the newly revamped London Arts Board. This body is responsible for the funding of the London arts scene to the tune of around £50m a year, without which support many of London's renowned cultural and artistic establishments would possibly fold. It is a role which fits Trevor Phillips well. His desire to do more in the civic and public arena, and his evident interest and pride in all things 'London', are both met admirably.

'London is probably the most important city in the world,' Trevor proclaims, 'and will be well into the twenty-first century.' He talks about London's unique spirit, which he sees as one of 'cosmopolitanism, openness and tolerance. Wave after wave of new migrants have been absorbed over the centuries into the fabric of the city and in doing so they too have become Londoners. London,' he adds, 'is one of the few major cities of the world where people of different ethnic backgrounds can live comfortably together side by side, rather than in segregated neighbourhood or areas.'

With Trevor Phillips talking so openly and passionately about London, I begin to appreciate why and how his name is so often mentioned as a possible candidate for the forthcoming election to select London's first Mayor. Probing to see if there is anything in the rumour, he responds rather coyly, but in good humour, 'My ambition remains to do something serious and useful in public life. What that might be we shall have to wait and see.'

I ask Trevor how he has managed to achieve so much and he is quick to acknowledge the help and support of others. 'Various people along the way have said "go that way and not this", or have shown me a door and invited me to open it. They don't do the work but they open the possibilities.'

His parents, he feels, were hugely influential, and he adds that to this day he always consults his mother and wider family before making any critical decisions affecting his life. He touchingly recalls one of his junior school teachers in Wood Green, North London, Ms Jean Gordon, whose intervention he feels was critical. She widened his horizons simply by taking an interest in his education and letting him know what he was capable of. He also acknowledges a number of professional colleagues, and cites amongst them Charles Clarke, now Minister of Education in the Labour Government, and John Birt, Director-General of the BBC.

Even negative but constructive feedback has its place, Trevor informs me. He recalls a discussion in 1975 when he was a new chemistry graduate (albeit also the outgoing President of the National Union of Students) trying to find work in the petro chemical industry. The corporate recruiter very matter-of-factly told him that as an older and more mature student, and especially someone already so well known through his involvement in radical student politics, he would find it exceedingly difficult to obtain a place in industry. With this candid advice ringing in his ears, Trevor Phillips set about finding an alternative career to that of a petro-chemical engineer, and he applied for a research position at LWT. The rest, as they say, is history.

Who knows whether consideration of a possible assault on the London Mayoral contest might have been possible from a position in the petro-chemical industry, but clearly the future burns brightly for Trevor Phillips. London will indeed eagerly wait and see what Trevor will do next.

Seen from the inner city

Heather Rabbatts

Chief Executive Officer, London Borough of Lambeth

The job advertisement for the position Heather Rabbatts occupies as Chief Executive Officer of the London Borough of Lambeth candidly declared in a banner headline, that it was 'arguably the worst job in local government'. Heather Rabbatts, who has now been in the post some four years, laughs as she says, 'Other than striking out the words "arguably", it was a fairly accurate description.'

For someone who has occupied such a hot and visible seat, albeit with the compensation of what is reputed to be the highest salary in local government, she is warm and good-humoured, and is exceedingly open about her work at Lambeth, and about her personal climb to the top. I was grateful that someone who is routinely in her office for twelve hours a day, would take time out to be interviewed for my *Millennium People* book. The meeting gave me a good perspective on why Heather Rabbatts was such an excellent appointment for this challenging position, and why she has earned plaudits for what she has already achieved.

Heather explains: 'Lambeth Council had an unenviable reputation for mis-management, poor delivery of service and even fraudulent and corrupt practices.' After years of being a high-profile 'political borough', some of the more basic service issues had been left unaddressed. This was characterised by poor systems for council tax collection, extraordinarily high levels of rent arrears, deteriorating housing estates, under-performing schools, sub-contractors who submitted grossly inflated bills, escalating and fraudulent housing benefit claims—some of which involved the Council's own employees—and so on. Heather says, 'The press were running weekly articles on the latest Lambeth horror stories,' adding ruefully, 'and in most cases they were true.'

A combination of factors lay behind Heather Rabbatts' decision to leave the Chief Executive position she already occupied with another of London's borough councils (in the more leafy and relatively sedate Merton), to come to Lambeth. Notwithstanding being headhunted because of her track record in management, Heather describes herself as 'thriving on challenges' and possessing 'a drive to make a difference'. She explains, 'There is much of me in the line "it is better to live one day as a tiger than 100 days as a sheep".' Moreover, as a black woman of Caribbean origin, she felt a strong affinity to the borough which includes Brixton within its boundaries. 'Somehow Brixton symbolises the black presence in the UK, so I felt I belonged there and that the

people of Lambeth, regardless of their ethnicity, deserved better.'

Heather Rabbatts describes her arrival on encountering the organisation as 'like pulling a lever only to discover it was not connected to anything—the machine had broken down'. She set about her agenda to turn Lambeth around, bringing with her trusted people from her previous job, making new and imaginative appointments to key management roles, establishing a corporate anti-fraud team, and improving the systems for council tax and rent collection.

She is both modest and realistic in her assessment of what has been achieved in her first four years. 'We have made progress but it's too early for satisfaction and pride. We have not done nearly enough and it is a long road ahead.' But there are signs which make her feel more confident about the future. Amongst these are the improving educational standards in Lambeth schools, with attainment going up and exclusions down; more positive feedback from tenants in council housing about the services provided; and the re-emergence of dynamism, enthusiasm and creativity amongst the managers and staff of the council.

Given the struggle she is actively engaged in, not forgetting the more regular responsibilities of a CEO in handling an annual budget of over £700m and a staff complement of some 9,000 employees, it came as a surprise to learn that Heather Rabbatts failed her Eleven Plus examinations and left school at the age of sixteen to work initially as a waitress. 'I did not have a career plan and certainly had no sense that one day I would be climbing the management or executive ladder. What drove me', she adds, 'was that I was determined not to just lie down and accept my fate. I wanted to make a difference.'

That same steely determination which has today made such an impact at Lambeth, coupled with the support of a mother whom Heather says warmly 'refused to allow me to be counted out', enabled her to get back into full-time study at a college of further education. From there she went on to the London School of Economics—where she now sits as a Governor—and completed her remarkable transformation by being called to the Bar in 1981. After a short period as a barrister in the private sector, where she was involved in representing many of the Greenham Common women protesting against Britain's nuclear involvement, Heather Rabbatts switched to local government.

Beginning initially as a policy officer with the Local Government Information Unit, and subsequently head of the women's equality unit in the London Borough of Hammersmith and Fulham, she rose rapidly to the top position of CEO with Merton Council before taking on the Lambeth job.

On a lighter note. Heather Rabbatts is renowned for her trendy designer clothes which provide a pleasant contrast to the usual 'grey suits' of most CEOs. She is also open about her fondness for good food and champagne, which are cited amongst her recreational interests in her entry in *Who's Who*. Heather says of these 'I've never been a puritan. If you work hard, you should play hard.'

She recalls encountering her first ever black teacher—Mac Johnson—whilst doing her A levels at college. 'He was hugely important to me in offering encouragement and reassurance that I could do it...especially since no-one had ever said that before.' Motivated by the experience, Heather Rabbatts acts as a mentor to a number of junior black managers and staff. While effusive in her admiration of Nelson Mandela, whom she met when he visited Lambeth, those whom Heather finds especially inspiring are the young people she meets in the borough and the many local people who work behind the scenes on a variety of local projects.

Describing the UK as 'home' Heather explains that she envies her mother's strong sense of belonging to her native Jamaica. In Heather's view, black people in the UK are still striving to create a sense of identity and a belonging that transcends nationhood and place. Looking to the future, she believes that whilst some of the social and economic indices are still pointing the wrong way—the higher levels of black unemployment and the continued exclusion of black pupils from school, for instance—on the whole things are moving in the right direction. She is particularly heartened by the very positive signs of hope shown in the enhanced relationships between young people of different ethnic groups.

Whilst her name has been mentioned as a possible future Mayor of London, Heather is herself unsure what, or where, her next career move will be. 'Lambeth', she says, 'is an exciting job and it is hard to see what could follow it.' I would contend, however, that wherever her future career may lead, one certainty is that Heather Rabbatts will bring to it the tremendous energy and drive for which she is renowned, and will not shrink from tackling the jobs which even the recruiters despair of promoting as attractive.

Scientifically speaking

Liz Rasekoala

Engineer

Liz Rasekoala is a black female engineer with a deep and infectious passion for science. She defies the more stereotypical conventions about prescribed occupational roles, and as someone who has dedicated much of her professional life to demystifying and breaking down the barriers of science and technology, she is actively engaged in the business of mould-breaking.

'Science', Liz Rasekoala says in her lovely mix of African and Mancunian accents, 'is a double-edged sword. It is a tool which can both de-humanise and empower. It empowers by opening the doors to jobs of status and power for those who understand it and know how to use it, but it can at the same time de-humanise by dis-empowering those without access to it'. Liz Rasekoala is on a mission to bring science more squarely into the realms of education for children of African and Caribbean origin in Britain.

Liz Rasekoala is by profession a chemical engineer. She received her education, including her first degree, in her native Nigeria and came to the UK to undertake a Master's degree at the University of Manchester Institute of Science and Technology (UMIST). Armed with her Master's degree she established a successful career for herself in industry in the UK in the latter part of the 1980s. Working initially as a process engineer with the pharmaceutical giant ICI, she later became the production manager for the Co-operative Whole-sale Society, where she was responsible for the company's food manufacturing and processing plant, and the manager of over 500 staff. Today she works as a successful consultant chemical engineer for a number of client companies.

Becoming a consultant, she says, was the best move she could have made. Not only is she able to work for a wide range of companies, but she is also able to give more of her time to other things, in particular to the African-Caribbean Network for Science and Technology.

To listen to Liz Rasekoala talk about the work of this organisation, which she founded in 1995, and of which she is presently the director—meaning, she says self-mockingly, 'its general dogsbody'—is like listening to a missionary expounding her faith to the non-converted. Here is someone who sees maths and science as the keys to unlocking the social, political and economic structures of the world. 'In Western technological society, the keys that open the door to jobs of power and status are maths and science.' The African-Caribbean Network for Science and Technology aims to give others access to those keys.

Whilst studying at UMIST, Liz explains that she was struck by the fact that in a city such as Manchester, with a large black population, there were hardly any local black university students, and of those she met even fewer seemed to be studying science or numeracy-based courses. Her subsequent research revealed that of all the black students at British universities, fewer than three per cent were taking courses involving science or numeracy.

At a conference she attended some years later entitled 'The Political Dimensions of Maths in Education', all was laid bare for Liz Rasekoala. The conference made direct causal links between issues of gender, ethnicity, socio-economic status and the respective groups' involvement with, or exclusion from, maths and science. 'It was not a coincidence', Liz declares, 'that the two subjects removed from the curriculum of black schools in apartheid South Africa were maths and science.' That conference confirmed for Liz what she wanted to do and she has been actively engaged in it ever since.

Through her contacts with other black scientists whom she had met during her years in industry, a small group gathered initially in Liz's Manchester home 'with nothing but our ideas and a wish to do something positive to address the issues affecting the education of black children especially in science and maths'. Of that beginning, the African-Caribbean Network for Science and Technology was born.

Today, the Network operates nationwide and has over 300 members. Liz explains that further recruitment is slow and painstaking. It has to be done by word of mouth, because, Liz says, 'there is no other group of black professionals so invisible as those in science and technology'. Operating as a registered charity, with seedcorn funding from local education authorities, scientific bodies and the European Council, the Network runs a string of 'Ishango' science clubs aimed at providing extra-curricular support in maths and science for black children through tutorials, mentoring, examination preparation and careers advice. At present, there are Ishango clubs in Manchester, Liverpool, Birmingham and Nottingham, and with funding having been agreed plans are well advanced for four more. The Network has set itself the target of establishing ten Ishango science clubs across the UK.

The Ishango science clubs are named after "the Ishango Bone", a carved bone discovered at Ishango, on the shore of Lake Edward in Zaire. Believed to be over 11,000 years old, it indicates early evidence of the use of a calendrical or numeration system. The name was adopted for the science clubs as a positive and, hopefully, inspiring symbol of the history of maths and science.

In addition to science clubs, the Network provides a schools outreach service, running workshops and seminars for teachers and academics, especially those teaching maths, science and technology subjects. The organisation's stature is such that it has been commissioned by the Department for Education and Employment to prepare a good practice guide for schools on raising the levels of achievement of black children in maths and science.

Liz Rasekoala regards her father, a UK-trained barrister who returned to Nigeria in the 1960s, as being something of a visionary. Despite his legal training and his great love of literature, 'he saw science and technology as empowerment', says Liz, and encouraged all his six children—including his four daughters—to go in that direction. With all her brothers and sisters now in successful professional roles in science and technology, Liz acknowledges that each sibling also acted as a role model for the younger ones in the family. She reserves special praise, however, for the person she describes as her 'biggest role model', the black television detective played by the late Greg Morris in 'Mission Impossible'. 'From the first moment I saw that programme I was inspired. He was a most unhip and uncool person, but he could do fantastic things with gadgets. It was the most powerful re-inforcement of my Dad's message,' says Liz effusively.

Looking to the new millennium, Liz expresses concern at the huge gap emerging in the UK, and globally, between highly skilled people at the top, a shrinking middle band, and a growing group of unskilled people at the bottom. She sees access, or lack of it, to science and technology as the main reason for this trend.

Having devoted much of her own time over recent years to the establishment of the African-Caribbean Network for Science and Technology, whilst continuing her professional consultancy on a part-time basis, Liz Rasekoala says of her own future, 'I do not judge my success on an individual level. It's about giving something back to my community. I am not fascinated by making lots of money or becoming a CEO. For me, it's about developing the next generation.' Liz Rasekoala has been doing just that to admirable effect, and is a powerful role model and spokeswoman for the very cause which she so ably espouses.

Commander Martyn Reid

Senior Officer, Royal Navy

With twenty-five years distinguished service behind him, Commander Martyn Reid is quick to point out that he did not hail from a long line of naval tradition, nor for that matter did he hold any childhood ambition of a naval career. It was rather, he says, pure chance that he ended up in the Royal Navy.

Commander Martyn Reid, who is one of the most senior black officers in the naval branch of the UK's Armed Forces, was born and brought up in Bolton in the northwest of England, where the closest seafaring towns are more usually associated with fishing fleets than with destroyers or frigates.

Leaving school equipped with A levels, but without any clear career ambitions, Martyn tried a variety of jobs, from administration in the civil service, to selling motor cars, to being a production controller on a factory assembly line, but none of these offered what he was looking for. 'The reality of my life prior to joining the Navy was one of absolute boredom,' is how Commander Reid candidly describes his early working years.

It was in this state of mind, and quite by chance, that he met up with some former school friends who had earlier joined the Services and he could not help but notice that they seemed to be having a much better time than he was, especially those who had joined the Royal Marines and the Royal Navy. Such was the impact of this encounter that it led to his immediate decision to join one of the services.

Chance would play a further hand on the day he went along to the recruiting station intending to join the Royal Marines. He arrived to find the office shut. The Royal Navy's recruiting station was, however open, and so began, in 1974, the start of Martyn Reid's naval career.

Unsure about whether he really wanted a long-term career in the Royal Navy, Martyn initially joined on a short career commission in the Navy's Fleet Air Arm. After attending Dartmouth Naval College, the Royal Navy's equivalent of the Army's Sandhurst and the RAF's Cranwell, he worked for the next few years of his commission with helicopters as a naval aviator, specialising in anti-submarine warfare. Whilst in the Fleet Air Arm, Martyn was awarded two Queen's Commendations for Valuable Service in the Air, the first for his part in pulling some thirty-five sailors from the burning deck of a ship on fire in the English Channel, and the second for a successful operation in the Caribbean.

No doubt prompted by my evident lack of naval know-how and puzzlement about the role of the Fleet Air Arm, Commander Reid took great pride in explaining to me the Royal Navy's special place among the three main branches of the British military service. Because Britain is an island nation, the Navy was the first— 'senior'—defence service to be established. The subsequent historical development of the Royal Navy resulted in it, unlike the Army or RAF, developing its own sea, land and airborne divisions within the fleet, including currently holding the United Kingdom's strategic deterrent.

Commander Reid explained that 'traditionally in a conflict situation the Navy's job is to open the door to allow the Army to march through. But', he proudly added, 'the Navy has within the service the capability for all open entry operations....It can take the force to where it needs to fight and can take the fight to the enemy on land, sea and in the air ...as we all saw during the Falklands Conflict.'

Realising that he did indeed enjoy life in the Royal Navy, and wanting to build a long-term career in the Service, Martyn Reid—by then a Lieutenant—decided to re-engage. He chose to transfer from the Fleet Air Arm to 'general service' because he felt this would give greater opportunity for promotion and, with it, the possibility of one day commanding an operational vessel. This decision meant that he effectively had to retrain. Instead of the principles of aviation and aeronautical engineering, he had to learn ship handling, navigation and maritime engineering. But it was a decision he has not regretted.

Martyn Reid has steadily moved through the naval ranks to become a Commander, which is the first senior officer rank in the naval officer corps. On the operational side, Commanders may be given full responsibility for operational vessels such as frigates or destroyers with between 200 and 300 seamen under their command.

Although Commander Reid has been operational at sea for the greater part of his naval career, including spells in the Persian Gulf escorting merchant ships through the Straits of Hormutz to prevent attacks during the Iran-Iraq War, and taking part in the UN naval blockade of the former Yugoslavia, his current role in the Royal Navy is serving in a 'Joint Service' appointment in the Ministry of Defence in Whitehall, London.

Intrigued by the concept of 'active service', I enquired about his feelings at such moments. Commander Reid responded robustly: 'The Royal Navy is all said and done a fighting Service and we are here to be able to fight if called upon to support Her Majesty's Government policies. Am I worried or concerned about it? No! If the team works and you have confidence in the team, the concept of losing does not enter the equation.'

On the issue of being a black officer in the Royal Navy, Commander Reid explained that life aboard ship is an interdependent existence, where everyone has to work together as a team and live at very close quarters. Professionalism dictates that people simply have to get along with each other. 'If you can do your job in the Royal Navy, you are accepted,' says Commander Reid, adding, light-heartedly, that 'arguably I have had more problems in the Navy for being an officer with a northern accent than for the colour of my skin!'

I was particularly gratified by the photographic record of our session together. Taken on the banks of the river Thames with HMS Belfast as the backdrop, the selected shot captures Commander Reid's mood and bearing: proud, strong and ever-willing to give loyal service to his country, much like the famous cruiser moored behind him.

The qualities which Commander Reid admires in others are supreme confidence, a competitive nature, the strength of character to stand up and be counted when the time comes, and the self-discipline to work hard to improve oneself. He particularly admires Mohammed Ali whose sporting career he feels displayed those qualities in abundance.

Looking to the future, Commander Reid acknowledges that the slimming down of Britain's Armed Forces and its impact on the Royal Navy—a reduction from 75,000 servicemen and women in 1974, when he joined, to a projected 42,000 by the year 2000—will, amongst other things, make competition to reach the ranks of Captain and above exceptionally fierce. Despite this, he retains a desire to move further up the chain of command.

Even with a slimmed down Naval Service, Commander Reid is of the view that the Royal Navy's role is no less crucial today than it ever was. With the vacuum created by the loss of a world superpower, the burgeoning of trouble spots around the globe, and major international crimes such as drug running, Commander Reid sees the Royal Navy continuing to be as active and important to Britain in the next millennium as it has ever been.

A commanding view

A good advertisement

Trevor Robinson

Director, Quiet Storm Creative Agency

Although Quiet Storm is the name of the creative agency owned and run by Trevor Robinson, it also serves as a rather apt description of the man himself. Cutting an imposing physical presence at one's first encounter with him, Trevor Robinson is actually quietly spoken, thoughtful, and altogether a rather reflective person, but one who has nonetheless succeeded in creating something of a storm in the advertising field with his creative talent and memorable output.

Trevor Robinson is both the managing director and creative director of Quiet Storm, nestled behind London's Carnaby Street, which he describes as a cross between an advertising agency and a production company, thus the term 'creative agency'. Trevor explains, 'there aren't other agencies around like us. We work across all the mediums— print, billboards, television, radio and film—offering our creative solutions and executions to client companies.' At Quiet Storm staff are selected on the basis of their multiple skills so that they, like Trevor himself, can offer an all- round service to clients. 'I don't want to be tied into just one discipline' says Trevor, 'because I am equally interested in all facets of our company. Plus it keeps us knowledgeable, excited and sharp.'

Prior to setting up his own agency, Trevor Robinson rose through the ranks of the advertising industry, working initially as a graphic designer and illustrator, then a copywriter, before moving on to make a splash as a director of some memorable commercials. But his career has not always followed a smooth, upward path. Indeed, his experience of getting into the industry and his early working life owe as much to his resilience, fortitude and self-belief as to his creative talents and skills.

As a youngster in inner city south London, Trevor was keen on drawing, and he soon found that his illustrations of friends and family gained him a certain amount of attention and popularity. Encouraged by an art teacher at school, he set his sights on going to college to study art. But he recalls, in trying to realise this goal be had to overcome discouraging careers advice at school. Because he was not particularly academically orientated, he was advised to be 'more realistic in his outlook' and to think about perhaps getting himself a job as a bus conductor!

Nonetheless, Trevor secured a place at South Thames College, moving later to Chelsea Art College, and finally to Hounslow Borough College where he studied graphic design and fashion together with advertising and fine art. Unsure which particular career direction to take on graduating —he so liked all the genres—he worked initially as a freelance designer and illustrator for newspapers and magazines. One project involved doing the illustrations for the then much publicised Jeffrey Archer High Court libel case, but despite other occasional high- profile work of this nature, Trevor felt restricted and unchallenged by this narrow range.

After a short stint as a visualiser with a small advertising company, where he admits that he was 'bitten by the bug of advertising', Trevor and a colleague—a talented writer by the name of Alan Young—decided that together they would present their combined talents and portfolios for consideration to the big name advertising houses. They would spend several months on 'the dole' while literally knocking on doors to show their portfolios to agency after agency.

Trevor remembers this period as 'exceptionally hard, to say the least. It was a merry-go-round of rejection, despondency and discomfort, as well as counting the pennies and eking out bus fares to get to interviews. But we knew that given a chance we would not only make it but also shine.' They landed short-term jobs with the advertising agency TVWA which gave them some limited exposure in the industry, before finding themselves back on the unemployment register during another six months of foot slogging and door knocking. Their next break came with the agency HHCL and was to prove decisive and where they did indeed go on to shine.

Perhaps their most controversial commercial, and the one which earned Trevor the accolade of being 'one of the gurus of guerrilla advertising', was for Tango drinks. Employing what Trevor describes as 'slapstick humour with a difference', the advertisement is seen as a classic of its kind. Of the guerrilla advertising accolade—a term used to describe advertisements which shock audiences— Trevor is philosophical and feels advertisers are caught in a double bind. 'At no stage do I set out to be deliberately provocative or to offend or alienate anyone, but I do want to make people sit up and take notice. Advertisers have to be interesting and entertaining because no one will view or remember something that is tedious or boring. But you are always treading a thin line between exciting some people while possibly offending others.'

Besides Tango, other commercials which have contributed to Trevor's reputation in the industry include one for Pot Noodles, a convenience food which was originally the butt of many comedians' jokes. Trevor's commercials helped to recreate and regenerate the image of this product. Similarly, his work for Martini the vermouth drink, reversed the sales trend of a rapidly declining product line, getting people talking about and purchasing it once again.

A project which Trevor derives a lot of satisfaction from, although it was not a strictly commercial proposition but rather something he did in response to an approach from a friend and because it touched a nerve of his own, was Operation Black Vote. Aiming to arrest the feelings of dis-empowerment and the non-voter registration of black people, especially younger ones. and get them out to vote in the then forthcoming 1998 general election, Trevor devised a campaign openly using the telephone numbers of the major political parties and their leaders in his advertisements. The campaign resulted in those telephone lines becoming deluged with calls, and prompted something of a major national debate about black voter registration. As Trevor proudly proclaims, 'every project we have worked on has greatly affected our clients' bottom lines, whether counted in pounds or people, and as long as we continue to do that and produce good work at the same time, that is all that counts for me.'

Trevor Robinson values his independence and feels that one of the big pluses of having his own company is that he can choose which projects to take on and the type of work he wants to do. Whilst he wishes to see his business grow, he does not want it to become 'big and fat', although having started his business with a capital of £30k, it turned over well in excess of a million pounds in its first year. On a personal level, having recently directed a television comedy series for the Paramount Comedy Channel, Trevor hopes one day to make a major feature film. As he looks to the next millennium, Trevor comments on how heartened he is to see 'more black people and women breaking through in numbers and doing good things in the advertising industry', and is gratified to know that he was and is part of that process of change. Recalling his parents' constant message to their children to be 'proud of themselves', Trevor Robinson can justifiably feel that he has heeded their words, observing, 'I have already achieved far more than some people ever gave me credit for.'

Chrystal Rose

Television Talk Show Host and Entrepreneur

To describe Chrystal Rose merely as a television talk show host, significant as that title may be since she is, after all, the first black person to host her own talk show on British television, would seem almost to do her a disservice. From the time she first appeared on screen presenting the 'Chrystal Rose Show', in 1993, she made an impact and was widely hailed as Britain's answer to America's Oprah Winfrey. Although this is the role in which she is best known, as my *Millennium People* interview revealed—much like the famous Oprah, who is Chrystal's mentor and role model—there is much more to Chrystal Rose than that slice of her personality which viewers see on her weekly television show.

Chrystal Rose is a gutsy and dynamic and yet elegant streak of energy, whose ever-growing list of credits and accomplishments defy simple categorisation. 'For me, there are no set boundaries. I do what I do simply because I enjoy doing it,' says Chrystal. She happily describes herself as being driven, and prefers the title 'entrepreneur' to sum up her varied interests.

Besides presenting her own television chat show, which has completed four series on Carlton TV, she designs clothes and has her own women's fashion boutique, 'Chrystals', in London's West End. She believes she is the first black woman to own and run a fashion shop there, and it is where we met for the interview and photo shoot. She also runs a highly successful nightclub in south London—Diamonds—and is awaiting release of her first music album— 'Chrystal Rose Persuasion', due out in October 1999—recorded with the help of leading pop music producers. Prior to this, Chrystal Rose has run her own PR and modelling agency, appeared as an actress on stage and screen, and has written and published a novel, which she quickly points out did not involve a ghost-writer.

All of this has been achieved by a woman who gave birth to a daughter at seventeen, whom she largely brought up single-handed. Indeed, Chrystal Rose's life and career path, with its struggles and successes, would make an excellent subject for a television chat show. In addition to being a good listener, sensitive and empathetic to other people's problems, she believes that part of the success of the 'Chrystal Rose Show' is that she can personally relate to the problems the show airs, like homelessness, racism, being a single parent, domestic violence, life on social security. The Chrystal Rose story is compelling, even if one focuses on just a single aspect of it as I have done here, namely the achievement of starring in her own television talk show, because it reflects the tremendous talent, remarkable self-belief and unstinting determination that lies behind the broad smile and immaculate attire for which Chrystal Rose is more usually noted.

'I always felt I was going to be successful,' Chrystal remarks, 'although I didn't know in which area or to what level.' Brought to the UK from Nigeria by her parents when she was eleven months, Chrystal and her two older sisters were encouraged to aim high. One sister is now an accountant and the other a lawyer. The plan was for Chrystal to be a doctor. In addition to lacking commitment to this professional direction, finding herself pregnant at seventeen did not exactly help.

After experiencing life on a council housing estate, and surviving with a young child on social security, Chrystal recalls returning home one evening in 1989 to see, for the first time, a black woman presenting a prime-time television show. She was greatly impressed by 'The Oprah Winfrey Show'. 'I thought she was incredible, cutting across issues and boundaries and especially broadcasting to a mainstream, multi-cultural audience. I knew immediately that that was what I wanted to do too.'

Chrystal laughs as she explains, 'The only problem was I had no production or presenting background and only a smattering of television experience at the time.' However, completely undaunted by this 'minor detail', through contacts, and on a shoestring budget, she put together a short, lighthearted video on the subject of tipping and gratuities and sent it to the BBC programme 'Open Air'. It obviously made the right impression because she was asked to come into the studio and do a live interview for the programme with the comic actor Richard O'Sullivan. 'When I got the letter, I thought it was a joke that someone was playing on me,' Chrystal recounts. But she did go and ended up also interviewing the entertainer and talk show host, Des O'Connor.

Although her appearance on the 'Open Air' programme led to a spell as a reporter and presenter with the BBC, Chrystal Rose was still not content. She remained determined to have her own show. 'I knew the opportunity would not come in a hurry at the BBC, so I decided to fund my own pilot programmes to prove to everyone what I could do.'

Once again, undeterred by lack of funds, she approached her bank for a loan and was instead given an overdraft facility. Chrystal hired the equipment and facilities she needed, persuaded friends in television to be her crew—at one stage as many as thirty-two people were working for her, giving up their Sundays in exchange for meals and drinks—and set about producing her own shows. Despite tight cost controls, her overdraft quickly escalated and the bank withdrew the facility before she had finished making the programmes.

Her response says everything about Chrystal Rose. 'I was already heavily in debt and could have gone bankrupt, but having gone so far there was no real difference in going yet further into debt. I knew I had to finish it. I could not stop, not least of which for my daughter. She was my inspiration. If I failed having tried my best I could live with that, but to stop before I had finished would be unforgiveable!'

Chrystal managed to finish the six pilot programmes by selling her car, television and other possessions, and borrowing from friends and family. Her gamble paid off. She presented her film package to a number of television companies all of whom wanted it. Chrystal Rose was set to become a national TV personality.

Chrystal believes that her success boils down to the fact that she kept going. Today she keeps a message on her mobile phone to remind herself to do just that, 'keep on going!' She applauds Oprah for giving her inspiration, and her parents for setting standards for her to follow. But most of all, she says, 'if it were not for my daughter, I would probably still be living on a council housing estate in Acton. I did it because I wanted to be a good role model for her. I hope that my work and life will in turn inspire her to find her own goal.'

It is a theme Chrystal returns to as she contemplates the issue of being a black woman in the position she occupies in British society. 'The black people who came before me made things easier for me, and I would like to think my generation has made it easier for my daughter's generation. There is still a lot of racism out there but I have never let it stand in my way. It is just another obstacle for us to get past.'

The interview ends with an enjoyable photo shoot of Chrystal modelling one of the stunning gowns available in her shop, while she talked about her ambition to one day explore a possible political career. If her other accomplishments are anything to go by, Westminster, be forewarned.

Sparkling Chrystal

A new future from the heart of tradition

Angela Sarkis

Chief Executive Officer, Church Urban Fund

'I would find it difficult to do this job without having faith. Strategically and managerially, it can be done, but making a success of the job on the ground, you need the faith element,' says Angela Sarkis, Chief Executive Officer of the Church of England's Church Urban Fund.

The Church Urban Fund, whilst established by the Church of England, is an independent grant-giving charity. It is an increasingly significant player in the field of inner-city and urban regeneration. Launched in 1987, the body provides funding to community-based projects in the most disadvantaged inner-city areas of England, seeking to address the issues of poverty, social deprivation and disadvantage.

Although the sum of money distributed annually by the Fund is not huge, totalling some £3.5m—a figure dwarfed in comparison to the various statutory and public sector agencies working in the field of urban renewal—the impact of its funding invariably makes a big difference to the local projects it seeks to help. Furthermore, besides hard cash, the Fund also provides its recipients with something less easily quantifiable, though often critically important to the projects it supports: access to a variety of local resources which only an extensive network like the Church can provide, access, for instance, to teams of volunteers and people on the ground to give practical assistance to the individual projects, use of local church buildings and a variety of other church facilities.

Angela Sarkis is now three years into her post as Chief Executive Officer of the Church Urban Fund, having been headhunted from her previous position as director of another voluntary sector national body, the Divert Trust. In speaking to her, one gets a clear perspective of the sense of mission which she brings to her work and which propels her as she seeks to make that 'big difference'. Her mission is essentially two-pronged. As a Christian, being able to give practical expression to her faith is important to her, she declares, but so is her strong commitment to social justice. Her current post brings these two core values together rather uniquely and offers Angela an opportunity to work at the national, strategic level towards realising her goals.

Underlining perhaps the level at which Angela Sarkis operates, the Patron of the Church Urban Fund, for example, is HM the Queen, and the Archbishop of Canterbury, (the leading member of the Anglican clergy), is the Chairman of the Fund's Trustees and in effect the person to whom Angela reports. Furthermore, Angela is also a part-time member of the Prime Minister's Social Exclusion Unit, a top-level think-tank reporting direct to the Prime Minister.

Angela Sarkis is greatly enthused by, and proud of, the achievements of the Church Urban Fund. She explains, for example, that although fund-raising remains an on-going task for the organisation, the millions of pounds now offered annually by the Church Urban Fund were actually raised through enormous campaigns and fund-raising efforts by the general membership of the Church of England. This is itself an impressive achievement, she believes, and a clear indication of the added dimension which faith and adherence to the social gospel brings to this issue.

The individual projects supported by the Fund—over 200 annually—Angela explains, often make a significant difference to people's lives at grass-roots level and can literally provide the catalyst to turn a community around. She cites the example of the Triangle Project in Manchester. This is a large housing estate which had virtually been abandoned by the local authority. Its shops and social amenities were either closed completely or seriously run down, and many of its housing units lay empty and decaying. Since the estate fell outside the area and scope for any form of statutory funding, it seemed destined for demolition. However, with money and support from the Church Urban Fund, a community worker was appointed to operate from one of the abandoned shop units, providing help and advice to people on the estate. As volunteers got involved, it quickly grew into a quasi-advice centre which gave renewed focus to the community and rekindled the estate's spirit, leading ultimately to the local authority putting resources back into the estate's infrastructure and deciding to regenerate rather than demolish it. Angela reels off a list of other similar projects where small, targeted interventions have produced large-scale outcomes.

One of the differences between the Church Urban Fund and other statutory and grant-giving bodies, says Angela Sarkis, is that it does not come with a string of conditions imposed from up high. Instead, it is given to local people to get them to help themselves in a practical way. 'It is important that people feel they have a stake in the regeneration of their own communities, and can take charge of the change themselves.'

As Chief Executive Officer, Angela Sarkis oversees the operation of the Fund's grant aid function, has responsibility for the eighteen professional staff it employs, and manages the Fund's investment assets of some £36m, in addition to her national-level strategic policy work. It is, therefore, surprising to learn that at school Angela Sarkis was

effectively written off as a non-achiever. 'At school I was regularly told I would not make it and that there was no point in my studying for O or A levels,' says Angela.

Angela came to Britain from Jamaica when she was seven, and particularly recalls how, despite ignoring such advice and successfully passing her O levels, she was the only person in her class who received subsequent careers advice directing her to a local sewing factory, whilst her white classmates were encouraged to continue studying for their A levels or to consider various professional career paths. 'But', she says, 'that sort of injustice only served to fuel my desire to succeed.'

Angela acknowledges the help she received in this regard from her parents— 'they had the vision to push me academically'—and from two elderly parishioners of her church. 'They were like second and third mothers to me. They constantly encouraged me and gave affirmation that I could do it.' Recognising the struggle and sacrifice made by her parents' generation and other early Caribbean migrants to Britain, who, says Angela, 'worked incredibly hard to give my generation its opportunities and a start', she adds, forthrightly, 'We owe it to them to take it to the next stage.'

Amongst the role models whom Angela Sarkis finds most inspiring is Dr Martin Luther King Jr. She cites 'his strong sense of social justice, and that he was ultimately passionate enough to die for his cause'. She also warmly refers to her own family, her husband and children, as providing a different, but no less inspiring influence. 'It's amazing what I get back from talking to my children.'

Britain is home for Angela Sarkis. 'I see myself as black British,' she says, 'and my contribution is here.' As a Christian, she believes she is always optimistic about the future, but it does not stop her from referring to issues which she feels still give cause for concern and which need to be addressed across Britain as we approach the third millennium. The persistence of long-term poverty and the criminalisation of young black men are two which she cites. 'What is needed', she declares, 'are sufficient mentors and role models to feed back into the community and to positively encourage young people.'

That said, there cannot be a better example of someone heeding her own words. Given her own struggles along the way and what she has since gone on to achieve, Angela Sarkis is a role model of high standing, and someone who is certainly at the forefront, as she herself describes it, of 'taking things to the next stage'.

Elegant eloquence

Rianna Scipio

Television Presenter and Journalist

Rianna Scipio has one of those warm, familiar and pleasing faces which puts people at their ease and makes them think they have known her for a long time. This may have something to do with the power of television, but it also explains why Rianna Scipio is such a popular and sought-after broadcaster.

For several years, many British viewers were treated to her charming smile and engaging personality as she presented the weekend weather reports on LWT. Rianna particularly endeared herself to her audience by being the first television presenter to remain on screen, visibly and happily pregnant almost to full term. She is today more familiar to viewers as the anchor presenter of BBC 2's weekly news magazine programme, 'Black Britain', now in its fourth series, which she has fronted since its inception.

Rianna's screen persona is bright and breezy, and while that was evident when we met, what came across more forcefully as she reflected on her success in the media was her enormous depth of character and inner strength, for Rianna Scipio's story is a moving one, characterised by great compassion, hope and courage.

We talked and I took pictures of her between takes on the set of the 'Black Britain' programme. It was quite amazing to hear her one minute expressing telling insights about her past and her ambitions for the future, and the next, delivering her lines to camera as a consummate professional right on cue. Only later did I discover that she had given birth to her second child only ten days before.

Rianna Scipio is one of those people who manage to work successfully and concurrently across all the main communications mediums. Besides being the lead presenter for the 'Black Britain' television programme, Rianna has her own multi-media and independent television production company. She also writes occasional articles for Britain's black press and for the music press and has a background in radio broadcasting.

During the course of our interview, she divulged that another current project is also in the field of music, but this one interestingly involves her taking centre stage as a musical artiste in her own right. Rianna modestly informed me that she has her own band and has been writing music for some time. 'My early childhood fantasy was to be a singer,' she declares. 'I still have musical ambitions and am very excited about the possibilities. Besides,' she adds, 'as a presenter you are really just a voice piece for other people's thoughts and expressions.'

This musical venture, she feels, will allow her to explore and express her own creative talents.

Whatever direction Rianna Scipio may decide to take in the future, she readily acknowledges that she has not always been in a position to choose. As the youngest of five children, with a few years between each, Rianna was the baby of her family. Her African father and Indian mother—both from Guyana—had a rather traditional approach to child rearing. 'Children should be seen and not heard, was their motto. I often felt unable to express myself as a child and had a longing for people simply to listen to what I had to say.' Finding an outlet to express herself may be a response, Rianna believes, to this early experience.

Two other events had an even greater impact on Rianna's life, influencing the person she has become today. Firstly, her parents divorced when Rianna was still a young child. When Rianna was just fourteen, the second and perhaps more devastating event occurred which, she says poignantly, 'changed my whole life completely'. Her mother was left incapacitated by a severe stroke, and Rianna and her brother effectively became her full-time carers. 'We moved from being *cared for* to being *the carers,* quite literally overnight. We became little adults who had to do everything from looking after our Mum to running the household.'

Because of the situation at home, and with no real parental control, Rianna did not go to school on a regular basis for almost two years. Returning to take her mock O level examinations, her results, not surprisingly, reflected her absence from school. Feeling that she could still get through the real examinations by working especially hard in the remaining months, Rianna was devastated when her head teacher told her it would be best if she left school as she had reached sixteen.

Rianna remembers feeling 'completely abandoned' at receiving this news, but explained how, even at such low points in one's life, fate can still take an unexpected turn. Ms Mudd, her English teacher—English was one of Rianna's favourite subjects—called Rianna at home that evening, telling her to 'get herself back to school tomorrow and she would try to sort things out.' Rianna recounts that Ms Mudd and another teacher, Ms Dargavel, personally vouched for her. 'They literally put their necks on the line for me because they believed I showed promise. To cap it, those two women phoned me every single morning for the next three months,

checking to see how I was, and to make sure I got to school. They really stood by me, and may not know to this day how grateful I will always be. I do not know where I would have ended up but for their intervention. I will never forget them.'

What Rianna believes she especially gained from this support—besides care and compassion—was the lesson that 'if they valued me the way they did, then I must value myself'. Rianna went on to take her O level examinations, passing five, before gaining two A levels at college. From this foundation she steadily built the career she has today. Sadly, Rianna's mother died when she was sixteen and never saw the success which her daughter has gone on to achieve.

Rianna Scipio's break in broadcasting came whilst she was at college where she became involved in pirate radio. This was at the time an exceedingly popular broadcast medium, especially with the young, because of the more limited choice and range of music played on the licensed airways. Rianna would later go on to find work and earn a reputation as a broadcaster of note on licensed radio, and it is clear that she still derives much pleasure from occasionally working in this, her first medium.

Perhaps influenced by her own experiences, Rianna is particularly inspired by women whom she sees as having great strength of character, for example, Mrs Doreen Lawrence, the mother of Stephen Lawrence who was killed in a racist attack. Rianna interviewed Mrs Lawrence for the 'Black Britain' series. 'Although she did not choose to be in the position she is, she is a powerful woman of great strength.' Rianna also admires Moira Stuart, Britain's first black female news presenter, who provided a role model for the young Rianna. 'I have only since come to realise through my own experience just how difficult it must have been for her over the years, being out there by herself.'

Besides her new venture in the music field, Rianna says poignantly of the future, 'I just want to be a good mother and role model for my children.' She expresses much optimism for the future of the country at large. Coming through a recession and all its uncertainty, has in some ways she believes, 'made Britain a much more self-confident and yet caring place to be'.

The poise and eloquence which define Rianna Scipio today are surely a testament to the ability to overcome adversity, given determination and an element of support, especially at crucial moments.

Peer into the future

Baroness Patricia Scotland

Peer and Queen's Counsel

'I believe every one of us is given a talent,' says Baroness Patricia Scotland. 'The challenge is to find out what that talent is and to hone it.' As a Peer of the Realm, an eminent Queen's Counsel—becoming in 1991 Britain's first black female barrister to 'take silk'—and a prominent member or chairperson of various high-powered committees and public bodies, it is evident that Patricia Scotland has found and honed her talents to a fine degree. From the time spent in her company and from my reading of other interviews which she has given, I would proffer, however, that the particular talent which she possesses in abundance, and which underpins many of her other achievements, is her skill in dealing with people. Baroness Scotland exudes warmth and compassion, and is so at ease with herself that in seeking to put others at ease her conversation is littered with self-deprecating good humour.

'I sometimes think it was a total miracle that I have got to where I am,' she says in response to an enquiry on what she aspired to be at the outset of her career and whether she sets herself career goals. Far from meticulously planning or driving her career, Baroness Scotland explained that she never set out to become, or even envisaged becoming, a QC or a Peer in the House of Lords. Her real 'heart's desire' was actually to be a modern expressionist ballet dancer. 'At sixteen, I only really felt alive when I was dancing,' she admits. But, she adds, once she had made the decision to go into law, her first and foremost ambition was 'to do every case as well as I possibly could'.

For the next fourteen years after being called to the Bar in 1977, she did precisely that. As a specialist in family law, local government and planning, and public and private enquiries, she sought to ensure that she was thoroughly prepared and ready and able to give her best to whoever she represented. Whether working on high-profile cases, such as the Jasmine Beckford child abuse enquiry, or lesser profile criminal defence matters, by focusing on 'what could be done today' and 'leaving tomorrow to the Good Lord to determine' (she is strongly committed to her Christian faith), Baroness Scotland feels that her career advancement was to some extent a by-product of this principle and its application.

Whether she is downplaying her own prodigious legal talents and years of dedicated application or not, Baroness Patricia Scotland today wears many professional caps, some quite literally. Since 1997 she has been a government- appointed working Peer in the House of Lords. In addition to participating in the full business of the House, she is the Chairperson of the Lord's Advisory Committee on Caribbean matters. Admitting that 'it is very difficult to balance one's outside professional interests with being a working Peer,' Baroness Scotland is still a practising QC (where she wears the customary barrister's wig with great aplomb). Having struggled to gain a pupilage when she was seeking chambers as a newly qualified barrister, she is now Master of the profession's esteemed Middle Temple. A former Commissioner of the Commission for Racial Equality, Baroness Scotland is also a Commissioner on the Millennium Commission, the national body set up to coordinate the many projects planned across the UK to mark and celebrate the new millennium.

Patricia Scotland was two years old when her parents took the decision to leave the Caribbean island of Dominica with their children—ten at that stage, with two more to be added later to the family—and go to England in order to enhance their children's prospects of a good education. Patricia and her brothers and sisters—all of whom have gone on to achieve success in their adult lives— acknowledge the tremendous sacrifice made by their parents. From being a well-off estate owner in Dominica, when he arrived in England in 1958, her father had to take work as a carpenter and builder in order to make ends meet. Beyond this immense sacrifice, Patricia cites her parents, and the rest of her family, as being of great importance to her for the support system they provide. She singles out two older brothers, Barry and Rudy, whom she says 'were like mentors to me; with all the time and encouragement they gave, they effectively challenged me to achieve.'

At school, where she was either the only black child in her class or indeed in the whole school, Patricia received careers advice based on the fact that since she worked in Sainsbury's supermarket on Saturdays, she should perhaps consider applying to the store for a permanent job where she might eventually become a supervisor. Instead, she left school with three A levels before going on to obtain a degree in English and sociology. It was only after working in a solicitor's office during a summer vacation that Patricia realised that the law struck a real chord in her. 'It combined all the things I liked: language, communication, being socially useful, a conduit for ideas and helping to express things for others, and generally sorting problems out in a creative and positive way.'

After her legal training and call to the Bar, Patricia briefly returned to the Caribbean where she contemplated settling down and practising law. 'It was like going home,' Patricia says, so taken was she by the warmth of the culture, the climate and the people. However, she describes having a 'tussle of conscience' about whether she should remain or return to Britain. 'It troubled me that if those black people brought up in the UK who achieve relative success don't stay, how will anything change?' Her father's bemused response to this dilemma was to ask, 'Are you Joan of Arc?'. In the end, Patricia decided that her calling was in the UK and on returning began her career and steady rise in the British legal profession.

Besides her family and her faith—which she describes as her 'greatest enabler'—she warmly acknowledges the many people who have helped her along the way. Lord Cross of Chelsea— 'a very special and wonderful man'—whom Patricia met when she was secretary of her college law society, was especially encouraging, as was her former pupil master, Paul Randolph. She believes that she was fortunate in belonging to a very creative and forward-looking chambers, and the friends and colleagues whom she met and worked with— many of whom have also gone on to be successful—were also very supportive.

Those who inspire Baroness Scotland are people who demonstrate great faith, courage, integrity and, above all, selflessness. She mentions two people in particular whom she feels 'epitomise everything one should aspire to',— Revd. Martin Luther King Jr and Mother Theresa. As she looks towards the new millennium, Baroness Scotland is both optimistic and hopeful but also aware of the challenges that lie ahead. On the position of black people in the UK she says, 'We cannot pretend that all the challenges have been met and all the demons overcome. There is still much to do, but we are getting there. Britain is no longer a mono culture and barriers to ethnicity and gender are being dismantled.' Amongst the pressing challenges that lie ahead, in her view, are the 'eradication of deprivation' and 'the need to value our children'. Of her own future, the modest Baroness simply says, 'I want to get a life! I feel I have so many hats you can't see me'.

Despite her concerns, her reputation, personality and achievements are such that one cannot fail to see what I saw through the lens of my camera: a woman who cannot be overlooked and who is giving so much to Britain and those around her.

The Right Reverend Dr John Sentamu

Bishop

My family's association with the Rt. Revd. Dr John Sentamu, Bishop of Stepney, goes back some years and is one which reflects life's ups and downs. Prior to his elevation to the bishophood, Revd. Sentamu was the minister of my family's local parish church—Holy Trinity in south London—and in this role he officiated at many of my family's major events. He brought joy in christening both my children. He also gave us all great spiritual comfort during my father's long illness, and officiated at the funeral on his passing.

When Revd. Sentamu arrived at the Holy Trinity Church, he inherited a dwindling congregation. It was largely due to his remarkable influence that, by the time he left to take up his position as Bishop of Stepney, thousands of pounds had been raised to finance a wonderful church restoration project and it had become almost impossible to find an empty seat in the church at Sunday services.

Revd. Sentamu is regarded with much affection within the Burnett family and is a man for whom I hold deep personal respect and admiration. It was, therefore, particularly gratifying that he kindly agreed to be featured in this book. Despite our long association, I was still taken aback to discover further depths and more inspiring insights about the man behind the collar.

Revd. Dr John Sentamu is only the third black person to be appointed a bishop in the Church of England. He is responsible for over 100 ministers covering the Diocese of Stepney, a large inner city area of east London. Prior to his appointment as Bishop in 1996, he held one of the leading lay clergy positions in the Church of England, sitting on the Church's governing body—the General Synod—where he served as chairman of the influential House of Clergy. Such is his standing and popularity, that he achieved the rare distinction of being elected to the General Synod totally unopposed.

Given his leading role in the Anglican Church, it came as something of a surprise to learn that theology was, in fact, John Sentamu's second career. Born one of thirteen children into a poor family in his native Uganda, John began his education by walking and, subsequently, riding a bicycle twelve miles to school each day. Despite his humble beginnings, he rose to become a prominent lawyer and high court judge in Uganda. He decided, however, in the mid-1970s to come to the UK to read theology at Cambridge University—he had always wanted to be able to read the Bible in Greek and Hebrew—but with the firm intention of returning home afterwards to continue his legal practice.

This was not, however, to be. At the point when he was about to return to Uganda, having completed his doctorate, the then Archbishop of Uganda was murdered and the changed political climate in his country made it impossible for him to go back. Dr John Sentamu decided to stay on in England. Although certified to practise law in the UK, he 'so enjoyed telling people about God and about faith' that he decided instead to enter the ministry of the church.

Ordained in 1979, he has held various parish posts and General Synod positions and has become a bishop, he explains, without having applied for any of these appointments. 'I've always enjoyed the things I have done and have done them with all my effort and energy. Fortunately for me, others have seen the gifts within me and tried to match these to positions where they thought I could make a contribution.' On this basis, I cannot help but wonder where else his talents may take him within the Church of England? Who knows, perhaps one day he may become the UK's first black archbishop!

Revd. Sentamu is not someone who courts high positions for the sake of it. He has been an active campaigner for the rights of women priests to be ordained in the Church of England. He is also very open about the issues of racism within British society and, indeed, in the church he serves. 'Every black person has experienced racism and the patronising attitude of others.' But he also acknowledges that, 'the Church of England has made great efforts and much progress in removing some of the vestiges of racism from its structure and way of operating.'

Looking to the millennium, Revd. Sentamu hopes that Britain will successfully complete its onward journey towards being a truly multi-ethnic and multi-cultural society, and that as part of this the Anglican Church will embrace a worship and theology that properly reflects this. He is also forthright about his hope that the millennium will bring with it the cancellation of the Third World debt which he feels will greatly contribute to the removal of poverty in Africa and in other parts of the developing world.

Tellingly, our time together ended as he departed to join his colleagues on the Home Secretary's appointed enquiry into the death of Stephen Lawrence, a young black man brutally murdered whilst waiting at a bus stop in South London, confirming Revd. Sentamu's passionate commitment and ongoing work in the field of racial equality and justice.

Above all, Revd. Sentamu attributes his achievements in life to his faith. 'The Christian faith has been very important in shaping who and what I am.' But he also acknowledges other major influences: the example and guidance of his mother (who had twelve other children to look after); the kindness and compassion of two Scottish missionaries, one of whom helped pay his fees to enable him to finish school and the other who provided him with a bicycle so that he could cycle to school instead of walk; and the inspiration of some of the older and past evangelists.

One of the people whom Revd. Sentamu most admires, however, is Nelson Mandela whom he feels has been one of the greatest role models of modern times. In my mind, the Rt. Revd. Dr John Sentamu is himself providing the UK with an impressive role model, that of a man of great faith and compassion, with the ability to lead and motivate others. The millennium, I believe, holds much more for this man who has achieved so much without actually putting himself forward for senior positions.

Faith

Dr Stephen Small

Professor

In spite of the discouraging words of his school's head teacher, Dr Stephen Small is today a professor at the prestigious University of California, Berkeley, in the United States. Given the American penchant for ratings and league tables, the University of California, Berkeley, is frequently ranked as the premier university for undergraduate education in the country, not withstanding its east coast rivals, Yale and Harvard. It is an extremely competitive university in which to gain entry as a student or, indeed, as a professor.

The words spoken by the headteacher of the grammar school Stephen Small attended in Liverpool in the mid-1970s were far from kind or encouraging. As one of only four black students in a student body of over 1,000, Stephen can still recall returning to school after completing his O levels to be met by his headteacher who enquired where he thought he was going in trying to do A levels. For good measure, he added, 'I hope you don't think you are going to get to university because it is beyond you.' Belittled and dispirited by this reception, Stephen remembers muttering that he was not planning to go to university, but just wanted the opportunity to do his A levels anyway. On this basis, the teenage Stephen was allowed to remain in school.

I am particularly pleased to feature Dr Stephen Small in *Millennium People,* not simply because of this story—which epitomises how someone can still succeed after being discounted so outrageously at an early age, but also because I believe that his academic achievements are to be admired in their own right. Moreover, he is a long-standing personal friend. Having met when we were both undergraduates at the University of Kent at Canterbury, we went on to do our Master's degrees together at the University of Bristol. We have shared many moments of friendship ever since, including his being the best man at my wedding.

Stephen was born and raised for the greater part of his pre-adult life in the city of Liverpool. Despite having spent the last fifteen or more years in the United States, he retains his trademark 'scouse' accent. Today, that accent is mixed in a charming, and at times amusing, way with a sprinkling of mid-Atlantic phrases. Stephen himself ponders the impact of this combination on his students. 'The fact that I have a British accent and am black certainly makes me stand out amongst the faculty members on campus. It is interesting to see the students' impressions—both black and white—when they first meet me and then hear me speak.'

After completing his Master's degree in the early 1980s, Stephen Small worked as a social policy researcher in London for the Policy Studies Institute (PSI), an independent research body. At PSI he authored and coauthored various research reports on a range of social policy topics. He decided after some years that he wanted to further his studies and was successful in being awarded a fellowship to study for a PhD in Sociology at the University of California, Berkeley. He quickly adapted to his new environment, gaining his PhD in seemingly double-quick time, and would have done so even sooner had his teaching skills not been spotted and utilised. Whilst only halfway through his PhD, he was offered a lecturing post at the University of Massachusetts. On being awarded his doctorate, he was headhunted by the University of California for a teaching appointment there. Today, he is Professor in the Department of African American Studies.

Stephen Small did not set out to be a lecturer. 'But', he says, 'I enjoy teaching because it gives me that certain critical and intellectual engagement, and I am also able to explore and analyse ideas, theories and situations. What's more, the young people I teach really keep me on my toes. It's very rewarding and fulfilling to know that you have helped the students develop intellectually, academically and even personally.' On route to academic tenure, he has published a number of books and articles— most recently a book entitled *Racialised Barriers* and another on *Blacks of Mixed Origins Under Slavery*—and has guest lectured and presented academic papers at conferences in the UK, Canada, the Caribbean, Europe and Africa. Indeed the selected photograph of Stephen for *Millennium People* was taken at London's Heathrow Airport with him about to commence another of his academic travels.

Reflecting on his career path, Stephen—whose father was of Jamaican origin and mother, white English— says that he draws greatest satisfaction from the fact that he did pass his A levels and became one of the first black men of his generation in Liverpool to go to university. 'Given my headteacher's view that I didn't have it in me, passing my A levels was even more rewarding than getting my PhD, because,' he says, 'by then I knew I had the ability.' He also takes pride not just in teaching at a prestigious university, but in giving lectures to community groups, institutions and speaking to black teenagers, some of whom may be in the same circumstances as he was at their age.

'I like to tell them, and show them, that they too can succeed.'

He recalls the encouraging words he received from the black youth and community leaders he encountered at the Charles Wootton Centre whilst he was growing up in Liverpool, who provided a counter view to that of his head-teacher. Stephen also warmly acknowledges the influence and support provided by his parents, and by a close friend in Liverpool. 'My parents', he remarks, 'virtually forced me to stay on and take my A levels, and willed me to go to university.' His best friend, he remembers, stood by him when others in the neighbourhood laughed at his commitment to education. Stephen explains that although he does not have heroes or role models as such, he very much admires the early African American sociologist, W. E. B. Du Bois, who also established his highly acclaimed career against all odds.

As a professor of African American studies in the United States, and a black man born and raised and still very much connected to the UK, Stephen Small is well placed to compare the position of black people in the United States and those in Britain as we approach the third millennium. 'On first inspection', he says, 'race and ethnic relations look distinctly different between the two countries—they have different histories, cultural circumstances, population sizes, etc.—but beyond these surface differences there are several similarities which show that the issues of race and racism remain central in both countries even today.' He admits to seeing both positive and negative indicators for what lies ahead. 'I see the pervasiveness and entrenchment of discrimination, on the one hand, whilst on the other, the increased levels of multi-racial alliances and cross-racial relationships.'

Whilst he is unsure where his career will eventually take him, he adds forthrightly, 'There are things I can do and achieve in America that I cannot do in the UK.' However, despite his years abroad, Stephen asserts that he remains essentially black British. 'I feel black British in ways that I do not and could not feel black American.'

In whichever direction, and wherever his career may take him, Dr Stephen Small has already achieved more than he was ever given credit for. Just as the other acclaimed black sociologist—Du Bois—reached great academic heights, I anticipate that this black British academic of growing international stature will attain yet more and even higher accomplishments in future years.

Professor on the move

Diplomatic diversity

Linbert Spencer

Senior Civil Servant, Foreign and Commonwealth Office and Equality Consultant

Linbert Spencer is one of those people who effortlessly manage to perform multiple roles and who are simultaneously involved in a wide range of activities and initiatives. His impressive resumé, his list of appointments to public and charitable bodies, and his business and professional involvements, leaves me wondering whether he operates on a different time cycle from those of us who work within the twenty-four-hour day.

Linbert is someone for whom I have high professional regard and much respect. At one stage I had the privilege of having him as my mentor and a wiser and more experienced mentor I could not have found. As a fellow black male and someone who operates at senior professional and managerial levels, Linbert was a great source of inspiration and support. Indeed, I recall discussing *Millennium People* with him when it was only the germ of an idea, and receiving his helpful and encouraging advice.

Linbert Spencer's professional expertise lies in the areas of equality and diversity management. He operates and manages his own business—the Linbert Spencer Consultancy—and its reputation is such that when major private or public sector businesses and organisations require top-level assistance in formulating and implementing strategies on equality and diversity, Linbert Spencer is invariably one of those to whom they turn for help. His client list includes some of the major UK banks, such as NatWest, HSBC and the TSB, the Cabinet Office and the Home Office, local authorities, educational institutions, a number of the UK police services, as well as the judiciary. Linbert Spencer is also a founding partner of Diversity UK, the publishers of the Diversity Directory, which lists and markets many other equality consultants across the UK, in addition to holding conferences, seminars and briefings on key topics for business executives and fellow practitioners.

Linbert also takes on appointments directly with organisations who seek his expertise from within their structures. It is in this capacity that he is presently engaged on a part-time basis with the Foreign and Commonwealth Office. Were he to occupy a permanent or established position with the department he would, de facto, be the most senior black staff member in the UK Foreign Service. Among other similar appointments, Linbert has been an advisor to the board of London First—a private sector-led organisation committed to achieving the resources, infrastructure and leadership required to secure London's position as a premier world city into the new millennium—and a member of the Police Complaints Authority, the body charged with investigating complaints made by members of the public against the police service.

I met Linbert for his *Millennium People* interview at the Foreign and Commonwealth Office overlooking Buckingham Palace in central London. His role there is to recuit and retain more black and minority ethnic Britons into the Diplomatic Service. Aware that the public perceive the department as being somewhat élitist in its selection and appointment of career diplomats and other staff, and in the light of the Secretary of State for Foreign Affairs' commitment to a more open and accessible Foreign and Commonwealth Office—and one which better reflects the diversity of modern British society—the department sought the help of Linbert Spencer to improve its profile in this area.

Linbert, who has now been in this part-time position for almost two years, and whose somewhat unique role means that he reports to both the Director of Personnel and to the Ministers responsible for the Foreign and Commonwealth Office, informs me that real progress is being made. Through a variety of targeted advertising, careers outreach, training and mentoring programmes, the number of black and ethnic minority applicants and recruits to the Foreign and Commonwealth Office is already well up on previous years. The day after our meeting he was due to fly to Islamabad to conduct training and briefing sessions for diplomatic and High Commission staff, and he has made similar presentations in many other British overseas missions and embassies.

Linbert Spencer's list of involvements with public and charitable bodies is equally impressive. He is, or has in recent years been: a member of the Home Secretary's Advisory Council on Race Relations; a member of the Archbishop's Commission on Urban Priority Areas; a member of the committee which appoints magistrates in the county of Bedfordshire; special advisor to the House of Commons Select Committee on Employment, and had involvement with both the Cabinet Office Public Appointments Unit and the Civil Service Final Selection Board.

Linbert identifies one or two of his yet other positions as ones which have given him great personal satisfaction. For example, he is co-founder and current Chairman of the highly regarded national training charity, the Windsor Fellowship, which seeks to prepare black and ethnic minority undergraduates for leadership roles in industry and commerce. Linbert takes immense pride in the achievements of the growing number of graduate fellows from the scheme. Similarly, as former CEO of the Fullemploy Group—which used to provide vocational training for young people with more limited educational qualifications from the ethnic minority communities—he believes that he and his management team members achieved a great deal for the project during his years as CEO, and is heartened that many of his former team have since developed highly distinguished careers themselves.

Linbert Spencer touchingly cites a friend and mentor, Bill Daniel, whom he acknowledges as a major guiding influence in his early life. 'I almost certainly would not be who I am, or where I am, had he not been in my life. Well over six foot tall, loud and full of life, Bill was a Christian commited to working with young people. I was one of a number he took under his wings, and he inspired me to become a community worker.' In appreciation of Bill's support, Linbert makes the point that he does what he can to mentor those who seek help and support from him.

Faith is important to Linbert, who relates the experience of his family's arrival in the UK from Jamaica. Unlike many other new black migrants, as members of the Salvation Army the Spencer family was met by fellow Salvation Army members in the UK who offered them care, concern and practical help. Today, Linbert remains an active member of the Bedford branch of the Salvation Army.

It is evident that the former athlete and one-time actor Linbert Spencer has already achieved admirable benchmarks during his multifaceted career. Knowing him as I do, I confidently predict that we shall see many further achievements and successful new ventures as we move into the year 2000 and beyond.

Making headlines

Annie Stewart

Editor, The Voice Newspaper

Annie Stewart is the editor of Britain's foremost black weekly newspaper, *The Voice*. As such, she is the person who manages the newspaper on a day-to-day basis, determining editorial content, ensuring production schedules and values are met, and supervising the journalists and other staff who work on the newspaper. Although it is a position which Annie Stewart achieved after moving up through the ranks of the newspaper, and one which she regards as 'more akin to a passion than a regular job', it is not without its difficulties and trying moments.

Founded by its publisher, Val McCalla in 1982, *The Voice* is an independent newspaper aimed at Britain's black community, which focuses on the issues, interests and perspectives of that section of the population. Indeed, one of the difficulties faced by Annie Stewart in trying to satisfy the newspaper's objectives, is that opinions and views about matters relating to Britain's black community are as many as they are varied. Besides having to contend with the differing views expressed about the paper within the black community, Annie Stewart and her colleagues also have to deal with occasional criticisms from the mainstream media. 'It sometimes makes this job very depressing,' admits Annie, recalling a recent example. *The Voice's* coverage of the death in police custody of Wayne Douglas, a black man from London's black community in Brixton, led to a hail of accusations and condemnations from sections of the mainstream press that *The Voice* had incited the riot which occurred when protestors confronted police. In defence of the newspaper, Annie explains that *The Voice* is, and will continue to be, a campaigning publication which often breaks stories affecting black people that are largely ignored by the mainstream press, and that *The Voice* is only doing the job it is there to do, but that it is often misjudged and misunderstood for doing it.

With steady weekly sales of about 50,000 copies, *The Voice* is undoubtedly the most influential black newspaper in Britain and the largest selling black newspaper in Europe. Certainly, one of its indisputable accomplishments over the seventeen years of its existence is that *The Voice* has been home to a good many black journalists, usually early in their careers, who have then gone on to establish and, in some cases, make names for themselves in the national press, television, or elsewhere in the media. The irony of this is not lost on Annie Stewart, who recognises that on one level this represents an endorsement of *The Voice* and the spawning of a diaspora of black media professionals by the newspaper. However, as a hard pressed editor trying to meet the needs of her own paper, ensure its continuity and retain her more experienced staff, she can also be excused for occasionally viewing this process through different glasses. Annie admits to being somewhat saddened that some of the staff do not always share her sense of mission, and do not see the newspaper as a valid career option in its own right rather than as a stepping-stone to other things.

Despite some of the more trying aspects of being editor of a newspaper such as *The Voice,* it is evident that Annie Stewart is still committed to her journalistic mission. 'I always wanted to be a journalist,' says Annie, adding that her long-term ambition is 'to go into television or radio'. In the meantime, she is full of ideas and vision for *The Voice* and what its future direction could or should be. '*The Voice*', she declares, 'is a very strong brand name, certainly in the black and ethnic minority communities across Britain, and has the potential to be treble the circulation it is now.' For Annie, a future step for the Voice Group is to widen its product range across the ethnic minority market and across all age ranges, from publishing comics for children, youth and music magazines for teenagers and young people, through to the existing newspapers. Annie's photograph shows her in 'Lou Grant' pose engaged in discussion with one of her journalists in the newsroom of *The Voice.*

Annie's passion for journalism was very nearly thwarted before her career even began. Despite expressing an interest in journalism, her school careers adviser steered Annie towards what he thought would be in her better interests—a career in retail management. Acting reluctantly on this advice, because, she says 'I didn't know any better at the time', one of her early jobs on leaving grammar school in east London was as a management trainee in a large central London department store. Although she gained excellent reports from the various supervisors and buyers with whom she worked, she was called one day to see the company personnel officer who very politely but pointedly asked her why she was seen out at lunch with a black man. Taken aback by the nature of the question, Annie's response was, 'but I am black myself'. To her amazement, the personnel officer told the light-skinned Annie, 'You did not tell us you were black when you joined! You do realise that you will not be able to have a career here?' Annie recalled being 'hit for six' by the blatant nature of this encounter, so much so that 'for about a year after leaving this job I did not do anything about my career, I just drifted.' Eventually, Annie resolved that she was not going to let this unhappy experience beat her and she was going to be what she had always wanted to be, a journalist.

To get into the industry, Annie Stewart took a variety of administrative jobs for the Mirror Group before gaining an opportunity to do a journalism course on her local newspaper, *The Walthamstow Express*. Even this long desired breakthrough was not without its challenges. In deciding to do the two year training she had to take a substantial salary drop at a time when she already had a young child, and a mortgage. It is a challenge she has not regretted taking. On completing her journalism training, Annie cut her reporting teeth with the same local newspaper and worked there for several years before eventually moving to *The Voice as* a reporter in 1987, where she moved steadily up the ranks to her present editor position in 1996.

In reviewing her career path, Annie recalls the encouragement and inspiration she received at school from one of her English teachers, Mrs Tomkins, who not only helped to instill in Annie a love of literature but whose 'you can achieve anything you want to' attitude had a profound effect on her. Annie also talks about her mother as 'a guiding light' in her life.

'Britain is definitely home,' says Annie Stewart, 'because I live and work here,' but she adds, aware of a possible ambiguity, 'although I was born in the UK I also consider myself Jamaican.' She laughingly points out 'the funny thing is that in Jamaica I am very definitely seen as British or English and certainly not as Jamaican!'

For the millennium, Annie hopes that more newspapers and publications across Britain will tackle wholeheartedly the issues of diversity rather than make token gestures, and that, as a result, the entry of black journalists into the profession and their progress within it will be easier than it has been in the past.

Lawmaker

Lord Taylor of Warwick

Peer, House of Lords

Lord Taylor of Warwick contributed to Britain's 'unsung history' in 1997 when he became the first black person to directly create law and add statute to the British legal system. While only in his first year as a life peer in the House of Lords, he introduced and carried through all its stages a legislative bill which now sits on the statute book as the Criminal Evidence Amendment Act, 1997.

In becoming the first black Lord to be created in over a decade, and only the second in the whole of British history, Lord Taylor has, as a result, been widely feted, especially overseas. He recounts how America, for example, has awarded him more honorary university titles than he can recall. He is, however, quick to point out that 'I am not here just to call myself "Lord Taylor of Warwick". I want to achieve something as well. I am conscious that we parliamentarians are making history.'

In fact, John Taylor, as he was known prior to the conferment of his life peerage, has, in his appealingly modest and unassuming way, been pushing back barriers and trying to break the mould throughout much of his adult life.

He was first catapulted into national prominence in the 1992 UK general election when he stood as a Conservative Party parliamentary candidate—itself something of a benchmark, since few black people had previously publicly associated themselves with the Conservative Party, and none had ever been selected as a parliamentary candidate for the party. John Taylor was selected to fight the long held Conservative seat of Cheltenham, but who would have predicted what was to follow?

The local party was virtually split down the middle in the full glare of the national media, with some members openly declaring they would neither work for a black candidate nor, as some are reported to have said, even vote for one. The ensuing intraparty squabble attracted massive media coverage with issues of race and John Taylor at the heart of the agenda, leading to his subsequent electoral defeat.

I recall my own feelings when this unsavoury event was splashed across the newspapers and television screens. As a black man close to John Taylor in age, I felt a sense of outrage on his behalf. I admired his fortitude and stoic dignity, but always wondered how he could endure such affront and ignominy from within his own party. Now, several years after the event, I have had a chance to ask him about his thoughts and feelings as he went through that bruising episode.

'My character was shaped greatly by Cheltenham. I could easily have been crushed. What people don't recall is that there was another black Conservative parliamentary candidate who also went through a similar experience at the same election, though in a less public manner, and he quit! It comes down to your inner resilience.'

'The best leaders in life are those who have encountered and dealt with setbacks, because they help form your character. You learn as much from the bad things in life as you do when everything is going well,' he added. But John Taylor is defined by much more than his Cheltenham experience. Far from being born with a silver spoon in his mouth, he recounts how his father was born in the tough neighbourhood of Trenchtown in Kingston, Jamaica, one of nine children. His father found his way out of poverty with a 'bat and ball', playing for both Jamaica and Warwickshire County Cricket Club in England—which accounts in part for John Taylor's choice of Warwick as the title seat of his peerage.

John acknowledges the key role played by both his parents in instilling certain core values which continue to guide him to this day. Central to these values is his strong adherence to the work ethic, a theme to which he frequently returns. 'You need to be focused and put in the hard work. There are no short cuts.... Often people want the end results but do not want to do the hard work to achieve them.... I am often asked what is the secret of my success and I always say hard work. There is no magic to it. You've just got to get yourself about, work hard and have a positive attitude to life.'

These are clearly principles which have guided both John Taylor's own life and his career decisions. Whilst still at school he decided that he wanted to be a lawyer, and in typical fashion 'set goals along the way, took it stage by stage, until the goal was achieved'.

He explains how he formed his own career goals, being driven by not wanting to fit the expected mould of becoming another black athlete or sportsman, although he loved football and still does. He felt that black people were under-represented in the professions, and that the law was where he should aim to go. 'It is still a vision of mine,' he adds, 'for other black people to get into areas where black people tend not to be seen or associated, such as business and especially in the corporate boardroom.' And this, he feels, is the best way forward for black people in the coming millennium.

As a barrister, he worked across the spectrum, from criminal defence, to acting as legal adviser and undertaking contract and commercial litigation work for large corporate concerns. He has also been chairman, director, consultant and patron to a variety of corporate, charitable and community organisations. He is Vice-President of the National Small Business Bureau, an area of interest about which he speaks passionately, pointing out that black-owned businesses are now the fastest growing sector across the UK small business market. He is also a long-standing committee member of the Sickle Cell Anaemia Relief Charity (SCAR). Lord Taylor has also presented and produced a number of television programmes and written articles for newspapers and other publications.

Britain is demonstrably Lord Taylor's 'home' and he attracted yet more attention and controversy a few years ago when he coined the phrase 'Afro-Saxons' to try and denote Britain's inextricable multi-racial, multi-cultural nature and black people's integral part in its society.

In his political career, Lord Taylor has shown that he is someone who is prepared to take the difficult, more arduous road, rather than opt for the easy, well-trodden path in order to achieve an objective. In my view, he has a clear vision of where he wants to be and what he wants to achieve, and is willing to back this up with self-sacrifice and a strong commitment to action.

Lord Taylor is also a family man as well as a politician, and as our meeting came to a close he told me an endearing anecdote about his young daughter which, in my mind, sums him up admirably. Curious to know why she was sometimes called 'The Honourable' (a title bestowed on the children of all peers), he told his daughter that she was only 'honourable' when she brushed her teeth and went to bed on time at night, or when she helped tidy her room and did other good deeds. Other than that she should simply forget about such titles.

Testimony indeed to his resolve to keep his own feet and those of his family firmly on the ground while he pursues his personal and political ambitions. With these qualities, Lord Taylor of Warwick is certainly someone to watch out for in the new millennium.

Samantha Tross

Orthopaedic Surgeon

My father recalls hearing me say when I was only seven years old that I was going to be a surgeon when I grew up,' Samantha Tross laughingly tells me, adding for good measure—'not just a doctor, mind you, but very definitely a surgeon!'

We talk as I am shown around an operating theatre in a London general hospital by orthopaedic surgeon Samantha Tross, who is taking great care to explain to me the extensive range of surgical tools and instruments she uses in her work. 'We use this one to cut off the head of the femur.... These are self retainers which are used if you are working on your own without an assistant.... Here are some artery clips to seal the blood vessels,' she says in a matter-of-fact way as if we were discussing everyday objects like books or CDs.

I fire off as many photographic shots as I can of this charming and obliging doctor, fully capped and gowned and surrounded by her surgical instruments.

Samantha Tross is one of the small but growing number of female surgeons now practising in Britain. Although nearly fifty per cent of medical graduates are women, most enter general practice. The figure for those going into surgery falls to below five per cent. I learn that the shortage of women at the top of their profession—the consultant surgeons—is even more acute. There are, for example, only seventeen female consultant orthopaedic surgeons in the country! The figures for black surgeons in the UK are no different; Samantha confides that she knows of only one black consultant orthopaedic surgeon.

I am intrigued to discover what it was that made a young girl know with such certainly that she wanted to be a surgeon and, just as importantly, what sustained her desire and ambition over long years of education and medical training.

Samantha is unsure what her ambition stemmed from. She acknowledges thal her parents, originally from Guyana, came to the UK and worked in the medical field, but adds that her mother was a nurse who went on to become a lecturer, whilst her father came to study accountancy but worked as a hospital porter to fund his education. Samantha Tross's parents played a vital role in helping her get to where she is today, through their repeated validation of her ambition and unstinting support. She still recalls her father's words of encouragement: 'If you want to be a surgeon, you make sure you study hard and I will make sure you have the money to go to school to realise your ambition.... My father was immensely encouraging. He was always stressing the virtues of academic achievement and in so doing he and my mother virtually propelled me through medical school. I felt almost obliged to achieve.'

Samantha Tross was educated in Guyana until she was eleven years old. She recalls one of her early headteachers taking the time and interest to help foster her career ambitions, talking to her about the practicalities involved in a career in medicine. Samantha did indeed make it to medical school, attending University College, London, where she recalls meeting her first female surgeon. This orthopaedic specialist so inspired Samantha that she determined to also make orthopaedics her surgical specialism. 'From that moment', she explained, 'it became a personal desire of mine to be the first black woman orthopaedic surgeon in the UK.'

I returned later in the interview to the issue of personal drive and motivation. Samantha Tross made a very telling observation, and one which touches the very heart of why *Millennium People* was conceived. In her view, 'What we lack in this country is a working environment where we see black people routinely moving in positions of authority. Coming from Guyana, wanting to be a doctor was not anything strange or unusual. I was so used to seeing not only black doctors but also black prime ministers, black presidents, black corporate leaders and the like. Young black people in the UK are not exposed to enough positive examples of black achievement or widely encouraged to believe that they too can become doctors if they want to.'

Samantha Tross has worked in various London hospitals and has recently been made a Fellow of the Royal College of Orthopaedic Surgeons. She admits that she is still adjusting to the heavy demands which her work, with its long and often stressful hours, imposes on her personal and social life, but she still finds time to act as a mentor for students and other would-be future medical practitioners through the Afro-Caribbean Medical Society.

Having achieved her first and long-held ambition, Samantha's new goal is to one day become a consultant orthopaedic surgeon, thereby enlarging the pool of female consultants in this medical specialism, and, quite possibly, once again becoming the first black female to break into this new territory. Given her clear focus, immense energy and unquenchable drive, I fully expect Samantha Tross to achieve her ambition sooner rather than later.

The operator

The business of fashion

Ray Walters

Product Director

Although Ray Walters left school at the age of fifteen to join the Army, he is today Product Director of a multi-million pound clothing manufacturing company Bentwood Ltd and, as I was to learn, soon to become Managing Director of another similar sized clothing manufacturer, Bagir UK Ltd, which is part of an international conglomerate.

As a management board member of Bentwood, he is one of a team of six directors who run the company, which enjoys a turnover of £150m per annum. The company has numerous factories spread across the UK as well as a site in Morocco, and altogether employs some 3,800 staff. It manufactures a range of quality clothing items, virtually all of which are supplied to the well-known high street retailer Marks and Spencer (M & S). Based at the company's head office in London, as Product Director Ray Walters' principal responsibilities involve sourcing the raw materials needed to supply the different product areas across the company, and, in conjunction with his production colleagues, overseeing these raw materials as they are developed into product ranges for sale to customers such as M & S. He also has specific responsibility for the company's menswear division. A stroll through the clothing aisles of any M & S store will take one past several lines of men's, women's and children's wear supplied to the firm by Bentwood. Indeed, it is quite likely that Ray Walters and his colleagues will have had direct involvement in the manufacture and supply of the many famous M & S lines.

Ray Walters takes pride in the senior management position he holds, especially when he reflects back on leaving school at such an early age. He confides, 'I did not do particularly well academically at school'—although he made up for this later. Now in his early forties, Ray is hungry for the ultimate challenge of the top position, and hence his impending move after two successful years with Bentwood to the Israeli-owned company Bagir UK Ltd as Managing Director.

There is no brashness or cockiness about him—Ray Walters' approach is rather one of studied assuredness—as he quietly makes the point, 'I feel I am behind my peers in terms of where I would like to be at this point in my career. I see myself as a leader and want to test myself in that capacity.' Of his new position, he says confidently, 'It's a good fit for me—to raise the profile and profitability of the company's business in the UK—it will be my biggest challenge yet.'

Born in Jamaica, Ray Walters joined his parents in the UK at the age of seven, after they had travelled there some years earlier. At fifteen and seeking independence he joined the Army, where due to his age, Ray's first two years were effectively spent in Army school—the Junior Leaders Regiment—where he went on to obtain his O and A levels before graduating to the regular Army. Ray Walters stayed for a further three years in the Army, advancing to Corporal, before leaving the Service in the late 1970s. Although he admits to not having any real career plan at that stage, he says firmly, 'All I knew was that I wanted to be somebody. I had a determination simply to do well.'

After a short period as a petrol station manager, Ray landed a job which he believes changed the direction of his life and put him on course to where he is today. That position was as a trainee manager with Marks and Spencer. It was not so much the particular job he had secured—although it did give him an across-the-board insight into the retail clothing business—but more the calibre of the company he was to work for. Ray Walters is effusive in his praise for M & S, viewing it equally as 'a model employer and of how to run a business. It is an excellent university of its type.'

Ray Walters spent almost twenty years working at various levels within M & S. In his latter years there he became Manager of the Buying Department, responsible for selecting the tailored clothing, underwear and leisure wear sold in its nationwide chain of stores. Not only did this product buying experience provide a thorough grounding for Ray and relate directly to the core business of clothing retail, and indeed to his subsequent roles at Bentwood and Bagir UK Ltd (both of which supply a large proportion of their output to M & S), but he believes, more critically, that the M & S experience developed his wider business management skills and self-confidence.

One of the most significant and personally satisfying highlights of Ray's M & S career was being selected as one of a group of senior managers for a study tour of Israel. Given the company's close historical ties with Israel and the fact that it does so much of its business there, the view was taken that M & S managers should know more about the culture and ways of doing business in that country. 'It was a tour you could not put a price on,' says Ray Walters emphatically. The busy itinerary included meetings with the President of the country and dinner with the internationally-renowned politician, Shimon Perez. For Ray, the trip was symbolic of how they did things at M & S, and a benchmark of how he intends to operate in his business and management capacities at Bagir UK Ltd. Ray is particularly proud of the personal acknowledgement and good wishes he received in a letter sent by the Chairman of M & S on his departure from the company. He also refers with pride to the classical music concert he organised for charity. Held at the Barbican in London, the concert attracted some 2,000 people and raised over £40k for Sickle Cell Relief charities.

Needless to say, amongst those whom Ray Walters acknowledges for the help and support he received in his climb up the corporate ladder are certain managers at M & S who not only recognised his ambitions but allowed him to flourish. He also cites a peer group of close black friends, all high achievers themselves, whom he describes as 'pillars of strength', providing a trusted and supportive network for talking through their professional concerns. Ray describes his mother as perhaps his biggest influence, not least for the inspiration she provided in raising five children and yet still finding the time and inclination to go back to full-time study in order to further her nursing career.

As Ray Walters prepares to take on the top position of Managing Director in his new company, he voices what he sees as the general position for black people in the UK in the next millennium. He says that he is both 'worried and optimistic at the same time'. He is worried about the position of young black people and the still iunbroken cycle of poverty and disadvantage that many face in the inner cities. On the other hand, he is heartened by the growing number of bright young black graduates he sees entering industry.

Ray Walters is in many respects a positive role model for both these groups. Given his own very modest start, his rise up the corporate ladder is a positive indicator both to those of lesser educational attainment and to the high flyers alike, of what can be achieved if, like Ray Walters, one has the self-belief and determination to succeed.

Verna Wilkins

Publisher, Tamarind Books

Fuelled by her strong passion to redress 'black invisibility in children's books', Verna Wilkins changed career direction to become an award-winning publisher of children's picture books. Today she is the Director of Tamarind Books which has, in the ten or so years of its existence, forged an important niche in a highly competitive market. When the demands of publishing allow, she is a successful author of children's books in her own right.

My meeting with Verna for *Millennium People* yielded not only an impressive subject for my book, but also gave me encouragement for the *Millennium People* project as a whole and helpful practical advice on publishing, for which I remain indebted.

For Verna Wilkins—who was born on the Caribbean island of Grenada but who has lived the greater part of her life in Britain— 'invisibility and omission' are two sides of the same coin. They are issues she was grappling with long before she became a publisher. As a college lecturer, and with two children at school, she observed first hand in the 1980s that even with much talk of multi-cultural education, most children's books in school rarely featured black children or any other black characters. Of the few that did, their underlying message was usually negative or gave exaggerated emphasis to the 'problems, pain and suffering of being black'. Verna felt that this strange invisibility, or negative portrayal, was damaging to black children because it sapped their self-confidence and lowered their aspirations.

Verna Wilkins also recalls that despite being a fairly forthright person, and certainly 'no weeping willow', as a lecturer she herself was not immune to this invisibility. She is able to laugh about it now, but explains how draining and annoying it was that whenever she walked into a lecture room to address new students, she would suddenly become invisible. 'They would automatically assume that as a black woman I could not possibly be the lecturer, and would just continue on with whatever they were doing or ask me where the lecturer was.'

Just as she had her method of making her presence felt in the lecture room to gain the attention and respect of her students, Verna Wilkins felt so strongly about the omission of black children in books that she resolved to try and fill this void herself. 'I decided to write for children, to put them into the picture, metaphorically and literally,' says Verna. Her view is that one needs to catch children early when their personalities and characters are still being formed so that black children gain self-esteem and white people gain greater awareness of the presence and capability of black people. She wrote her first three children's books whilst maintaining her day job. When she eventually gave up her salaried lecturer position, she expected to become a full-time writer.

However, she soon discovered it was not going to be easy getting her books published. Since publishers were so unused to seeing black characters and images they believed that such books would not sell if they put them on the market. She smiles ruefully, saying, 'I was virtually forced into publishing. If existing publishers were not going to do it, I decided I would do it myself.' Thus, she set up Tamarind Books on a shoestring budget.

Tamarind was the company name she bought 'off the shelf', but she says, 'It has a definite Caribbean connection. I did not have any prior knowledge of publishing but I knew what schools needed.' Armed with a bank loan of £25K— she laughingly describes the initial business plan to secure this as her 'best piece of fiction to date'—Verna Wilkins, with her family members giving invaluable support, set about getting her books into the market and addressing the issue that lay at the heart of her business enterprise. 'It was about giving black children something to be proud of,' she says. 'I set out very deliberately to change the status quo, and I am still writing and publishing for change.' A factor which helped, says Verna very firmly, 'is that I realised early on that publishing'—which she feels still needs to be demystified— 'is essentially about risks, and I am a risk-taker.'

Ten years later, Tamarind Books has an impressive reputation. The books neither stress colour nor deal with multi-cultural themes. Rather, they simply show black children and their families living ordinary lives. They cover topics common to all children, such as having a birthday, learning to walk, and losing one's milk teeth, but in so doing they portray—through beautiful illustrations—positive and enhancing images of black children, and black people generally. Indeed, my own children have Tamarind's books amongst their collection and have found them attractive and endearing.

Although Verna commissions and publishes the works of various authors, the most successful Tamarind book to date, *Dave and the Tooth Fairy,* was, in fact, written by herself. It was the winner of a children's book of the year award and has sold over 150,000 copies. The BBC has recently purchased television rights to the book. Other Tamarind books have also won awards. *Mike and Lottie,* for instance, won a children's book of the year award in the early 1990s. Although she still enjoys writing, Verna explains that it is the process of publishing which gives her the greatest satisfaction and sense of achievement. It has allowed her to attend book fairs and to be invited to speak at conferences and to groups worldwide. In 1999, a further twelve new titles were added to Tamarind's growing list.

Verna Wilkins acknowledges the support of her family from the outset. 'Everybody pitched in.' She adds with good humour, 'But they can also be my hardest critics if they feel I have not got something quite right!' She also received helpful advice from a group to which she belonged when she first started— 'Women in Publishing'. However, she reserves special praise for her father 'whose influence was absolutely tremendous. He instilled in me and my four sisters and our brother great self-confidence.' It is this, she feels, which has been the real reason for all she has achieved in life. Looking to the future, Verna Wilkins anticipates an expansion of her business. Of the next millennium and the position of black people in the UK, she describes herself as optimistic. 'I have seen many things change for the better over the last ten or so years. I now see young black British people in positions of authority, and there are many more black executives than there were even five years ago. Their presence is noticeable, and the future looks much brighter,' says Verna.

Perhaps the cloak of black invisibility has at last been lifted. If so, someone who has played, and continues to play, a significant role through her books in developing and moulding the young minds to be receptive to change, is Verna Wilkins, Publisher.

Literary lady

Profiles in brief

Paul Boateng MP

Minister of State

Paul Boateng, Member of Parliament for Brent South in north west London, quietly made history when, with the election of the new Labour Government in 1997, he was appointed Parliamentary Under Secretary of State at the Department of Health, thus becoming the first black person to hold ministerial office in Her Majesty's Government. He consolidated his position a year later when, in October 1998, be became the Minister of State for Home Affairs.

Born in Ghana, Paul Boateng is himself the son of a former Ghanaian Cabinet Minister. Following a military coup in Ghana in 1966, Paul Boateng, then fourteen, found himself with his family abruptly becoming refugees and living on a British council housing estate. Despite this setback, he nevertheless graduated from the University of Bristol, and after training to be a solicitor switched to the Bar in 1989.

Noted as a highly articulate and astute politician, Paul Boateng is also one of the Commons' snappiest dressers, purchasing his suits from, amongst others, the black couturier designer who shares his name but is no relation— Ozwald Boateng. With his reputation as a fighter for injustice, Paul Boateng is a devout Christian who first came to public attention in the early eighties as an elected member of the radical Greater London Council, and later through his advocacy in some of the prominent legal cases of the period.

Given his present ministerial responsibilities and his acclaimed political skill, Paul Boateng is considered a strong bet to become Britain's first black Cabinet Minister.

Naomi Campbell

Model

Naomi Campbell is one of an élite group of models in the fashion world who are seen as 'supermodels' because of the international celebrity status and huge fees they enjoy. Born in Streatham, south London, Naomi Campbell is one of the biggest names on the catwalk, and reputedly earns well over US$1 million a year.

Naomi was 'discovered', aged fifteen, in London's Covent Garden shopping mall. Within a few short months she was to become the first black model to grace the covers of some of the world's most renowned magazines, and has continued in much the same vein ever since.

During several years in the modelling business—an achievement in itself, since by the industry's very nature modelling careers tend to be short-lived—Naomi has periodically broken new ground. She has debuted in films, appeared in numerous music videos, released, her own musical recording and co-authored a novel. She has even had the distinction of being honoured with a waxwork at London's MadameTussaud's Museum.

Given the press coverage that supermodels like Naomi invariably attract, often of an intrusive nature, what is little known about Naomi Campbell is the considerable amount of charity and humanitarian work she does. The Red Cross Somalia Relief Fund and UNESCO efforts to support children in poor communities worldwide are but two causes to benefit from her personal support.

Naomi Campbell will no doubt continue to reinvent herself in many guises as she utilises her celebrity status to build her multi-faceted career and lend her support and influence to those who can benefit from a touch of her stardust.

Jenni Francis

Public Affairs and Media Relations Executive

Jenni Francis is a dynamic black businesswoman who runs her own public relations company, the Jenni Francis Agency, specialising in arts and entertainment, tourism and leisure promotion. She provides marketing and communications expertise for an impressive range of corporate clients, public bodies and well-known individuals. Recent contracts include the Victoria and Albert Museum, the Theatre Museum and the Royal College of Art.

However, Jenni Francis's activities extend well beyond PR and marketing, She established her first company, Networking PR, at the age of twenty-five, without any real business support—earning the title of 'Black Businesswoman of the Year' for her efforts. As a firm believer in helping business people to help themselves. Jenni is particularly active in the business development field. For example, she is a member of the Princes Youth Business Trust Ethnic Minority Advisory Group and was formerly Chairperson of the Women's Enterprise Development Agency.

Jenni also has long-standing involvements in the radio and television industries. She served for many years on the Radio Authority and on the Independent Television Commission's Advertising Advisory Committee, and is today one of the prime movers—along with the boxer Lennox Lewis—behind the bid to establish a black radio station, Irie FM, for north London.

When Jenni Francis started her career as an office junior on a local newspaper she very quickly started to climb the corporate ladder, but she held onto her dream of setting up and running her own business. Today, the successful and highly talented Jenni Francis serves as an excellent role model, particularly to young women who similarly aspire to run their own businesses.

Peter Herbert

Barrister

Peter Herbert is a well-known and respected black barrister. Called to the bar in the mid-1980s, he has earned a reputation not only as a leading counsel – notwithstanding the more senior black barristers to be found in the British legal profession – but also as an outspoken advocate and former chairman of the Society of Black Lawyers (SBL).

Under Peter Herbert's stewardship during the 1990s, the SBL as the collective body for black lawyers and law students in the UK, would challenge and often make major in-roads in its struggle against perceived racism and injustice within the legal profession and beyond. In doing so, the SBL became a respected champion in addressing issues affecting Britain's black communities.

Peter attributes his legal career to the influence on him as a youngster, of the political advocacy of Dr Martin Luther King Jr. and Malcolm X. 'Through these influences I developed a consciousness and willingness to challenge orally any perceived unfairness or discrimination, so by the time I was looking for a career, law seemed the most logical extension.'

Outlining his personal philosophy, Peter proclaims, 'I am a believer in self-help. I see change as something dependent on what you do to help yourself, rather than what others do for you.'

Peter Herbert was appointed, in 2000, chairman of the Metropolitan Police Authority, the newly-established body which oversees policing policy and expenditure in the capital.

Denise Lewis

Athlete

Denise Lewis is ranked as the world's most outstanding heptathlete, and is Britain's undisputed golden girl of athletics. Heptathletes compete in seven combined and punishing athletic disciplines: hurdles, high jump, shot put, sprinting, long jump, javelin and middle distance running. To excel in this multi-discipline event, one has to be a tremendously talented and tenacious all-round athlete. Denise Lewis is all this and more.

Born and raised in the west midlands, Denise combines awesome athletic power with natural pin-up beauty—she has graced calendars and magazine covers— but remains refreshingly unpretentious and down to earth. Having started serious training at the age of fourteen, her athletic ascendancy began in 1994 when she won the gold medal for the heptathlon at the Commonwealth Games in Victoria, Canada.

Successfully retaining her Commonwealth title at the Kuala Lumpur Games in 1998, she also became European Champion, took the bronze medal at the 1996 Altlanta Olympics, and the silver at the 1997 world championships. More recently she was awarded an MBE by the Queen in recognition of her sporting achievements.

Her eyes are now very firmly set on winning gold at the Sydney 2000 Olympics thereby confirming her status as the number one female heptathlete. Denise readily admits that she would like to dominate the event in the style of another British Olympic legend—Daley Thompson—and effectively make it her own property, much as he did, well into the new millennium. The ever popular Denise Lewis is on course to do just that.

Lennox Lewis

World Heavyweight Boxing Champion

Lennox Lewis has twice held the world heavyweight boxing title. But for a dubious decision in early 1999 when he fought the American boxer Evander Holyfield, he would now be the undisputed heavyweight champion of the world and the first Briton to hold that status in over a hundred years of boxing.

Born in London's East End, although partly educated in Canada, Lennox Lewis is fiercely proud of being black and British. He is immensely popular across the whole spectrum of British society, as seen by the cross party receptions extended to him at the House of Commons through to the enthusiastic greetings he receives from youngsters in the street. Having personally contributed some £2.5m to help establish a college of further education for the East End of London, Lennox Lewis is held in especially high regard by Britain's black population.

Lennox Lewis does not fit the image of the 'typical' boxer. He is university educated, highly articulate and carries himself with dignity and grace. Since winning the gold medal as an amateur boxer at the Seoul Olympics in 1988, Lennox Lewis has been nothing short of a credit to his sport and to himself, and has reaped the just rewards of his endeavours. He is for example, the highest placed black person on a national newspaper's list of the 500 richest people in Britain.

Since a re-match has been set with Evander Holyfield for late 1999, Lennox Lewis could yet enter the new millennium as not merely 'the people's champion' but the undisputed champion of the world.

Wayne Marshall

Organist, Composer and Conductor

Wayne Marshall is acknowledged as Britain's leading virtuoso organist. He is also an accomplished pianist and composer, and has more recently added conducting to his repertoire of musical skills. In 1997, he became the first organist in recent history to perform solo at the prestigious 'Last Night of the Proms' concert, following this up a year later by becoming only the third black musician to conduct at the Proms in its 104-year history.

Wayne Marshall's first introduction to the piano was at age three, sat at his mother's side, in Oldham, north west England, where his parents had settled after leaving Barbados. He would regularly be asked to play the piano at his primary school assemblies. He went on to attend music school at eleven—it was here that Wayne acquired his love of the organ—before graduating from the Royal College of Music.

For a period, Wayne was organist at St George's Chapel, Windsor, where he played at one time or another for all members of the Royal Family. His current post is as organist-in-residence at Manchester's Bridgewater Hall which houses the largest organ in the UK. Wayne Marshall's musical talents have taken him around the world, with regular overseas recitals in the USA, Europe and the Far East.

One of Wayne's stated missions is to raise the profile of organ music and to spread the pleasure of it. With his reputation for being an innovative showman—he occasionally mixes organ music with jazz, rock and other genres—there could be no better exponent to take organ music into the new millennium than Wayne Marshall.

Chris Ofili

Artist

Chris Ofili is one of the rising stars of British art and his paintings are amongst the most talked about works on the British art scene. In 1998, he won the Turner Prize, a highly prestigious award given to the artist whose work has been judged the most impressive during that year. He is undoubtedly the most famous and successful black British visual artist.

Hailed by many as one of the most creative talents in Britain, Chris Ofili's paintings are nonetheless controversial, and are considered by others to be bordering on the profane.

Although difficult to properly categorise, Chris Ofili is essentially a figurative painter who creates distinctly colourful abstractions which pack a strong visual punch. His works have a three-dimensional quality made up of layer overlaid upon layer and pattern lurking within pattern. What makes his work controversial is that Chris Ofili attaches to the surface of nearly all his pieces his trademark pats of elephant dung! The dung is used in a variety of ways and his works are often given colourful titles to match.

Born in Manchester of Nigerian parents, Chris Ofili was surprisingly first introduced to painting at college —he studied at the Chelsea School of Art and the Royal College of Art. Now just turned thirty, he has since had solo exhibitions in New York, London and Berlin. His works adorn the walls of a variety of prestigious galleries and are sold at Christies, the auctioneers, for more than £10,000 a piece. For all that, Chris Ofili simply says that all he is looking for 'is to have fun'.

Courtney Pine

Jazz Musician

Courtney Pine taught himself the tenor saxophone when he was fourteen, and within the space of a few short years was hailed as one of the leading exponents of contemporary British jazz. Some would argue that he and a coterie of contemporaries, like Julian Joseph, were directly responsible for the resurgence of jazz in Britain, expanding its base and creating interest in a musical form previously regarded by many as esoteric and inaccessible.

Courtney Pine made his breakthrough in the mid-1980s when his debut album sold over 100,000 copies, becoming the first jazz album to crack the British top 40 record charts—a phenomenal achievement for a jazz album and the envy of many pop groups. Although the jazz boom has peaked since then, Courtney Pine nevertheless continues to pack concert halls worldwide, has released a number of other popular selling albums, and has performed and recorded with major artists such as Art Blakey, Elton John and Mick Jagger. Acknowledging his Jamaican parental influences, and the musical preferences of his peers, he has never been afraid to fuse jazz with other musical forms and in doing so has expanded the repertoire of jazz.

Still in his mid-thirties, this accomplished saxophonist and composer has already succeeded in realizing two of his strongly held objectives—to achieve longevity in a field noted for its transitory nature and to bring jazz to the masses.

Heather Small

Singer

Heather Small is the lead singer and front person for the highly successful band 'M People'. Since its formation in 1991, when the band would play to perhaps a few hundred people in smokey clubs, 'M People' has risen steadily to become one of the most popular British bands of the nineties, selling millions of records worldwide and playing to audiences in their tens of thousands in stadiums and arenas. 'M People' produce what might be described as 'feel good music', and their upbeat and soulful dance tunes have become so popular that some have been widely used by major advertisers as well as political parties to sell their products and messages.

At the heart of 'M People's' music are the trademark vocals of Heather Small who has one of the most distinctive and finest voices in the music industry - gutsy, soulful and with a towering presence. While growing up in west London's Ladbroke Grove, the petite Heather was too shy to sing in public until she reached eighteen although she always wanted to be a singer. Despite her prodigious talent and the years of success behind her, she still suffers from stage fright prior to a performance. Nonetheless, she and the band are noted for their stunning performances, where Heather's extravagant theatrical gestures admirably match her powerful vocals.

Heather Small, like the other members of her closely knit band, is a rather shy and reluctant superstar but one whose star qualities are shining brightly into the new millennium.

Gary Wilmot

Entertainer

Gary Wilmot is one of the biggest names in British theatre today having taken the lead role in a number of acclaimed West End and repertory theatre musical productions. From *Oliver, The Goodbye Girl, Me and My Girl,* to *Copacabana* and *Carmen Jones,* Gary Wilmot has been attracting full houses and leaving a huge mark on the genre of stage musicals.

Yet, when south London born Gary Wilmot started off in the entertainment business more than twenty years ago, it was as a comedian. He steadily rose to prominence through guest appearances on television. Not only did he win the television talent show 'New Faces', but he later stole the show at a memorable Royal Variety Performance in 1985.

However, in 1989, when his celebrity status was at its peak Gary took the radical step of changing course to

pursue a career on the stage and has never looked back.

Multi-talented Gary Wilmot is seen as a consummate all-round entertainer because of his singing, dancing, acting and comic performances. He has also successfully tried his hand at stage directing and has debuted in films. Having achieved so much with no formal training, he points to the early death of his Jamaican father—who came to Britain on the famous 'Empire Windrush' and who passed away when Gary was six—as the source of his qualities as an actor and entertainer. Humour was Gary's release from the sadness of losing his father, his way of being noticed and his shield from being taunted. That shield has certainly stood Gary Wilmot in good stead and will no doubt continue to serve him into the future.

Ian Wright

Footballer and Television Presenter

Ian Wright, or 'Wrighty' as he is also affectionately known, is something of a phenomenon both on and off the football field. An England international footballer and one of the high-profile characters of the game. he has more recently also become a successful television chat-show host with his debut series, 'All Wright' on London Weekend Television.

Ian Wright was a late starter in football, not turning professional until twenty-six when most players are reaching the mid-point of their careers, but he has more than made up for it since. At his best, Ian Wright manages to combine the sublime skill and record-breaking scoring of basketball's Michael Jordan, with the snarling aggression of the same sport's Dennis Rodman, but all with the boundless enthusiasm

and passion of a perennial schoolboy.

His so-called 'bad boy' image has not stopped him from being revered by fans—at his previous club, Arsenal, he achieved near icon status—and he continues to be sought after by corporate advertisers eager to secure his name and endorsement for their products.

Despite his status and the trappings of wealth, Ian Wright has retained his down-to-earth black south London persona and is recognised and respected for it. He is someone with oodles of street credibility.

As he approaches the twilight of his football playing career it is evident that there is much more still to be heard from Ian Wright in the new millennium, given his broad appeal and fearless approach to life.

Epilogue

In response to feedback and growing requests received from readers of the first edition of *Millennium People-the soul of success* (published in 1999), this Epilogue is intended to provide a brief update, some three years on, of those individuals previously featured.

Given the relatively short intervening period, entries here are focused primarily on those persons for whom some notable change, or significant professional achievement or accomplishment has occurred in their chosen careers/ business paths since the publication of the first edition. Where there is no reference or entry in the Epilogue on a particular individual previously featured in *Millennium People*, this would mean either there was nothing substantive to add to the existing profile at this point in time, or else, and in a small number of cases only, no additional information was gained.

Entries in this Epilogue section are grouped in generic categories for ease of reference, and are as follows:

The political arena

Paul Boateng MP after a spell as Deputy to the Home Secretary, became the first black Cabinet Minister of any British Government in history when he was appointed Chief Treasury Minister in 2002.

Baroness Patricia Scotland became the first black female Minister in Her Majesty's Government when she was appointed Junior Minister at the Foreign and Commonwealth Office in 1999.

Baroness Valerie Amos after initial appointment as a government whip, was promoted to Junior Minister in the Foreign and Commonwealth Office, before being elevated in 2003, to the Cabinet post of Secretary of State for International Development—becoming the first black woman Cabinet Minister.

Oona King MP has since founded and is chairperson of the All Party Parliamentary Group on Rwanda, and remains a member of the International Development Select Committee. She is also Vice-Chair of the London Labour Group of MPs and Vice-Chair of the British Council.

Trevor Phillips was elected in 2000, as a representative to the then newly-established Greater London Authority. He subsequently became the chairman of the Authority, a position he occupied for the next three years until he was appointed in 2003, Chairman of the Commission for Racial Equality.

Lord Herman Ouseley stepped down as Chairman of the Commission for Racial Equality in 2000, after six years in the job. He continues to be active in the field of race equality as a director of a leading consultancy. Sir Herman was made a life peer in 2001 and is now Lord Ouseley, an active member of the House of Lords.

Armed services

David Case earned the coveted star on his shoulder when he was promoted in 2000 to the rank of Air Commodore (the airforce equivalent of Brigadier). He is now a member of the RAF HQ Management Board with responsibility for general planning.

Major Eze Ugwuzor was deployed in 1999 to Kosovo, where he commanded a squadron of British forces responsible for logistics and supplies for the British forces serving as part of the NATO peace-keeping mission in the troubled province of the former Yugoslavia.

Commander Martyn Reid joined Britain's flagship aircraft carrier, HMS Invincible, in May 2000, as Commander Air Fleet, an appointment which puts him in command of the carrier's group of fighter aircrafts and helicopters.

Sports

Lennox Lewis did, indeed, see in the new millennium as boxing's undisputed world heavyweight champion after defeating America's Evander Holyfield in a celebrated fight in late 1999. He would go on to make several successful defences of his titles and remains the world heavyweight boxing champion.

Denise Lewis fulfilled all the early praise and predictions made of her that she would be one of Britain's key medal contenders at the Sydney 2000 Olympics. Her gutsy performance in the heptathlon at Sydney did indeed secure her an Olympic gold medal, to huge national and international acclaim.

Sol Campbell was transferred in a high profile move to Arsenal football club in summer 2001, after several top English and overseas clubs competed for his services. In his first season at his new club they would win the rare and coveted 'double' of league championship and F.A. Cup. He remains a mainstay in the England international football team.

Viv Anderson left Middlesbrough football club, along with his managerial pal, Brian Robson, in summer 2001, after eight eventful seasons which saw them achieve two promotions and three cup final appearances. He was awarded an MBE in 2001.

Wayne Otto retired from competition as the undefeated world Karate champion in 2000, and was honoured with an OBE in 2001. He is now a coach with the British Karate governing body.

Business

Fitzroy Andrew left the Windsor Fellowship in 1999, and is now working in the private sector as a consultant with a leading UK recruitment consultancy.

Sky Andrew was closely involved in the high profile negotiations and subsequent transfer of his principal client, footballer Sol Campbell, to Arsenal football club in summer 2001. The transfer made his client one of the highest paid professional footballers in English football.

Jim Brathwaite was appointed by the Secretary of State for Trade and Industry, in 2002, as the chair of the South East England Development Agency, becoming the first black person to hold the top position in a regional development board. He was awarded an OBE in 2000.

René Carayol achieved his sought-after goal in 1999, when he founded and became Managing Director of IPC Electric, a subsidiary of IPC Magazines. He has since diversified his interests becoming CEO of an e-business consultancy, chairman of a dotcom business, a regular contributor on radio and television as well as to the e-business press. His first book *Corporate Voodoo,* was published in 2001.

Julianna Edwards is now one of the managing consultants of Future Steps, the global internet recruitment arm of Korn Ferry International.

Malcolm John after a spell as the Head Chef of Terrance Conran's flagship private members' club restaurant, Bluebird, is now a partner in Niksons restaurant and bar in London. Plans for more Niksons outlets are already being considered.

Kanya King was awarded an MBE in January 2000, for her contribution to the music industry and the MOBO Awards continue to reach an audience of millions worldwide.

Dej Mahoney left Sony Music in 2000, after eight years as Vice President to pursue wider media and leisure projects. Prior to his departure from Sony he sat on the Music Industry Forum, chaired by the Secretary of State for Culture, Media and Sport. He is today a director of Visual Track Software consultancy.

Val McCalla deceased 2002.

Trevor Robinson continues to make award winning television commercials for multinational companies such as Sony (Playstation) and Coca Cola (Coke). He directed his first full length feature film *Hour Glass Boys* in 2001 and produced one of the big budget advertisements for the much coveted US SuperBowl television slot.

Ray Walters after a period as Managing Director of Bagir UK Ltd., was headhunted in 2000 by the Worldwide Retail Exchange – the world's largest electronic business to business marketplace exchange – to join its development group as a textile supplier consultant.

Michael Fraser has since branched out from his business interests to explore a new genre, that of being one of the presenters on a new BBC television programme, *To Catch A Thief.*

Public Affairs

Keith Ajegbo remains a school principal. In 2000, he became Governor of the National College of School Leadership. He was previously awarded an OBE in 1995.

Karlene Davis' national and international contribution to health issues continues unabated. In 2000, she was appointed by the Secretary of State for Health to the NHS Modernisation Board – the committee set up to oversee the implementation of the NHS Plan for England. She is now also Director of the WHO Collaborating Centre for Midwifery, and Regional Representative for Europe in the International Confederation of Midwives.

Peter Herbert was appointed in 2000 chairman of the newly-established Metropolitan Police Authority, the body which oversees policing policy and expenditure in the capital.

Dr Terry John has since been appointed to various influential BMA and other medical forums This includes his chairmanship of the BMA's Education and Audit Sub-Committee of GPs and membership of the Appraisal Board of the National Institute for Clinical Excellence—the body which advises the Secretary of State for Health on new drugs and technologies to be made available on the NHS.

Heather Rabbatts resigned her position as CEO with Lambeth Council in 2000, initially to run her own consultancy company. She was subsequently appointed a Governor of the BBC and moved from this executive postion in 2002, to become the Managing Director of the 4Learning television programme division at Channel 4.

Liz Rasekoala continues to steer the development of the Ishango Science Clubs. In recognition of her work in this area, she was honoured in 1999 with an Innovation Award from the Commonwealth Association of Science, Technology and Mathematics Educators, and in 2000, with an Honorary Doctorate from Sheffield Hallam University.

Angela Sarkis was awarded a CBE in 1999, and later appointed a Governor of the BBC in 2002.

The Rt. Revd. John Sentamu was inaugurated as the Bishop of Birmingham in 2002. His new diocese covers Britain's second most populous city. He also chaired the high profile public enquiry into the murder investigation of Damilola Taylor.

Prof. Stephen Small achieved tenure at the University of Berkeley, California—the coveted next step on the American academic career path.

Linbert Spencer has since stepped down as chairman of the Windsor Fellowship. He remains highly active in the UK equality field.

Lord Taylor of Warwick alongside his parliamentary work as a peer in the House of Lords, was appointed Chancellor of Bournemouth University in 2002.

Cultural

Marianne Jean-Baptiste continues to expand her acting career in the US, where she has appeared, amongst others, in feature films with Robert Redford and Brad Pitt (*Spy Game*, 2001), and Jennifer Lopez (*The Cell*, 2000). She has also been a regular cast member of two US television drama series—*Without a Trace* and *Men Only*.

Angie Greaves now broadcasts for BBC Three Counties radio, in addition to her regular show on BBC London Live. Her voice can also be heard as one of the central characters in the highly acclaimed children's animated television programme Construction Site, as well as on numerous voice-overs for television, radio and corporate videos.

Julian Joseph has continued his efforts to raise the profile of jazz music in the UK, with his presentation of the *Jazz World* series on television, his *Jazz Legends* series on BBC radio, and through performances at the prestigious *Proms* concerts.

Wayne Marshall besides touring Europe, North America, Australia and the Far East with his solo recitals, released in 2000 two CDs of his virtuoso organ music, one of which—*Symphonie*—was recorded on the much vaunted Bridgewater Hall's Marcussen organ.

Revd. Bazil Meade's commitment to the promotion of gospel music has seen him set up and run regular gospel music workshops in schools across London. In June 2001, the London Community Gospel Choir achieved a new milestone when it performed a concert in its own right at London's St Paul's Cathedral.

Chris Ofili's reputation as an acclaimed and yet highly controversial artist was maintained, with his *Holy Virgin Mary* exhibit at the Carnegie International art exhibition, which toured the US in 2000.

Mike Phillips published his ninth novel in 2000, to great critical acclaim. *A Shadow of Myself*, a crime thriller, was set in post-Cold War Eastern Europe.

Courtney Pine was awarded the Gold Badge by the British Academy of Composers and Songwriters in 2002, in recognition of his services to jazz music in the UK. He became the youngest ever jazz musician to receive this honour. He was awarded an OBE in 2000, as well as receiving an Honorary Fellowship from Leeds College of Music.

Rianna Scipio is presently a reporter/presenter for BBC News in London. She continues to pursue her declared desire for a music publishing deal and has recently finished writing a cinema screenplay.

Heather Small still an active member of the chart-topping M People, released her first solo album *Proud,* in 2000, most of the songs of which she had co-written.

Annie Stewart left *The Voice* newspaper in 1999, having been commissioned to write a book.

Verna Wilkins continues via her publishing company, Tamarind, to be one of the leading UK publishers of multicultural picture books for children. Amongst her more recent titles was the authorised biography on *The Life of Stephen Lawrence*.

Ian Wright retired from professional football and was honoured with an MBE in 2000. He has since gone on to become a media personality as his career in broadcasting breaks new ground. He was headhunted by the BBC to present a series of television programmes on its networks, such as *Wright Here Wright Now*. He remains a regular radio broadcaster.

The Millennium People Series includes

Millennium People – **the soul of success** – *Book*

Millennium People – **the soul of success Poster Series** – *Set of 6 posters*

Millennium People - the motivators – *Set of 3 Posters*

Millennium People – **the soul of success Wall Calendar**

Black People Achieving Amazing Things – *Poster*

Dream Create Excel Personal Planner

Millennium People Image Banks – *Set One and Set Two*

Dream...Create...Excel – *Poster and Mounted Print*

Best of British – *Poster and Mounted Print*

Achieve Your Potential...it's up to you! – *Training Resource Pack*

Dream...Create...Excel Bookmarks

Dream...Create...Excel Notecards

Millennium People Series Lesson Plans

For details of the Millennium People Series send your name and address to

hibiscusbooks@hotmail.com

Acknowledgements

A book of this nature cannot be produced without the input and involvement of many people and *Millennium People* is no exception. A great many individuals and organisations provided invaluable help and assistance in countless ways, both large and small, and I would like to express my sincere gratitude to all who gave their kind support to this project.

In particular, the book would have been a very different concept without the co-operation of the individuals profiled. I am indebted to them for their generosity of time, patience and openness in sharing their career and, in some cases, their life stories with me. Appreciation is also extended to their assistants, management staff and agents who helped make the necessary arrangements to facilitate their involvement.

A special note of thanks is due to Professor Chris Mullard for contributing the book's Foreword, and for his warm and encouraging words of support. It was a privilege to have him lend his learned wisdom and experience to the project.

The following organisations are thanked for the assistance provided in offering recommendations of possible subjects for the book—namely, the Ministry of Defence, the Metropolitan Police Service, the British Medical Association, the Cabinet Office, the Institute of Personnel and Development, and several of the subjects who also made helpful suggestions in this regard—and to those who provided help in other equally supportive ways, such as the Imperial War Museum, Barratt East London and Steinway Hall, London, who kindly allowed access to their premises for photo-shoots.

The creative and professional input in helping turn the material into this *Millennium People* book, was provided on the photography by Mr Teik Teo of Sungrafix and Lingo Sdn. Bhd., Malaysia, on the text by Datin Noor Azlina Yunus, Malaysia, and the Art Revo Studio and Interactive Marketing, both of Malaysia, on typesetting.

Without doubt, however, my greatest debt of appreciation is owed to my wife, Susan. She not only shared my dream—with all, besides, that went with it—and offered untold encouragement for me to see it through, but her myriad of practical and unsung roles in supporting the project helped turn a long-held vision into reality. Without her support it would not have been possible.

The following photographs are reproduced with kind permission:
Sol Campbell (uhlsport), Andi Peters (Channel 4 Picture Publicity), Lennox Lewis (Media Machine), Wayne Marshall (Askonas Holt), Courtney Pine (Tickety-boo), Heather Small (The Voice), Gary Wilmot (Francis Loney, and Dee O'Reilly Management), Lenny Henry (BBC Picture Archives), Jazzie B (Jamie Morgan, and Soul II Soul), Ian Wright (London Weekend Television Picture Publicity), Naomi Campbell, Denise Lewis and Chris Ofili (News International), Paul Boateng MP (personal office), Jenni Francis (the Jenni Francis Agency), Lord Taylor of Warwick (personal office).

All other photographs were taken by Derek Burnett with kind sponsorship provided by Paterson Group International, suppliers of Paterson Acupan black and white film.